Corporate Finance Law

A GUIDE FOR THE EXECUTIVE

Bruce Wasserstein

McGRAW-HILL BOOK COMPANY

*New York   St. Louis   San Francisco   Auckland   Bogotá
Düsseldorf   Johannesburg   London   Madrid
Mexico   Montreal   New Delhi   Panama
Paris   São Paulo   Singapore
Sydney   Tokyo   Toronto*

Corporate Finance Law

To Chris

Library of Congress Cataloging in Publication Data

Wasserstein, Bruce.
  Corporate finance law.

  Bibliography: p.
  1. Corporations—United States—Finance. I. Title.
KF1428.W38   346'.73'0662   77-14376
ISBN 0-07-068423-5

1234567890   DODO   7654321098

*The editors for this book were W. Hodson Mogan and Carolyn Nagy,
the designer was Naomi Auerbach, and the production supervisor
was Teresa F. Leaden. It was set in Baskerville
by University Graphics, Inc.*

Printed and bound by R. R. Donnelley & Sons Company.

Contents

Preface   *vii*

PART ONE   *Starting a Business*

1. Introduction   *3*
2. Forming a Business   *6*
3. The Role of Directors   *22*
4. Capital Structure   *34*
5. Legal Requirements for Selling Securities   *60*
6. Venture Capital and Private Placements   *76*
7. Alternative Means of Financing   *96*
8. Bringing the Deal Together   *111*

PART TWO   *Public Financings*

9. Preliminary Considerations in Going Public   *117*
10. Public Offerings under the 1933 Act   *131*
11. Public Offering Documents and Expenses   *143*
12. Timetable for a Public Offering   *162*
13. An Overview of the Securities Laws   *174*

PART THREE   *Mergers, Acquisitions, and Tender Offers*

14. Mergers and Acquisitions   *183*
15. Tax, Corporate Law, and Accounting Considerations   *202*
16. Tender and Exchange Offers   *222*

PART FOUR   *Bankruptcy Law*

17. Bankruptcies and Reorganizations   *255*

Appendix A: Sample Certificate   *269*
Appendix B: Bylaws   *271*
Bibliography   *285*
Index   *291*

Preface

The purpose of this book is to provide a sophisticated guide to the realities of corporate finance law for executives, investment bankers, and investors as well as for attorneys without substantial experience in corporate practice.

Because the scope of the book is so broad, it cannot purport to be exhaustive. The intent is rather to provide a sensitivity and a context so that the right questions can be asked at the right time. A bibliography supplements the text for further reference.

This book evolved from my work with corporate clients who wanted to know more about the legal problems they were facing every day in making corporate finance decisions. Mergers, public offerings, private placements, venture capital deals, tender offers, and reorganizations are all of vital concern to the executive; yet it is impossible to operate effectively in these areas without a fundamental understanding of the legal principles and issues involved. This book attempts to fulfill that need.

The preparation of the book was aided by the considerable help of friends and colleagues. I would like to express my appreciation to some of my mentors in corporate law: John F. Hunt, Jr., George T. Lowy, Allen H. Merrill, David Ormsby, and William J. Schrenk, Jr., and particularly to Richard M. Allen, Samuel C. Butler, and Benjamin F. Crane. In addition,

I would like to thank some of the many friends who devoted substantial effort and time commenting on drafts: Betsy Carter, Peter C. Canellos, Richard H. Kelly, Joseph R. Perella, Pamela and James R. Silkenat, David Shakow, and Philip M. Young. None of them, of course, is responsible for the contents of the book. Finally, a debt of gratitude is owed to Nancy Baran Kordell, who on her free time skillfully typed the manuscript, and to my wife, Chris, who tolerated the intrusion of my work on this book during our weekends and vacations.

Bruce Wasserstein

PART ONE

Starting a Business

I think it was Gertrude Stein's cousin, according to Miss Stein, who said that money is always there, but the pockets change; it is not in the same pockets after a change, and that is all there is to say about money. Well, maybe.
— "ADAM SMITH," *Supermoney* (Random House 1972)

Introduction

In 1720, the shares of the South Sea Company were all the rage. This diversified conglomerate had interests in the glamour sectors of the economy: slave trading, whaling, exploration, and government finance. An investor who bought these shares with "sex appeal" in January 1720 would have made a tidy 800% profit by July. Everybody seemed to be in on the action. Imitation being the sincerest form of flattery, other speculators nudged their way into the game by bidding up the shares of more than 200 new stock issues to a level greater than the estimated worth of all the land in England.

Among the worthy ventures being financed were exploration for a shipwreck, making oil from seeds, the conversion of salt water to fresh, and the importation of jackasses from Spain "for carrying on an undertaking of great importance, but nobody to know what it is." As a reaction to the widespread speculation, Parliament passed the Bubble Act of 1720 to control the unauthorized new issues market, but the effect was, in fact, to burst the South Sea Bubble and quickly deflate many a fortune and reputation.

In the late 1920s, history repeated itself. From 1920 to 1933, some $50 billion worth of securities were sold in the United States. By the end of 1933, half of these securities were worthless, and many investors were wiped out. In September 1929, the aggregate value of all stocks listed on the New York Stock Exchange was $89 billion; by 1932, the aggregate value was $15 billion, a crashing decline of some 84% in value. The public demanded retribution, and the Senate Banking and Currency Committee began a searing investigation into the abuses of Wall Street, which led eventually to the federal securities laws.

Recently, we have all seen the stock averages go back and forth between the canyons of despair and the lofty spires of rampant speculation. No law by itself can curb avarice, and even if it could, perhaps it would be a mistake. Amidst all the flimflam, there is sometimes a good idea generated by a vision of Eldorado.

However, today, whatever their effectiveness, the web of laws regulating corporate financial transactions, or deals, is intricate and ever changing. Any particular vehicle and the applicable legal considerations may vanish tomorrow. For this reason, no book can hope to keep completely current with the passage of time; however, the central issues and themes have a remarkable consistency. And one clear rule of thumb has prevailed: Whatever the changes or reforms in the laws, the paperwork will grow.

A European client carrying two bulging briefcases once asked why American deals involve so many documents. His attorney replied, "Because we charge by the pound."

Maybe so. Deal documents sometimes contain page after page of irrelevant boiler plate blindly lifted from precedents. Jeremy Bentham, the English utilitarian philosopher, once had the incisive idea that all contracts should be categorized into standardized basic types; each class of contract would be colored differently, so that all parties would be clear about what they signed. Lately, some progressive banks have taken a tip from Bentham and eliminated the gobbledygook of consumer loan contracts and replaced them with readable short forms, and some enlightened state insurance commissioners are insisting on policies which are comprehensible. Not quite green and orange contracts, but certainly a step in the right direction.

Unfortunately, simplification is not always the answer. The tangle of securities, antitrust, and tax laws grafted onto a common-law tradition of individually tailored agreements indeed produces bulk and complication. But, for example, when the Justice Department commences an inquiry before an assets acquisition transaction can be closed, a client wants to know why there wasn't an "out" in the contract. If something goes wrong, clients are not interested in the excuse that the lawyer kept the papers simple.

The deal business is unfortunately replete with dangerous minefields. Hurtling roughshod over the intricate layers of governmental regulations is a prescription for disaster. The trick is to tiptoe lightly and not get blown up. Disciplined creativity, a very precious commodity, is required.

It has sometimes been said that a bad lawyer is one who fails to spot problems, a good lawyer is one who perceives the difficulties, and the excellent lawyer is one who surmounts them. As J. P. Morgan is said to have remarked about his attorney, Elihu Root, "I have had many lawyers who have told me what I cannot do. Mr. Root is the only lawyer who tells me how to do what I want to do."* Unfortunately, too many lawyers seem incapable of stepping back from the papers and thinking in economic terms about a transaction: Does it really make sense? Can it be done a better way? But it is also true that for a lawyer to be effective, an understanding and perceptive client is a must.

This book, then, is meant to be a guide to both the law and the spirit of deals, an area of vital and everyday concern to the financial executive, corporate director, or investment banker. The curious thing about deals is that they generate an interest, an excitement, and a personality all their own. To the outsider, a financial transaction may indeed seem a huge stack of jargon-filled paper. But to the active participant, the transaction lives and breathes. This book is dedicated to the South Sea Bubbles and the Xeroxes, the Equity Fundings and the IBM's, the LTV's and the ITT's, the Penn Centrals and the Polaroids, that make life hazardous but interesting.

The approach taken in this book is to start at the beginning with the formation and capitalization of the corporation, then move toward a consideration of public financings and mergers and acquisitions, and finally to analyze corporate bankruptcies and reorganizations. Necessarily, this volume is not concerned with purely legal matters; the financial considerations are inextricably intertwined with the legal issues. Executives who blindly defer to lawyers or think that an analysis of the applicable law is not their concern are fundamentally mistaken. As is clear from the considerations entering into the choice of business organization and its structure, to which we now turn, law by itself only indicates the permissible options; it cannot dictate the economic sense of a transaction.

---

*P. Hoffman, *Lions in the Street* at 96 (Saturday Review Press 1973).

TWO

Forming a Business

CHOOSING THE FORM OF BUSINESS ORGANIZATION

A corporation's distinctive characteristic is its ability to insulate its stockholders and management from personal liability for its obligations. Managed by a board of directors elected by its stockholders, a corporation generally has a perpetual existence and must comply with formalities of state law to be established. Ownership interests in a corporation are evidenced by stock certificates which are readily transferable, subject to state and federal securities laws. Generally, the corporation itself is subject to taxation of its profits at a rate of 20% on the first $25,000 of taxable income, 22% on the next $25,000, and 48% on income above the $50,000 level.

By contrast, in a partnership, each general partner is personally liable for all the debts of the partnership. Although a partnership can be started with hardly any formalities, a partnership agreement may also be extremely complex. Management control, share of the profits, whether the partnership survives in the event of the death of a partner should all be specified in the partnership agreement. If there are no specific provisions, the Uniform Partnership Act, which most states have adopted, provides that unless otherwise specified in a partnership agreement, control and profits are split evenly among the partners and the partnership terminates whenever a partner dies. Generally, no federal income tax is assessed on the profits of the partnership as such; each partner is taxed individually by his or her share of the partnership income.

These general characteristics of corporations and partnerships are, however, only the beginning of a thoughtful analysis because there are a number of situations where the distinctions become blurry. For example, under Subchapter S of the Internal Revenue Code, a corporation with a limited number of stockholders may elect to be treated like a partnership for tax purposes. Specifically, a corporation with one class of stock, having no more than 10 stockholders (15 if a corporation has elected Subchapter S treatment for 5 years), with no shareholders other than individuals, estates, or certain trusts (all of whom must be United States citizens or residents) may elect to have its shareholders taxed on the taxable income of the firm in proportion to their stockholdings; the corporation itself pays no federal tax. Similarly, losses are reflected on the stockholders' returns, not the corporation's.

On the other hand, the limited liability feature is not unique to corporations. Under the Uniform Limited Partnership Act, which has been adopted by most states, limited partners may share in the profits of a partnership with limited liability as long as they take no role in the management of the partnership. To form a limited partnership, a formal state filing must be made containing certain key facts about the partnership; usually, there is also a partnership agreement which contains the more detailed business provisions which the partners may not want as part of the public filing.

Conversely, there are also certain circumstances in which stockholders of a corporation can be held personally liable. In New York, for example, the ten largest stockholders are liable for the accrued but unpaid wages of employees. Also, if a corporation is grossly undercapitalized so that it is essentially a mechanism designed to bilk potential creditors, courts may "pierce the corporate veil" and hold the shareholders personally liable.

Tax factors are certainly among the most important elements in making a decision about the form of business organization. It should be noted that major aspects of the tax code are in the process of being revised and tax authorities should be consulted as to the latest developments. An investor in a corporation is currently subject to two levels of taxation: As noted, the corporation itself is generally taxed at a rate of 48% of its profits after the first $50,000, and then the investor is taxed in turn on any dividends paid out. If nearly all profits are going to be paid out as dividends, a partnership avoids an additional layer of taxation. In addition, tax shelters are generally partnerships because of the flow through of losses generated by deductions such as depreciation or depletion allowances, which can be used to "shelter" other income of the investors. There may also be other reasons for favoring one form of business organization. Some law and investment banking firms, for example, point to the unlimited liability of partners as a source of pride to them and of confidence to clients.

But, whatever the tax advantages of partnerships, Subchapter S seems to make the tax advantages of a partnership readily available to stockholders of a corporation. Furthermore, Section 1244 of the Internal Revenue Code allows a recently formed corporation with net assets of less than $500,000 to issue all its stock under a plan whereby any losses to investors on the stock will be considered a deduction against ordinary income rather than, as usual, a capital loss. Section 1244 limits the availability of the ordinary loss to a maximum of $50,000 on a joint return.

For an investor in a high tax bracket, a Section 1244 plan vastly changes the nature of the risk taken by investing in a small business. For example, assume that the probability of a given venture's doubling in value is about equal to that of its going bankrupt. A Section 1244 plan allows a taxpayer to take an ordinary deduction if the investment fares poorly, but to pay only a capital gain tax if it is successful—a dramatic shift in financial risk. So if a new venture is unsuccessful, the combination of Subchapter S and Section 1244 may result in a corporation's producing more beneficial tax results for the investor than a partnership. In addition, a corporation may also deduct for tax purposes the cost of certain employee benefit programs, which a partnership can't do.

Furthermore, there are a number of serious drawbacks to the limited partnership form. The general partners are still exposing all their personal assets to the risks of unlimited liability, and the limited partners are completely eliminated from any management role. Simply stated, these arrangements cannot approach the subtlety of the corporate structure and still maintain limited liability.

Why then ever use a partnership? The reality is that Subchapter S has a number of practical limitations. First, there are a number of technical reporting and election requirements which have to be complied with, and some attorneys and accountants are either unfamiliar with the mechanics of the Subchapter or don't wish to bother with them. Second, there are often situations where the technical requirements of Subchapter S can't be met. For example, there may be more than fifteen investors, one of the future stockholders may be a corporation, a noneligible trust, or a foreigner, or there may be a desire to create a more complex control structure than only one class of stock.

So incorporation is not necessarily a panacea. In fact, start-up situations are often begun as partnerships and later shifted to corporate status. But as a general rule, no other form of business organization allows parties exercising control to limit their liability to such a degree, and because corporations are generally the vehicles for larger enterprises, they will be the focus of this book.

THE EVOLUTION OF THE CORPORATE FORM

Spontaneous collective organizations existed in England before the 1500s. The earliest groups were the peace guilds—neighbors or workers in a trade who were pledged to stand by each other for mutual protection. Eventually, the peace guilds among trade workers evolved into the medieval trade guilds, associations of goldsmiths, tailors, vintners, and even fishmongers, which governed the conduct and protected the rights of the craftsmen. With the rise of foreign trade during the sixteenth century, merchantmen banded together in organizations like guilds to carry on their enterprise. Members of these trading companies, like members of guilds, had the exclusive right to carry on the trade and, of course, apprentices and sons of members were admitted to the trade, as was customary in the guilds. However, for the more adventurous explorations, such as the East India trading proposed by the Company of Merchants of London, more capital was needed than could be provided by the merchants themselves. Therefore, opportunities were open to the public to subscribe and jointly hold the stock of the company. At the end of the voyage, the profits would be split in accordance with the percentage of stock ownership.

Over time, the membership notion became vestigial, and joint stock companies began to be formed without the state sanction of the early trading companies for financing projects involving high risks or large amounts of capital. By the 1600s, the Stuart kings attempted to assert their control over these entities as part of their royal prerogative, but with little long-term success. With the boom in the early 1700s, unsanctioned joint stock companies became commonplace, and state-chartered companies, such as the South Sea Company, worried that the speculative abuses engendered by these firms would adversely affect the more legitimate businesses. Thus, firms already having charters sponsored the reform South Sea Bubble Act of 1720, which substantially prohibited the further formation of corporations in England without a royal charter. Ironically, as has been discussed, the immediate result was a general crash in the market—including the securities of chartered companies. The impact of the Bubble Act was, however, relatively long lasting. As Blackstone's *Commentaries,* the classic restatement of common law, noted in 1776, "The King's consent is absolutely necessary to the erection of any corporation."*

The Bubble Act antipathy toward the formation of new ventures widely prevailed in the colonies. At the time of the American revolution, there was only one chartered corporation in the country, a Philadelphia fire insurance firm. Indeed, when, in 1781, James Madison proposed at the

*W. Blackstone, 1 COMMENTARIES ON THE LAWS OF ENGLAND at 472 (1776).

Constitutional Convention that Congress be given "a power to grant charters of incorporation," the provision was roundly defeated by an 8 to 3 vote. The states felt both that the concept was irrelevant—at that time, there were fewer than fifty chartered companies in the whole country— and that it was dangerous because of the prospect of creating state monopolies like the old British trading companies.

With the coming of the industrial revolution in the early nineteenth century, state legislatures began to bend to the pressures of the growing commercial interests by issuing special state charters in the style of the old royal grants. Practically all of these state charters specified strictly limited powers, which were quickly outgrown. The nemesis of the nineteenth-century corporate lawyer was that the actions of a corporation functioning beyond its specified powers (ultra vires) were subject to challenge; therefore, constant expansions of corporate purposes had to be cajoled out of the legislature. As a result, politics and corporate law were inextricably, and often scandalously, intertwined.

Finally, in reaction to the corruption incident to the granting and amending of special-purpose charters, states, starting with New York, began enacting more statutes authorizing corporations with general rather than special purposes. But even these statutes were severely restrictive. Often there was a maximum limit on capitalization and indebtedness, charters were generally limited to a specific term of years, and frequently the activities of corporations were limited geographically. As business became increasingly interstate in character, corporations began to shop for the most "modern" statute, the law giving management the most flexibility.

New Jersey acquired the nickname "Mother of Corporations" by passing a series of incorporation acts, which by 1896 gave the widest powers to management and eliminated most of the traditional limitations on the activities of corporations. It has been estimated that by 1900 more than 10% of the country's largest companies were incorporated in New Jersey. However, in 1913, under Governor Woodrow Wilson's sponsorship, the New Jersey legislature passed a series of reform acts, subsequently repealed, with various antimonopoly provisions. The business community did not take kindly to Wilson's reforms, and began to look for an alternative. Delaware, which in 1899 essentially adopted the New Jersey statute, welcomed America's corporations with open arms and over time has emerged as the most popular state in which to incorporate. Today, about 50% of the country's 1000 largest companies are chartered in Delaware, and more than 20% of the state's revenues come from taxes related to corporations.

To get a practical sense of the advantages of the Delaware statute from management's point of view, it is instructive to compare some of its provisions with New York's:

- Delaware's law is more flexible as to the sources of funds used for paying dividends.

- New York's statute permits stockholders to initiate amendments to the certificate of incorporation; Delaware's does not.

- New York law generally requires a two-thirds vote of outstanding shares to authorize a merger, and a majority vote of any class whose rights are being altered; the Delaware statute generally requires only majority approval and no class vote, and, indeed, for some transactions involving the issuance of new shares of stock equaling less than 20% of the then outstanding common stock, no stockholder approval is required at all.

- New York gives a broader right to stockholders who dissent from a merger to have the value of their shares appraised and paid for by the corporation.

- New York law requires stockholder approval of loans to officers and grants of stock options; Delaware's does not.

- Delaware's statute permits somewhat broader indemnification of directors than New York's does.

Critics of present corporate law, such as Ralph Nader, contend that the forum shopping by American corporations has led to the lowest common denominator in state corporate laws: Management is relatively insulated, and shareholders have few rights. As one distinguished commentator has pointed out, "The absurdity of the race for the bottom, with Delaware in the lead—tolerated and indeed fostered by corporate counsel—should arrest the conscience of the American bar."*

One specific proposal supported by Nader would involve the federal chartering of all firms listed on a national stock exchange which have more than $250 million in sales or employ more than 10,000 workers, some 700 corporations. Among Nader's suggested requirements for corporations which are federally chartered are the following:

- revised election procedures so that incumbent management can't directly nominate directors

- tighter limits on the ability of corporations to indemnify directors for wrongdoing

- more extensive disclosures of major stockholders and data regarding the social impact of the firm

- an employee's "bill of rights" including protection against dismissal if the worker reveals unethical or illegal company conduct

---

*W. Cary, *Federalism and Corporate Law: Reflections upon Delaware*, 83 YALE L. J. 663, 705 (1974).

- a built-in deconcentration bill which would compel the divestiture of assets if concentration in the concern's industry reached specified levels

Since Madison, the notion of federal chartering or licensing has periodically emerged without much lasting impact. However, Congress has already reacted to the present clamor for federal chartering by conducting a series of hearings on the current state of corporate law. Many witnesses agreed with Nader's fundamental critique, but suggested that a preferable alternative would be a federal minimum standards bill which would establish criteria for internal corporate regulation.

There is much to be said in support of the general concept of the need for reform of the state corporation laws. The crazy quilt pattern of state statutes makes little sense, especially as applied to large billion-dollar interstate operations. On the other hand, realistically, the most vital areas governing the regulation of corporations were, until recently, increasingly becoming subject to the developing notion of a common law emanating from the federal securities acts. Antitrust issues perhaps should be explicitly dealt with rather than tied to bills fundamentally aimed at the internal workings of a corporation. However, the arguments for federal chartering regulating the fairness of corporate procedures have been bolstered by recent Supreme Court rulings which, as will be discussed, have cut back the scope of the impact of the federal securities laws. Inevitably, Madison's old idea of federal chartering, especially for the largest companies, will be debated for years to come.

There are, however, reasons other than management favoritism for the popularity of Delaware law. The statute is among the most streamlined procedurally and is periodically modernized. Directors can hold a meeting by telephone; shareholders and directors can take actions through consents; the case law on permissible actions is clearer, more comprehensive, and, critics argue, more favorable to management than most states; and New York corporate lawyers are often willing to give opinions on Delaware law without consulting and paying for local counsel, while, generally, they feel obligated to engage local counsel in other states. A recent indication of the ability of Delaware to adapt to changing circumstances is the new tender statute. When other states, such as Indiana and Ohio, began writing state laws protecting incumbent management from tender offers, the Delaware lawyers, with a mind to business, hastened their own tender bill through the legislature in a month.

What must be remembered is that a key reason for the popularity of flexible statutes such as Delaware's was the archaic restrictions of their nineteenth-century predecessors. In revising the corporate laws, the inculcation of broad public policy and fundamental fairness is laudable, but care must be taken to assure that the well-intentioned, benevolent provision of today doesn't become the anachronistic straitjacket of tomorrow.

In corporate law, the current general presumption is that a large public corporation should be incorporated in Delaware. If a company is not publicly held, it may well not be worth the effort, and the local statute may be perfectly adequate. In the past, if a major stockholder was a foreigner, New Jersey's law was often preferable to Delaware's, because under the Delaware statute, the ownership of stock certificates itself created jurisdiction in the Delaware courts over the foreigner. Recently, however, that provision was found to be unconstitutional by the Supreme Court. Therefore, in fact, Delaware incorporation is the most common for a public concern and is likely to continue to be so for the foreseeable future.

SETTING UP THE CORPORATION

The Certificate of Incorporation

To establish a corporation, the incorporator files the certificate of incorporation, the basic document on which the very existence of a corporation rests, with the secretary of state of the appropriate state. In some states, such as Delaware, the certificate must also be filed in the county in which the corporation's registered office is to be located. Under Delaware law, an incorporator, although usually an attorney, may be any individual or even another corporation. The chief function of the incorporator is, generally, signing the certificate. Although there are service companies which will do the actual filing for a fee, one can also mail in the certificate (which, in some states, is called the articles of incorporation or the charter), making sure to include the applicable fees.

The truth of the matter is that there is no reason why incorporation as such has to be an expensive process—particularly if standardized provisions are used. For example, in Delaware, there is a $25 fee for filing and indexing the certificate, a minimum tax of $10 upon incorporation, and an annual franchise fee of $20 if not over 1000 shares are authorized and their par value is $100 or less. In addition, there are minor copying fees. What does take time and cost money are documents tailored to the unique facts of a particular situation.

A key problem is the name of the corporation. First, under many state laws, including Delaware's, the name must contain words such as "Inc.," "Incorporated," or "Limited." Most state laws also prohibit new companies from having names similar to existing firms. For that reason, before actually filing a certificate, some lawyers will check with the local office of the secretary of state to see whether a given name will encounter problems. Many a lawyer has been quite embarrassed by having a certificate bounce.

Regardless of a firm's state of incorporation, if it does conduct activities in other states, it must qualify to do business in those jurisdictions. For example, a Pittsburgh-based company, incorporated in Delaware, with a New York sales office, will have to qualify to do business in both Pennsylvania and New York. Essentially, this involves a simple filing which puts authorities in those states on notice of the corporation's presence. Once a firm gives notice that it is conducting activities in a state, it may, of course, be subject to local taxation. Many larger firms are qualified in all fifty states. It makes sense to check a name in the states a firm has to qualify in to do business as a "foreign" corporation, because the name can be rejected for use in any one of them.

A story is often told to young lawyers about a *Fortune* 100 corporation which had changed its name and was gradually qualifying across the country. A smart aleck, however, beat this industrial giant to the punch by incorporating his own firm under the new name in California. This entrepreneur was bought out, and is said to be enjoying the sun on the Riviera.

A certificate will sometimes name the initial board of directors. At their first meeting, these directors will adopt bylaws and appoint officers. Alternatively, if directors are not named in the certificate, the incorporator may elect directors and officers and adopt bylaws even before any shares of stock are sold.

Well-drafted certificates may be quite simple, stating principally the name of the corporation, its registered office in the state (usually, in effect, a mailbox), its purpose, the authorized capital stock and the names of the initial directors, if any, and the incorporator. (A sample simple certificate for a Delaware corporation is included as Appendix A to this book.) Some eager beavers, working from old precedents, like to write long descriptions of the powers of the corporation, but this can easily lead to trouble if some unforeseen future purpose is omitted. At least for a Delaware corporation, it's generally preferable to state broadly, as is permitted by statute, that the purposes are to engage in any activity permissible under the Delaware Corporation Law. In some states, such as New York, some specific purposes must be stated. It is imperative in those cases that a general "basket" clause be added at the end of the list to pick up unforeseen situations. Under Delaware law, a certificate may be generally amended by the holders of a majority of shares acting upon the recommendation of the board of directors.

The certificate is also the best place to formulate any complexities in the management or ownership structure of the corporation. For example, the relative rights and privileges of all classes of stock in a corporation are specified in the certificate, or, pursuant to a provision in it, directors may be allowed to designate the specifics in an instrument called a "certificate of designation." Thus, the terms of a preferred stock would either be part of the certificate or be included in a certificate of designation. If there is a desire to structure a balance in the directorships or to require cumulative voting, as will be discussed, the certificate is an appropriate place for such provision.

Copies of a corporation's certificate are available at the offices of the pertinent secretary of state. In connection with financial transactions, lawyers often will ask for the certificate, as amended (which would include all certificates of designation), certified by the secretary of state, a long-form, good-standing certificate listing all amendments to the certificate (with tax advice about the paying of local corporate taxes) and a "bring down" telegram updating the good-standing certificate through the close of business of the day before the closing of the deal.

The Bylaws

Unlike the certificate of incorporation, bylaws are never filed with state authorities. They may range from brief statements to comprehensive treatises. Often, bylaw provisions repeat the existing state law in great detail, which can be needlessly restrictive if the statute changes. The alternative approach is to have very terse bylaws, relying on the applicable provisions of state law, which govern many situations anyway. However, bylaws are much easier to change than certificates because usually the directors themselves may amend them. On balance, detailed bylaws can be quite helpful in guiding corporate officers who, realistically, do not have at hand annotated corporate statutes about what should be done in particular circumstances.

A typical set of bylaws might have, among other provisions, sections on (1) how meetings of stockholders are called and conducted; (2) the duties of the board of directors: how and when they meet, how they can be removed, how vacancies are filled and how they are elected, and what committees of the board, such as the executive committee, may perform its functions; (3) the duties of officers; (4) how books and records are kept; (5) how share transfers are made; (6) indemnification provisions for officers and directors; and (7) requirements for amendments. (Sample bylaws for a Delaware corporation are included as Appendix B to this book.) The drafting of bylaws may, however, become quite intricate when there are allocation-of-control problems: the functions of various officers, the power of directors in various situations, the ability to call meetings— all require thoughtful analysis.

A typical problem in bylaw draftsmanship is the seemingly simple issue of how a board of directors meeting may be called. If there are competing factions, the mechanics become complex. For example, usually the description of the functions of officers is quite sparse, and the president alone or a high quorum of the directors has the power to call a meeting. But suppose the president is the entrepreneur, and the other directors are wary that they may not be kept well informed. It may be desirable for these directors initially to select the chairman of the board and give that officer, as well as the president, the right to call meetings. In addition, the number of directors needed to call a meeting may be kept at a low level, and longer notice of a meeting, perhaps by registered mail, may be required.

Similarly, care must be taken in the standard provision authorizing committees of the board. Under Delaware law, a committee of the board, such as an executive committee, may generally have all of the power of the board, if authorized in either the bylaws or a specific enabling resolution. An executive committee, however, may not amend the bylaws or the certificate of incorporation, adopt a plan of merger, recommend the sale or liquidation of the concern, or, unless the bylaws otherwise state, authorize new securities. Thus, a board majority may be able to get around the blocking power of a pesky minority by stacking a powerful executive committee.

Minutes

Specific actions of a board, such as approval of a given contract, are reflected in the minutes of the corporation. After incorporation, the initial board of directors meets and first approves the bylaws, elects officers, and authorizes the initial sale of stock. Then the routine aspects of starting a business are dealt with: approving the form of seal (if a seal is desired), authorizing qualification in certain states, and authorizing the opening of a bank account. Under Delaware law, there is no legal requirement that any minimum amount of money be invested in a corporation. Indeed, no stock need be sold. In fact, some corporations exist for months purely as shells until stock is sold.

Companies have varying styles about what is included in minutes. Some want a record of the contents of discussions. Most larger companies seem to prefer very sparse minutes which reflect conclusions rather than the arguments about an issue. In financial transactions, lawyers often read the past 5 years' minutes; the experience is rarely edifying. Occasionally, however, the minutes give clues to incidents or documents not otherwise brought to the lawyers' attention.

In deciding whether a corporation is entitled to take a particular action, lawyers first examine the state statute, then the certificate, the bylaws, and the specific minutes authorizing the action. Surprising as it may seem, one repeatedly runs across examples of actions which were not duly authorized. For example, the old California corporation statute, replaced as of January 1, 1977, stated that all directors' meetings must be held at the principal place of business of a corporation unless otherwise specified in the bylaws or by a resolution. Needless to say, many meetings were invalidly held, simply because the bylaws were poorly drafted and did not state that meetings could be held anywhere. Similarly, if the corporation existed at the turn of the century, you might find its life of limited duration—say 75 years from 1896—which is not very helpful after 1971. So, unfortunately, lawyers fumbling through stacks of paper are quite necessary in checking out a deal—because other lawyers may well have botched the job.

Even though formalistic in nature, resolutions are also, unfortunately, often badly done. The most common problem is that they are too narrow. For example, a particular draft of contract may be approved; then, because of an unexpected event, a term changes. If the resolution does not give officers broad powers to be flexible on terms within the general parameters approved by the board, another meeting may have to be called.

In summary, the basic instruments for forming a new corporation may range from the simple to the highly complex. Unfortunately, no rule of thumb is appropriate; careful thought about the particular circumstances is required.

THE ALLOCATION OF CONTROL

In structuring a new corporation, there are two fundamental allocation issues: power and money. Obviously, the division of control and the split of the profits or losses are related, but they are not necessarily congruent. The most obvious example is in large corporations where management with relatively small stockholdings may, in fact, be in control. In a small venture, the entrepreneur may feel that control is imperative, even though other investors have a large economic stake.

Alternative Control Devices

There are a wide variety of alternative control mechanisms. To put this discussion in perspective, however, the availability of these devices does not necessarily mean that it's wise to use them. All parties have a common interest in a smooth-running company, and too intricate a mechanism of controls tends to degenerate into a corporate obstacle course.

Classes of stock   Share ownership by itself in a firm with one class of stock represents a system of allocation, but it has serious limitations. First, with one class of stock, the holder of 51% of the shares generally has absolute control. Second, the system is not responsive to changing events: Whether the firm is doing poorly or is booming, the control pattern remains the same. A more explicit way of handling the problem is setting up multiple classes of stock, each having specified control rights. For example, a firm might have Class A and Class B common stock with identical features except that Class A holders are entitled to elect two directors and Class B, one. Similarly, the preferred stock of a corporation can have the power to elect certain directors, with the rest chosen by the common stockholders. Sometimes, however, multiple classes or types of stock are undesirable. For example, a corporation with multiple classes of stock would not meet the requirements of Subchapter S. The classification of stock may also have an undesirable permanence.

Voting agreements   An alternative to classes of stock is shareholder voting agreements, whereby certain shareholders agree on whom they will vote for as directors. Under Delaware law, a voting agreement is enforceable as long as it does not have a term longer than 10 years; however, an agreement may be renewed in the last 2 years of each term.

There are two fundamental difficulties with shareholder agreements: They are not self-executing, and a shareholder's bankruptcy may make them ineffective. For example, if embittered shareholders should decide to breach the agreement, they could vote for an opposing slate of directors—and the deed would be done, agreement or not. Certainly there are legal remedies for breach of contract, but they may be too late if the vote has already been taken. A damages suit may also be futile. Conceivably one party to a shareholders' agreement could have assets of little value but could cause a great deal of harm. Furthermore, if the shareholder should go bankrupt, the obligation to comply with the agreement may be disaffirmed at the option of the bankruptcy court. Disaffirmation is actually likely, since the restrictions of an agreement would probably limit the marketability of the bankrupt's stock.

Incidentally, it is quite common to see agreements signed by all the directors of a company, assuring the investor a slot on the board. These contracts are often prime examples of dangerous legal overkill. Under Delaware law, such an agreement may very well be unenforceable because it represents an abdication on the part of the directors of their fiduciary responsibilities. As individual stockholders, directors can agree how their votes will be cast. But in their capacities as directors, they cannot limit their scope of action.

Irrevocable proxies   A different approach is an irrevocable proxy. Essentially, a proxy is a simple legal document, often a card, which authorizes another party to cast a shareholder's vote. As a general rule, proxies, unless stated otherwise, are revocable. In any event, proxies are generally effective for a limited time—in Delaware, 3 years. However, if a proxy is "coupled with an interest"—for example, given as security for a loan or an obligation in a shareholders' agreement—it can be made irrevocable in most states, including Delaware. Through the means of an irrevocable proxy, an allocation of control can become self-executing. In the event of the bankruptcy of the shareholder, however, a court may still attempt to revoke the proxy.

Mechanically, there is a rich variety of alternative ways the proxy can be used. For example, in a corporation with cumulative voting, the proxies added to an investor's own shares will, in effect, give him a particular representation on the board. If additional flexibility is desired, such a proxy can be made revocable upon certain conditions—for example, a repayment of a loan or a year with earnings above a certain level.

Voting trusts   Another possibility is a voting trust. Participants in a voting trust deposit the shares of stock they own into a trust in return for voting trust certificates. For the life of the voting trust, the trustees vote the deposited shares in the manner specified in the voting trust agreement. A voting trust under Delaware law can have an initial term no longer than 10 years but, like stockholder agreements, can be renewed 2 years before the expiration of the term. The advantages of a voting trust are that it is self-executing and the bankruptcy of a depositor does not affect it. On the other hand, voting trusts are complex, and stockholders dislike the idea of surrendering their shares.

Restrictive covenants   A different approach, which will be discussed later in detail, is to have agreements called covenants embodied in debt or preferred securities banning specified corporate actions, such as dividends above a certain level or mergers or investments above a stated dollar amount, without the permission of certain security holders. Alternatively, it is not unusual for preferred stock to specify that in the event certain conditions occur, such as the failure to pay dividends for a period of time, a reallocation of directors will be triggered, with the preferred holders getting additional representation; but if management is doing well, it has complete control.

Close corporation statutes   Incorporation under a special close corporation statute, designed for companies owned by a small group of stockholders, is another possibility. Unlike large public corporations, which are relatively liquid and in which ownership is often separated from control, small businesses often have control conflicts which can deadlock the board, devastate the business, and lead to gross abuse of minority stockholders. The premise of close corporation laws is that there should be flexible mechanisms for resolving these disputes.

For example, under Delaware law, a close corporation can be established by filing a certificate of incorporation which specifically states that the firm is a close corporation. Among other requirements, there can be no more than thirty holders of the corporation's stock. This type of close corporation has a number of unique attributes. First, agreements restricting the powers of directors are enforceable. Second, if desired, the certificate may state that the firm is being managed by its stockholders rather than a board of directors. Third, there can be a number of deadlock-breaking provisions. For example, the Delaware Court of Chancery may appoint a provisional director (who cannot be a stockholder or creditor of the company) for a concern if its directors are deadlocked and one-half of the existing directors and the holders of one-third of the stock, assuming one class of voting securities, request the appointment. Or, if the business is specified to be managed by the shareholders, the Court of Chancery may, upon the application of any stockholder, appoint a custodian or a principal director.

Informality governs; the Delaware statute specifically states that the corporation can operate internally like a partnership, including the division of profits. To add further flexibility, the statute allows a certificate to have a provision stating that the corporation can be dissolved upon the petition of a given number of shareholders or a certain percentage of the stock.

General Considerations

Whichever system of allocation is used, care should be taken to make sure it really works. For example, assurance about a certain number of directorships means little if the size of the board can be expanded. Of course, if one's objective in getting board representation is to acquire the ability to block certain key actions, the quorum required for board decisions should be carefully examined. For example, if all decisions can be made by a majority vote of the board, having two out of five positions has little practical impact; but a requirement of a two-thirds vote for any mergers, employee contracts, and major expenditures would give the investor effective veto power. Finally, it is important to make sure that the bylaws or certificate cannot be amended to alter the agreed-upon allocation.

Establishing a system of controls which works effectively is not enough, however. The more fundamental question has to be asked whether a truly unbreakable mechanism is sought or whether, in the event of deadlock, a means of arriving at conflict resolution is desired. The close corporation laws, recognizing the problem, feature stalemate breakers. A lawyer with a little ingenuity can think of a whole flock of additional possibilities of breaking deadlocks. For example, arbitration clauses are among the more popular possibilities.

The key point is that tying a corporation up in order to allocate control without a readily available mechanism to resolve or compromise disputes may well be senseless. Unfortunately, the story of the stockholder in a growing, poor-dividend-paying small venture, who cannot get out, while the majority stockholder receives a handsome but arguably reasonable salary, is an often-repeated tale. The best way to solve the problems of the future is to think of them today.

OTHER TAX CONSIDERATIONS IN INCORPORATION

Tax law is quicksand, minefields, and barbed wire all in one, and must be handled with the utmost care. Even the relatively simple transaction of incorporating a new business may contain tax problems.

The purchase of stock for cash is a nontaxable transaction. But if property or services are being transferred to a corporation in exchange for stock, the tax situation becomes more complicated. As a general rule, property transfers to a corporation in exchange for stock are tax-free, under Section 351 of the Internal Revenue Code, provided that the owners of the property are in control of the corporation. Control, for this purpose, is defined to be at least 80% of the outstanding voting stock and 80% of all other outstanding stock. However, if cash or other property is received by the property exchangers, gain will be recognized to the extent of those assets. On the other hand, stock issued for services rendered, or to be rendered, to the corporation is ordinary income to the shareholders and is deductible by the firm. The services are not considered a contribution of property, and therefore an employee is not included as a member of the control group for purposes of the 80% test.

These tax requirements necessitate careful planning before incorporation. For example, if a partnership were to bring in outside investors and give them 25% of the stock at the time of its transformation into a corporation, the incorporation transaction would be taxable to the partners. However, new capital brought in after the formation and not part of the original incorporation plan will not result in a taxable transaction. Similarly, a partnership that is being incorporated with employees receiving stock may be surprised not only to have the employees taxed at ordinary income rates on the value of the stock they receive, but also to have the partners taxed on their property contributions.

However, a taxable transaction as such is not always a bad thing. If the partners, for example, have a loss on the assets they are contributing, they may prefer a taxable transaction in order to recognize the loss at an earlier date. The lesson: Even simple transactions may have unexpected tax consequences. Consult an accountant or lawyer about the tax situation before there is a lot of unnecessary grief.

The Role of Directors

MECHANICS

According to Delaware law, "The business and affairs of every corporation . . . shall be managed by or under the direction of a board of directors . . ."; other states have similar provisions.

The initial board of directors of a company is usually named in the certificate of incorporation, and in Delaware may consist of one or more individuals. Subsequently, directors are generally elected on an annual basis at stockholder meetings. In companies subject to SEC requirements, a proxy card and statement are mailed to the stockholders every year with information about the nominees including their background and their transactions with the company and the stockholders.

At the annual meeting, the chief executive usually gives a prepared speech and answers inquiries. Sometimes corporate gadflies such as Wilma Soss or one of the Gilbert brothers will ask piercing questions, but usually meetings are calm, family affairs. A few years ago, various social reform groups such as Campaign GM attempted to turn annual meetings into debating forums, but the transformation was not long-lasting. However, there has been a long-range beneficial effect. Some of the standard proposals of the Gilberts, such as audit committees, are being increasingly adopted, and the SEC, by rules, has forced management to put responsible positions to a stockholders' vote. Nevertheless, it is still true that management's control over the proxy machinery and the annual meeting itself is usually absolute.

Directors will usually meet at least quarterly, to declare dividends if for no other reason, and frequently more often. Under Delaware law, meetings may be held anywhere and, indeed, can be convened by means of a conference telephone call. Alternatively, all the directors may execute a form of unanimous consent, and the effect is the same as if the action had been taken at a regular meeting of the board.

Frequently there are committees of directors, such as an executive committee or a finance committee, composed of selected directors, which are authorized by the bylaws and can perform nearly all the functions of the board. These committees are often composed of "inside" directors—officers of the corporation or lawyers or investment bankers who are regularly retained by the corporation. There has been a trend toward also establishing audit and compensation committees of "outside" directors to review with the corporation's auditors its financial record and the salary levels of executives, and, recently, an "outside" audit committee has been made mandatory by the New York Stock Exchange for all companies listed on it. The functions of directors can vary widely from active management of the firm to passive enforcement of the executive teams' recommendations.

GENERAL RESPONSIBILITIES: THE THEORY

In theory, directors may not abdicate their basic supervisory function. Even though management may make the day-to-day decisions and, in effect, run a firm, the directors are supposed to make active efforts to be aware of the performance of the enterprise and to bring about change if necessary. Directors are deemed to be fiduciaries for all the stockholders of a company: they have a public trust to protect diligently the broad interests of the firm rather than representing the block of votes which elected them. The classic formulation of the applicable standard was stated by a Delaware court in 1939:

> Corporate officers and directors are not permitted to use their position of trust and confidence to further their private interests. . . . A public policy, existing through the years, and derived from a profound knowledge of human characteristics and motives, has established a rule that demands of a corporate officer or director, peremptorily and inexorably, the most scrupulous observance of his duty, not only affirmatively to protect the interests of the corporation committed to his charge, but also to refrain from doing anything that would work injury to the corporation, or to deprive it of profit

or advantage which his skill and ability might properly bring to it, or to enable it to make in the reasonable and lawful exercise of its powers. The rule that requires an undivided and unselfish loyalty to the corporation demands that there shall be no conflict between duty and self-interest.*

The corporate opportunity doctrine evolved by the courts establishes at a practical level the principle of a director's undivided loyalty to a corporation. Essentially, directors may not avail themselves of business opportunities which a corporation would have a reasonable expectancy of taking for itself. Thus, signing contracts with customers of the corporation for goods it could have produced, buying property the firm would have been interested in for a plant, or making profits on assets or products purchased from the company if it could have made a deal itself might well result in liability. However, if the corporation could not reasonably have taken advantage of the opportunity itself or did not have a prior involvement in the field, the doctrine is inapplicable. Unfortunately, many of these situations are ambiguous, and counsel should be consulted. In any event, it is prudent to try to build as clear a record of impartial judgment as possible.

All this is not to say that directors may not make errors. Indeed, the courts have developed a "business judgment" rule which protects directors from liability if they used their best judgment as to an issue, even though the decision was a mistake. They must, however, use that standard of care that a prudent man would use in handling his own affairs.

DUTIES AND RESTRICTIONS

In addition to the duties imposed by state corporate law, directors have specific responsibilities and potential liabilities under the federal securities laws. Furthermore, they are subject to restrictions on their activities and must comply with reporting requirements.

The Sale of Securities and Filings with the SEC

Under the Securities Act of 1933, offerings to the public of corporate securities must be registered with the Securities and Exchange Commission in the absence of a specific exemption. If any part of the prospectus used in connection with a public offering contains a material misstatement or has a material omission, every director of the issuer at the time of filing, among others, is personally liable to a purchaser. The standard is quite strict: Directors are liable even though they never signed the filing. Indeed, directors may be liable even though they never read the prospectus or even knew about it.

*Guth v. Loft, Inc., 5 A.2d 503, 510 (1939).

There are, however, limited defenses provided by the 1933 Act. A director will be able to establish a due diligence defense as to a part of the prospectus not based on the authority of an expert, such as an accountant, only if after reasonable investigation, the director had reasonable ground to believe and did believe that the statements were true and there were no omissions. So in an unexpertized portion of a prospectus, the fact that a director knew of no error is not enough to establish a defense; a reasonable investigation had to be made, and there had to be a positive belief in the truth of the material. A director's liabilities and defenses regarding the sales of securities will be dealt with in more depth later in this book. The pertinent point for now is that the statute is quite severe.

Other documents filed by a corporation with the SEC subject directors to similar liability. Section 18(a) of the Securities Exchange Act of 1934, which deals with the trading of securities, states that any person who causes any proxy statement (both statements used for annual elections and those used for mergers and other special actions), a tender offer filing, a periodic company report, or a personal holdings report to contain untrue statements or have material omissions will be liable to those relying on these documents. Furthermore, Section 20 of the 1934 Act states that persons who, directly or indirectly, control a corporation which has liability under the 1934 Act shall also be liable unless the controlling persons can show that they acted in good faith and did not directly or indirectly induce the violation.

Reporting Requirements

Each of a public issuer's directors, officers, and beneficial owners of more than 10% of any publicly owned class of security is regarded as an insider and is required under Section 16(a) of the 1934 Act to file with the SEC and the pertinent stock exchange a Form 3 statement, which, essentially, discloses the holdings of the insider. Form 3, which is required even if no securities are owned, must be filed within 10 days after a director is elected to office. After the initial filing of a Form 3, any changes in ownership must be disclosed on a Form 4 filed with the SEC and the pertinent exchange within 10 days after the end of the month in which the change occurred.

In addition to reports on Forms 3 and 4, the annual proxy material sent to stockholders contains information about the directors, usually provided by the directors in response to a company questionnaire. Among the items covered in a proxy statement are employment for the last 5 years, ownership of securities, any arrangement or understanding with any person regarding the director's election, remuneration of the director if compensation exceeds $40,000, any money owed the company, and any transaction between the company and the director or any relatives. In addition, if the company should make a tender offer for another corporation, the employment background of each director would have to be listed for the past 10 years on the schedule required to be filed with the SEC. Much of this information is also contained in registration statements filed by the company, as will be discussed. All this information is public, readily available at the offices of the SEC.

Liability for Short-Swing Profits

Directors, as insiders, are subject to the provisions of Section 16(b) of the 1934 Act, which expunge any profit made by a director, among others, as a result of purchases and sales of a company's stock within a 6-month period. Any recovered profits are paid over to the company. The objective of the section is to deter insiders from trading in and out of a stock on inside knowledge, and the provision has been strictly construed by the courts.

This 6-month period is calculated from the date of any transaction and may be carried backward as well as forward. For example, suppose a director purchases 100 shares of company stock on January 1 and 100 additional shares on February 1, and then sells the first 100 shares purchased in January on July 15. Even though the particular certificates sold were held for more than 6 months, the director would be liable under Section 16(b), since the sale was within 6 months of the February 1 purchase. Similarly, a sale in February followed by a purchase in July would fall within the ambit of Section 16(b).

If Section 16(b) is violated, any security owner of the issuing corporation may sue on behalf of the corporation to recover the full amount of the profit realized by the insider from the short-swing transaction. In determining the amount of profit recoverable in such a suit where more than one purchase and sale within a 6-month period is involved, the purchase and sale prices are not matched on the basis of the purchase and sale prices of particular stock certificates. Rather, the profit is computed on the basis of matching the lowest purchase price with the highest sale price within the 6-month period. As a result, the short-swing profit recoverable may be sizable even when the insider has actually incurred a loss in the overall transaction.

Short Sales and Arbitrage Transactions

Under Section 16(c) of the Exchange Act, it is unlawful for directors to sell equity securities of a public company they do not own or, if a director does own the securities sold, to fail to deliver the certificates representing such securities within 20 days after the sale or to fail to place such certificates in the mails or other usual channels of transportation within 5 days after the sale (with certain limited exceptions).

In addition, under Rule 16(e)-1, it is unlawful for any director of a public company to effect any foreign or domestic arbitrage transaction in any equity security of that issuer unless the director reports the transaction as required by Section 16(a) of the Exchange Act and accounts for any profits as provided under Section 16(b). In essence, arbitrage must be reported and no profit can be made.

Trading on the Basis of Inside Information and Tipping

Section 10(b) of the Exchange Act and Rule 10b-5 make unlawful all fraudulent practices in the purchase or sale of securities. As will be discussed later in connection with public offerings, the judicial interpretation of Rule 10b-5 is constantly evolving. In recent years, the Supreme Court has narrowed the potential scope of the rule, but the situation is still very much in flux. However, the courts and the SEC have consistently taken the position that if an insider purchases or sells securities on the basis of material information not available to the public, the insider will be liable in damages to the other party to the transaction.

The information not disclosed, or disclosed inaccurately, must be material, a fact to which a reasonable investor would attach importance in determining whether to buy or sell the security. Examples of such material information are knowledge of an impending change of dividend rate or capital structure, a stock split or stock dividend, an important financing, tender offer, a major licensing agreement, a joint venture agreement, a substantial change in stock ownership, a shift in the control of the company, a proposed merger or acquisition, and other important developments affecting the business, including quarterly or annual income information.

Rule 10b-5 is not an absolute bar to directors' trading. All it requires is that, if a director knows or reasonably should have known of material facts that have not been publicly disclosed or of material facts that have been inaccurately publicized, the director must not trade in the securities of the corporation until the public disclosure has been made and absorbed by the market or the inaccuracies have been publicly corrected.

What constitutes public disclosure of inside information before an insider may trade depends on the factual situation. However, the principle which should be followed is that before an insider trades, dissemination of the news item must have been sufficient to provide the investment community with a reasonable opportunity to assess the materiality of the news item. For example, the American Stock Exchange Company Manual suggests that insiders should wait for at least 24 hours after the general publication of the release in a national medium.

An insider also violating Rule 10b-5 may be subject to money damages if material information is disclosed to third parties, tippees, who trade on that information, even where the insider in no way personally profits from the information.

Great efforts must be made by directors to avoid a tipping violation, since it is easy to transmit inside information inadvertently. Even where the tipping takes place in a casual conversation and there is no intention that the tippee profit from it, the tipper may incur personal liability.

The leading decisions dealing with insider trading and tipping grew out of the discovery of major deposits of copper, silver, and zinc in Canada by the Texas Gulf Sulphur Company.

In November of 1963, samples were taken which indicated the possibility of rich ore deposits. Texas Gulf acquired the neighboring property and resumed drilling in March. In early April it issued a press release downplaying its findings, but by late April it announced that it had, indeed, discovered a rich mine. In November, the stock was selling at $17 per share, in early April at $28, in late April at $37, and in mid-May at $58.

Various employees and directors bought shares of Texas Gulf before the public release was made of the discovery. A flurry of litigation followed, with both the SEC and private claimants suing the insiders and Texas Gulf for violations of the securities laws. In the end, Texas Gulf was held to have violated the law in issuing its overly pessimistic early press release, and the insiders were forced to disgorge their profits and, in some cases, the profits of the persons to whom they gave tips. In addition, nearly $3 million was paid by Texas Gulf in settlement of the claims of traders who claimed they were adversely affected by the misleading series of press releases. The law in this area is still not crystal clear. Whatever the precise nuances, however, it is certain that the scope of exposure is broad.

Misleading Public Statements

A related problem involves misleading public statements by corporate insiders which affect the market price of a company's securities. It has been held that Rule 10b-5 is violated whenever statements are made in a manner calculated to influence the investing public if such statements are false or misleading or so incomplete as to mislead. This is so whether or not corporate officials contemporaneously trade in the securities of the corporation. However, it may be better not to say anything than to rush into print with a statement that contains inaccuracies.

Forms of Proceedings

In addition to actions taken by the SEC, private parties may sue directors for breach of their responsibilities. There are basically two forms of civil lawsuits: individuals suing for damages themselves and stockholders suing on behalf of the corporation.

Since the revision of the Federal Rules of Civil Procedure in 1966, a great deal of litigation on behalf of individual parties has been cast in the form of class actions—suits in which relief is claimed for the benefit of a whole class of individuals allegedly injured by the same act or omission. A typical class action might involve a claim that all those who had purchased a particular security during a specified period had done so in reliance on a material misstatement and that consequently each such individual was entitled to damages. Although in recent years the federal courts have tended to be less receptive to class actions than was originally the case, including the imposition of stiff notice requirements, the mechanism still exists by which a large number of relatively small claims may be aggregated in a single lawsuit.

Derivative lawsuits are brought on behalf of the corporation by stockholders who assert that the corporation as an entity has been harmed as a result of the wrongful actions of the defendant officers or directors and that consequently the defendants should pay damages to it. Again, the amount in controversy can be far in excess of any damages suffered by the stockholder who initiates the litigation. If the complaining stockholder wins, the court may order the payment of attorney's fees. Since in determining the size of the legal fee the court considers the size of the total recovery by the corporation, there are significant financial incentives for a lawyer to undertake a stockholders' derivative suit.

Insurance and Indemnification

Under Delaware law, a corporation is entitled to indemnify directors in a private party suit if the directors acted in good faith, in a manner which the directors reasonably believed to be in, or not opposed to, the best interests of the corporation, and if the directors had no reasonable cause to believe their conduct unlawful. If the suit is a derivative action on behalf of the corporation, the same standard applies except that if a director is adjudicated liable for negligence or misconduct, a court will have to approve any indemnification. The determination for eligibility for indemnification must be made on a case-by-case basis by disinterested directors, by the stockholders, or, under certain circumstances, by independent legal counsel.

Most Delaware corporate bylaws have indemnification provisions which essentially track the state statute. However, it is conceivable that the concern would not have sufficient assets to pay the indemnification even if applicable, and, of course, these provisions do not cover all situations.

As the potential liability to outside directors has increased, there has been a growing insistence by potential directors that they be covered by liability insurance. Today, more than 80% of New York Stock Exchange companies carry directors' insurance in an average amount exceeding $8 million. However, in the wake of major recent payments on these policies, the insurance companies, led by Lloyd's of London, the largest firm in this field, have begun to tighten up the coverage. First, the deductible amount is increasing. Second, the policies have become loaded with critical loopholes, including ones excluding claims related to foreign payoffs. Furthermore, insurance companies have increasingly disputed their liability for payments when fraud is alleged or criminal actions are involved. Yet, the costs for this diminishing coverage is very high. For example, a $25 million policy excluding foreign payments for one major corporation has a premium exceeding $500,000 annually, and some companies have difficulties obtaining a policy at all. As a result, insurance and indemnification are comforting but not absolutely certain protection.

DIRECTORS: MYTHS AND REALITIES

In the abstract, the corporate form seems a model for a capitalistic democracy, a popular rule of dollars. That, at least, is the theory. The courts and the SEC rely to a heavy extent on directors to assure that the system functions in the intended manner. The eye mists with the judicial vision of the selfless director, guardian of the small investor, poring over an infinity of documents, verifying all facts, ever skeptical of management's analysis, and periodically offering pearls of sage advice.

In fact, however, most corporations are governed by top management. Indeed, management often selects the candidates proposed for the board. Even when matters are decided by board members, it may be by the committees authorized to have nearly the full power of the board, such as the executive or the finance committees, which may be dominated by inside directors.

For example, Professor Myles L. Mace of the Harvard Business School made a detailed empirical study of directors and came to the conclusion that the myths and realities of the role of directors are quite disparate. Despite legal doctrine, Mace finds that directors do not generally establish basic corporate strategies or ask discerning questions. However, Mace concludes that the background of directors may be useful in considering corporate problems of a generalized nature: alternative means of financing, for example. Mace also argues that however pro forma the gestures, the mere fact of having a board tempers the inclinations of company management. The board, in effect, acts as a corporate conscience. Finally, Mace points out that in certain crisis situations, the board may be forced to act—for example, at the death of a president who has not designated a successor.

One reason why directors of large corporations often do little has been that they have no constituency other than corporate management. As a practical matter, their election has been engineered by the present chief executive officer—not by the amorphous public stockholders. As was pointed out in the 1932 classic, *The Modern Corporation and Private Property,* by Berle and Means, ownership and control have become quite different concepts. In most large corporations, there is no single shareholder or group of related shareholders with more than, say, 20% of the stock.

However, the days of directorships as sinecures may well be ending. Economic conditions have changed. When executives assumed never-ending and consistent prosperity, the risks of nonfeasance seemed limited, whatever the SEC's position. But the events of the turbulent seventies have already altered that perspective. As the courts and the SEC increasingly demanded a higher standard of diligence from directors, the shifting economic climate all of a sudden made the theoretical risk of liability a realistic fear.

The new dilemmas of directors is indicated in the SEC's July 1975 report on the role of directors in the Stirling Homex fraud. Stirling Homex was a manufacturer and installer of modular dwelling units. In order to keep the stock price up, Stirling recorded fictitious sales, earnings, and assets. Among Stirling's two "outside" directors, not members of management, was Theodore W. Kheel, a noted labor attorney.

In examining the fraud, the SEC found that over a two-year period there had been only seven meetings of the board and most had been perfunctory. Several were conducted by phone, and few questions were asked. No memoranda, agendas, or detailed financial reports were presented to the board. The SEC concluded that Kheel did not obtain a sufficiently firm grasp of Stirling's business or accounting practices to make an informed judgment as to its business affairs or the integrity of its officers. When Kheel did ask questions, he accepted superficial answers without further inquiry. Therefore, in the SEC's opinion, Kheel did not provide the shareholders with any significant protection.

The Stirling Homex situation is important because the SEC complaint was generic: it dealt with Kheel's entire performance, not a specific incident, and said the performance did not meet their standards. Kheel, however, has a reputation as a particularly able attorney, and if he did an unsatisfactory job, there are many other directors in this country doing even less. The realization hit many directors: Stirling Homex tolls for thee.

At the same time, however, that the SEC is demanding a higher standard of care from outside directors, it is also pushing companies to have more of them. The SEC has urged the New York Stock Exchange to require listed companies to have a majority of outside directors on their boards, and the Exchange responded by requesting that at least audit committees dominated by outside directors be established. Also, in several situations involving litigation of corporate behavior, the SEC has insisted that, as part of the settlement, boards contain additional outside directors. According to a survey done by *Business Week,* corporations are facing a worsening problem as they try to fill directorships. The combination of bad business conditions and disclosures of corporate scandals increases the need for outsiders, but the growing threat of financial liability and of public censure make potential board members reluctant to join.

In fact, the composition of the board has been changing recently. Fewer investment bankers and lawyers providing services to companies are board members, while more women, academicians, and members of minority groups are directors. The new importance of outside directors is vividly illustrated in the Gulf Oil bribery situation, where the board fired the chief executive officer: a key vote was cast by Sister June Scully, president of a local Pittsburgh college.

Nevertheless, the American concept of a director's role is still quite ambiguous. Of the 200 largest American companies, the average company has fourteen directors, of which more than half are outside directors. A survey by Korn/Ferry, an executive recruiting firm, indicates that directors are paid approximately $10,000 for their services and claim they spend 100 hours a year on their business as directors. Those hour figures may or may not be bloated, but the income for the work is still attractive. But without a staff and budget, the tough board suggested by the SEC may be little more than wishful thinking. It is simply impossible in that 100 hours to acquire an in-depth understanding of a complicated business which is constantly changing.

Professor Detlev Vagts of Harvard has pointed out that a heightening of the level of care and diligence expected of boards must be accompanied by a rational and comprehensive redefinition of their functions. Nothing could be more disastrous, according to Vagts, than making a directorship too dangerous and unattractive for precisely the capable people needed to give corporations effective guidance.

A *Forbes* survey of a number of chief executives to find out their reactions to developments regarding directors provides some interesting insights into the realities of the situation. As J. Peter Grace, the president and chief executive of W. R. Grace & Co., has said about his board: "No matter how smart you are, if I work 100 times harder than you on a given subject, you have no way of catching me. No way." Ingersoll-Rand Chairman William L. Wearly, however, perhaps raised a more fundamental point: "I think if the board does very many of the things that the writings and the charters say they're supposed to do, you'd have a mess."

But staff resources and greater devotion of time in themselves are also not enough because the fundamental question arises: To whom are directors responsible and for what? Leaders of the United Auto Workers, for example, have proposed that Chrysler include employees on its board.

Similarly, reformers have argued for representatives of consumers and the government. In Europe, employee representatives and, in some instances, government representatives are common.

Over the next few years, the issues of the purpose of a corporation—is it simply profit-oriented, or is there a larger social responsibility; what are the duties of a director; and who should be a director—will be increasingly in controversy. Certainly, a sharpening of the vision as to the role of directors is long overdue; it is a question which goes to the very heart of the assumptions of our economic system. The task of this book, however, is to examine directors' decisions and liabilities as they relate to legal aspects of financings. The essential message is the need for great care— perhaps more than it is reasonable to expect of directors under the existing system.

FOUR

Capital Structure

The essential problem of devising an appropriate capital structure for a new firm is meshing the financial prospects of the venture with the individual needs and preferences of the investors. Many businesses have come to the realization that an ill-conceived capital structure can have a devastating effect on a firm's future.

To get a rough handle on the situation, an attempt should be made at projecting the financial characteristics of the corporation. How much money will it need? Will it be capital or labor intensive? How large an inventory will be required? What are other working capital needs? Will plant and machinery be purchased or leased? How risky is the business? If it should fail, what would its liquidation value be? Does it have a high upside potential? What are its alternative means of financing? Can the receivables be pledged? Can the assets be easily mortgaged? What are the likely earnings before interest and taxes and cash flow?

The threshold task for management thinking about capital structure is to determine the corporation's goals. For example, a conservative management of a mature company or a management of a new firm or of a concern subject to major uncertainties may have as the prime focus the avoidance of risk. To implement that strategy, a minimum of debt would be logical. Another company may be seeking to increase the firm's stock price and has to guess what combination of policies will appeal to the market. Once a company has a concept of its own needs, it then has to try to mesh its ideas with the perceptions of potential investors and lenders.

LEVERAGE

Perhaps the most fundamental decision management must make is the degree of desired leverage—that is, the relationship between senior securities and common stock. The basic concept of leverage is simple. For example, take a company with $1 million in earnings after taxes but before any interest costs. If it had 1 million shares of common stock which had been sold at $10 a share, and no other stock or debt, its total capitalization would be $10 million, and earnings per share would be $1. But if, instead, the company decided to finance itself with 50% debt, its results would appear quite different. The total capitalization would still be $10 million, but there would be only 500,000 shares of common stock and $5 million in debt. Assuming a 10% interest rate on the debt and a 50% tax bracket for the corporation, the after-tax cost to the firm of the $5 million in debt is $250,000. So earnings allocable to the common stock are reduced from $1 million to $750,000. However, since there are only 500,000 shares of common stock, earnings per share increase to $1.50—a 50% increase.

Leverage, however, presents downside potential as well as upside opportunity. For example, assume that the same company has earnings after taxes of $250,000 before any interest costs. With the all-stock capitalization, earnings per share will be 25 cents a share ($250,000 divided by 1 million shares). But with the 50% debt capitalization, earnings per share will be zero ($250,000 in earnings minus $250,000 in after-tax debt costs). In essence, although leverage may boost per share earnings, it also has the effect of making them vary more widely. The effects of leverage will be discussed in more detail later in this chapter, but simply stated, for the same business risk the financial risk changes with the degree of leverage.

In addition, as a firm continues to lever itself by increasing debt, the possibility of cash insolvency increases because the debt has to be serviced by the payment of interest and principal. If a firm's cash flow can be predicted with great certainty, it can afford a heavier load of debt—for example, certain utilities which will generally get rate increases if there is substantial danger of the debt not being serviced.

The Theory of Leverage

A simplistic view of capital structure, sometimes known as the net-income approach, argues that a firm can increase its value by increasing its leverage; with fewer shares of common stock, income per share increases and at a given price-earnings ratio level, the value of the firm will increase. There are a number of critical assumptions in this perspective. First, the assumption is made either that earnings are to be constant or that volatility of earnings does not matter as long as there is the expected average of earnings over time. Second, it is assumed that there is no risk of insolvency. Third, it is assumed that lenders and stock purchasers will not change their evaluation of the company enough because of the increase in leverage to offset its advantages.

An alternative point of view, sometimes known as the net-operating-income approach, states that a company is valued on its capital structure as a whole and, therefore, the breakdown between senior securities and equity is unimportant. The theory is that the cost of debt to a firm has two elements. First, there is the explicit and obvious cost of the interest rate. But, just as important, there is also a hidden cost; as the debt-equity ratio rises, the common stock is seen as more risky, a higher return is demanded by investors, and the value per share drops. Conversely, if there is less debt, the common stock is less risky and the value rises; however, since there are less earnings per share, the total value of the enterprise doesn't change, so there is no optimal capital structure.

This theory, made famous by academicians Franco Modigliani and Merton Miller, has some interesting insights. The key point, that as debt increases the price-earnings multiple should decrease, is sensible and also has some empirical support. However, the majority of academicians and business persons think the Modigliani and Miller model is a theoretical nicety with little relevance in the commercial world.

The majority approach is that an optimal capital structure can be devised through an appropriate use of leverage. As a firm becomes more levered and therefore more financially risky, the price-earnings ratio will decrease, but not enough to offset the benefit of using debt instead of equity for financing. At some point, however, increasing leverage becomes so risky that the disadvantages in terms of its implicit costs—a lower price-earnings ratio—more than offset the advantages of using debt. The optimal capital structure is, therefore, one in which the marginal cost to a firm of selling equity is equal to that of selling debt. Cost, of course, would include explicit and implicit costs, both interest and the penalty the market places on a firm's stock with too much debt. At that theoretical point, the market price of the company's stock should be maximized in the long run. Depending on the business risk of the company, the level of ideal leverage can vary widely. For example, utilities can be more highly leveraged than manufacturing industries because their earnings are more predictable.

The difficulty with even this model is that it assumes a constant market perception and steady economic conditions. In fact, in good times and with low interest rates, increasing leverage may be sensible, while in difficult conditions, a higher proportion of equity would be prudent. Depending on the economic environment, any one of these approaches to leverage may be correct. Flexibility is a must. No one course is right for all winds.

Some Analytical Techniques

These theoretical concepts are helpful to keep in mind in creating a capital structure. But they are certainly not enough. In finance, "pumping the numbers" is a necessity and is a prerequisite for understanding the practical impact of legal restrictions.

The EBIT diagram   For example, a number of numerical exercises can give a feeling for possible outcomes. As a start, the relationship between earnings per share (EPS) and earnings before interest and taxes (EBIT) should be examined. Frequently, finance managers plot the relationship to dramatize the effect of leverage on earnings per share above and below certain levels. This practice does not, however, focus on the implicit costs of overusing debt. Although an EBIT diagram will illustrate the impact on earnings per share of leverage past given points, it does not reflect the market's evaluation of the increased financial risk from the increased debt.

To plot an EBIT diagram, write earnings per share on the vertical axis and earnings before interest and taxes on the horizontal axis. On the horizontal axis, plot the before-tax impact of any financing alternative. For example, if one alternative is $5 million in debt at 10%, the pretax charge of $500,000 is plotted on the horizontal axis. This is another way of stating that at a level of earnings before interest and taxes of $500,000, earnings per share under the debt alternative will be zero. Since the equity option has no impact on total earnings, it is marked at zero on the horizontal axis. Assume there are now outstanding 500,000 shares, the tax rate is 50%, and the alternative to debt is another 500,000 shares at $10 a share. Therefore, if before interest and taxes, the company earned $2 million, the earnings per share for the debt alternative would be $1.50 ($2 million minus $500,000, the debt cost, times 50% equals $750,000, which, divided by 500,000 shares, equals $1.50) and for the equity alternative $1 ($2 million times 50%, equals $1 million, divided by $1 million shares equals $1 per share). A point should then be plotted on the intercept of the debt alternative's EPS, $1.50 per share, and EBIT, $2 million. Similarly, a point can be plotted at $1 per share in earnings and $2 million EBIT for the equity alternative.

A line can now be drawn between the two plotted points for each of the debt and equity alternatives. For each alternative, the line indicates the relationship between EBIT and EPS. As can be seen in the diagram which

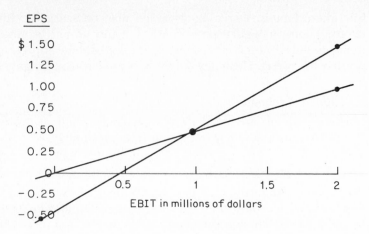

illustrates this example, the two lines cross when EBIT is $1 million and EPS is 50 cents. This is the indifference point. With EBIT above this point, the debt will bring a better EPS result; below this point, the debt actually lowers the EPS.

An EBIT chart analysis is useful in illustrating the acceleration effect leverage has on EPS, but it is only a beginning. Having found the indifference point, it is useful to determine the probability that EBIT will fall below that level. If the EBIT is only slightly above the indifference point, particular care must be taken because increased debt may well have a negative effect on EPS.

Ratio analysis   It must be remembered, however, that earnings are not cash flow. Management should also be concerned both about the risk of insolvency, not having the cash to meet its obligations as they come due, and about the inability to take advantage of attractive investment opportunities, including repairs and improvements of capital equipment.

The traditional ratio analyses regarding liquidity, coverage of fixed charges, and debt structure give management a fix on its own situation and is also useful in appraising the likely reaction of investors and lenders to financing alternatives.

Obviously, the more liquid a firm's assets, the more easily they can be used to pay off fixed charges, including debts which are due in the near future. For example, owning real estate, which takes time to sell, will not help in meeting the cash need of paying an interest installment due next month.

A common but very rough method of computing liquidity is a current ratio. Current assets, cash and near-cash items, accounts receivable, inventories, and prepaid expenses are divided by current liabilities, accounts payable plus principal installments of any debts due within a year. The higher the current ratio, in theory, the easier it is to meet cash obligations.

There are, however, a number of problems with a current ratio. First, one has to remember that interest costs or fixed lease payments due within a year are not reflected as current obligations. Second, the ratio only reflects the situation as of the date of the balance sheet upon which it is based. Next year there could be a large installment of debt due, and the ratio could dramatically change. Third, one has to look behind the figures and analyze two key questions: How fast could the money really be obtained, and what price could the assets bring if they had to be sold on short notice?

An alternative and more rigid test of liquidity is the quick ratio, which is current assets, less inventories, divided by current liabilities. The theory is that inventories are the least certain of current assets, both in terms of their value and in the time it would take to sell them.

Instead of excluding inventories, they themselves can be analyzed. An inventory turnover ratio can be computed from the cost of goods sold divided by the average inventory. A high turnover indicates that the inventory is relatively liquid. But this analysis too must be used with caution: there could be strong seasonal trends, or the inventory level could be too low, resulting in "stockouts."

Similarly, the accounts receivables can be analyzed. The average collection period can be obtained by dividing the receivables times 365 (the days in the year) by the amount of annual credit sales. A low figure may be the result of an efficient collection policy or of a too-restrictive credit program. An alternative is to age the receivables by months due.

Coverage tests are another measure of determining liquidity and are used by investors, banks, and credit-rating agencies. The most frequently used test of this type is to divide EBIT by interest and principal payments, adjusted for their before-tax cost. A broader test would include all mandatory cash obligations, lease payments, essential capital investments, and preferred stock dividends.

Often, analysts will examine the debt ratios of a company, dividing the total debt by the net worth or dividing the long-term debt by the total capitalization. Like other ratios, these must be used with some sensitivity. If the interest rates are low on the long-term debt, for example, the coverage problems may be much less than those of a company with a better ratio. Similarily, the pattern of principal maturity is important.

With any of these ratios, the numbers by themselves must be massaged to be useful. Comparisons should be made against other firms in the industry and the past performance of the company being studied.

SECURITIES: THEIR TERMS AND CHARACTERISTICS

Having made some judgment as to the ideal capital structure of a firm, management must negotiate with investors to see whether its ideas are acceptable and what particular form the securities will take. Whatever a financial manager's analysis and perspective, if investors can't be persuaded, the logic is irrelevant. In reacting to the demands of potential investors, management should be particularly careful to avoid a common mistake: unduly encumbering the future in order to get money today. For example, excessively restrictive provisions in debt instruments may haunt a company later, or issuing excessive warrants and options may limit its ability to issue common stock in the future.

Devising a capital structure is a little like dividing a pie, but not very much. The pie concept assumes a static object. Dividing it up is what economists call a zero sum game: the more any one party gets, the less anyone else receives. A corporation, however, is dynamic; its future is fraught with uncertainty, but the possibility of growth is also present. Some investors will want more security than others, and will be willing to sacrifice some upside potential. Thus, the particular securities a concern issues not only determines the financial risk for the venture as a whole but also allocates risk and return among the investors. The trick is to find investors who mesh well with the company's business profile and to carve out securities which balance risk and return in a manner satisfactory to the investors and the concern.

Common Stock

The ownership of shares of common stock entitles the holder to a proportionate share of the profits, assets, and voting power of a concern not otherwise allocated to senior securities such as debt and preferred stock.

If a company is successful, the common stockholder shares in its upside potential. On the other hand, the risk is greater on the downside than for debt or preferred stock. In the event of a liquidation, the senior securities would generally come first.

Terms   There can be more than one class of common stock, but the relative rights of each class must be clearly designated in, or pursuant to, the provisions of the certificate of incorporation. As has been discussed, it is quite common in joint ventures or other corporations in which control has been carefully allocated, to have classes of stock, for example, Class A and Class B, with identical rights, except that each class is entitled to vote for a specified number of directors.

Occasionally, common stock of a particular corporation will have other unique features. For example, some stock has preemptive first rights to purchase any new stock being offered by a company. Another example is cumulative voting, which is optional in most states and mandatory in a few.

Any share of stock, common or preferred, can have either a par value or no par value; no-par stock may itself have a stated value. Par value is a curious relic of the gilded age; in law school, one learns that it is irrelevant, but it does have some practical impact today. Two considerations go into its determination: tax factors and dividend restrictions. Many states limit the ability of a corporation to pay dividends out of paid-in capital, which is defined to be the cumulative total of the par value for all shares of stock issued. With too high a par value, dividend flexibility may be limited. Taxation is a factor because in some states a corporation is taxed on the par value of its stock, while in others, if no par value is stated, the market value of the stock is used, resulting in a very high rate of taxation. Therefore, before deciding on the par value, if any, of a security, the tax laws of the states where the business has been incorporated, as well as those in which it needs to qualify as a foreign corporation doing business, should be carefully examined. On the other hand, for psychological reasons, corporations have a tendency to dislike an extremely low par value: it seems to make the security chintzy.

Pricing   In setting up a new venture, an entrepreneur must be careful in planning a realistic price for common stock. It is all too easy to make plans predicated on high multiples of nonexistent earnings because this new-born company is going to be another Xerox. This attitude will only bring disappointment. Yet, venturers understandably do not want to be diluted out of their own businesses by selling too much cheap stock.

On the other hand, an investor naturally wants a return from his stock investment in a new venture which justifies the added risk over such alternative investments as IBM stock or government bonds. One mode of analysis, very popular in textbooks, is to discount the expected cash flows (including future dividends and, at some terminal date, an expected sale price) at a rate which reflects the business risk of the venture. This discount is nice in theory, and it looks great to budget justification committees in large corporations; but the method is very unrealistic. Most new ventures need a shakedown run, and estimates are very soft. For this reason, many investors try to pump the best numbers they can get and then discount by high factors in order to compensate for the uncertainty.

In addition, to the degree that any of the three key attributes of common stock are significantly impaired—voting, share of profits, and share of assets—the value of the stock diminishes. For example, a voting trust for a company that effectively locks out minority shareholders from any role in deciding future policies decreases the value of the stock.

If small business persons are realistically optimistic about the prospects of the new firm and wish to limit dilution, there are three practical possibilities. First, limit financing until there is a performance record. Second, for initial financing, use sources that are familiar with the business person's record, such as relatives and friends. Third, reduce uncertainty through devices such as getting signed purchase contracts and firm cost bids on construction projects.

Preferred Stock

Preferred stocks are really contracts blending debt and equity elements, whose key attributes are determined by the negotiating parties; the precise proportion of these features varies widely among differing preferreds because there are few bright-line rules as to the terms of preferred stock. However, in order to be listed on national exchanges, preferreds may be required to have some key provisions such as voting power in the event of the continuing nonpayment of dividends. Preferred stocks' popularity seems to wax and wane in the financial community. Recently, preferreds have been quite popular for utilities and other companies having financing problems. In addition, "cheap preferreds," preferred stock offered under the conventional figures of $100 or $1000 a share, are gaining vogue because they are apparently more marketable.

On the face of it, preferred stock has severe disadvantages to a corporation over other means of financing. The preferred dividend is not tax deductible, and because there is a claim on assets only after debt, the yield rate has to be generally higher than that of debt. As a result, the cost to a corporation of servicing preferred stock is usually more than twice that of debt on an after-tax basis.

Despite its disadvantages, there are certain benefits to its use. First, if corporations are investors, 85% of the preferred dividend may be tax exempt. Therefore, the yield on preferred stock likely to be purchased by other corporations may not be much more and in some cases may be less than the debt of the same firm. More important, however, are its implications for a corporation's flexibility and debt capacity.

Commonly, a preferred issue has no final maturity, has a dividend that cumulates if not paid but doesn't have to be paid, and does not require gradual repayment over a specified term. As a result, if a company should be temporarily tight on cash or if it wishes to preserve its cash for investment, preferred stock offers great advantages over debt. Debt servicing, principal and interest, must be paid or there will be a default; there is generally no built-in flexibility like that in a preferred stock. Of course, to individual investors, it is precisely this flexibility which is unattractive about preferred stock. While the corporation is being flexible, the preferred stockholder is not being paid.

Furthermore, to a corporation, the explicit cost of the preferred is not the only factor to consider. Additional preferred gives an additional equity cushion to debt in the event of insolvency; debt-equity ratios look much better; and the ability to finance additional debt is increased. Thus, the total cost of a preferred issue must be analyzed in terms of its benefit in increasing debt capacity as well as of its explicit costs.

Because the terms of preferred can vary widely, it is useful to examine carefully the provisions of the preferred contract, which are either part of the certificate of incorporation or are adopted by resolution of the board pursuant to an authorization in the certificate. Among the common terms in a preferred stock are the following:

Dividends Most preferred stocks state a specific dividend rate, such as 6%, and have a provision which says that such dividend will be paid when and if declared by the board. In short, the payment of a preferred dividend is generally not guaranteed; the board may or may not declare it.

However, preferreds can utilize a number of provisions to increase the likelihood of eventual dividend payments. First, unpaid dividends usually cumulate, and the unpaid dividends in any period are carried forward to the next. Second, no dividend may be paid on common stock until all current and all past payments on the preferred stock are paid. Third, in the event of liquidation, the amount preferred holders are entitled to receive usually includes accrued but unpaid dividends.

Unfortunately, these provisions are often ineffective. If a management is willing not to pay dividends on common stock, it can pass the dividends on the preferred with no practical consequences. Meanwhile, the firm is getting the use of the money. Eventually, the preferred can be paid off, having, in effect, given the company an interest-free loan, or the preferred can often be purchased by the company for bargain prices from individual holders or from the preferred owners as a class. Furthermore, even the terms of the security may often be modified by owners of two-thirds of the outstanding preferred. As a result, the rights of the individual preferred holder can be crammed down by the majority. Therefore, a standard preferred is from an investor's point of view a very "soft" obligation of the business; in bad times, or at the whim of management, holders can find themselves with a meaningless dividend provision.

Preferred contracts can, however, be drafted with stronger provisions, although they usually are not. For example, the dividend can be made mandatory, although the security then becomes very close to being a junior form of debt. More commonly, an arrearage in dividends over a period of time will trigger additional powers for the preferred holders. For example, if dividends were not current in the last six consecutive quarters, the preferred holders may be entitled to elect a specified number of directors. Or if the preferred is convertible, the arrearage can be used to reduce the conversion price. Similarly, there may be a provision prohibiting any repurchases of preferred if there are any dividend arrearages unless all outstanding preferred shares are bought.

Usually, the stated dividend rate is the maximum dividend preferred holders can get because the residual earnings belong to the common stockholders. However, there are occasionally participating preferreds, which allow the preferred to share in income in accordance with a specified formula.

Liquidation   One key advantage of preferred stock over common stock is that it usually has a stated liquidation preference over the common. For example, a preferred may have a liquidation preference of $100. This means that in the event of a voluntary liquidation or a bankruptcy, the preferred is entitled to $100 before the holder of a share of common stock is entitled to a dime—but after the creditors, including the debtholders, have been fully satisfied. Usually, any unpaid but accrued dividends are added to the stated dollar amount of the liquidation preference.

Call and sinking fund provisions   A call provision, quite frequently used in preferreds, allows a company to repurchase the preferred at its option at specified prices; thus, if there is a dramatic shift in interest rates, a company retains its flexibility by being able to repurchase the preferred. Usually, there is a provision barring a call for a number of years to protect investors if the dividend rate turns out to be high. However, it should be noted that some of the recent preferreds issued by companies with high risk and high interest rates have contained minimal call protection. Once the ban provision is no longer applicable, the call price starts out at a premium and gradually decreases to the face value of the preferred. Since, unlike with debt, there is generally no final maturity date, a call provision can be quite useful.

A sinking fund is a device whereby a given proportion of the outstanding preferred is retired on a specified schedule. Although a sinking fund is advantageous to the holders of the preferred, it reduces the security's flexibility from the company's point of view and is therefore not very common. An alternative which adds some flexibility is to make the triggering of sinking fund payments dependent on the earnings level of a firm.

Convertibility   Often, especially in small ventures, the preferred is convertible into common stock. The conversion mechanism will be discussed in detail later. The point for now is that to a powerful, sophisticated investor, a convertible preferred, with voting power equivalent to the number of shares of common stock into which it is convertible, is quite a useful investment vehicle. Basically, it combines most of the advantages of a junior debt security, yet adds to the equity base of the company and has the upside potential, and possibly the voting power, of common stock. For these reasons, convertible preferred stock is quite common in venture-capital deals.

Debt

There are many permutations of debt securities. Long-term debt, often called "funded debt," is usually defined as debt due more than 12 months from the date of issuance. Debt with the longest maturity commonly takes two forms: debentures, which are unsecured by property, and bonds, which are secured. Debt with a term of less than about 7 years is often called notes. If the notes are due within 12 months, they are short-term debt, often referred to as unfunded debt. Within these broad categories, there are wide variations indicated by the title of the issue. Often, for example, the term "refunding" is used in a title of an issue to indicate that the purpose of the issue was to retire other long-term debt. Sometimes the nature of the secured interest is highlighted, such as in First Mortgage Bonds, or, if personal property such as stock is pledged, the issue may be called Collateral Trust Certificates. Similarly, emphasis is sometimes given to key features of the issue in instruments such as a Subordinated Convertible Debenture. Debt owned by more than a few individuals or corporations is usually issued pursuant to a contract, or an indenture, between a firm and a trustee who represents the debtholders' interests.

In 1939, the Trust Indenture Act was passed by Congress in reaction to a study by the SEC, conducted by William O. Douglas, that concluded that trustees for public debt issues were often doing little to protect investors, even in the event of default. The 1939 Act's most important section explicitly requires that all public indentures contain a provision stating that in the event of a default, the indenture trustee must act to protect the debtholders as a prudent man would act under the circumstances in the conduct of his own affairs. In addition, by limiting the eligibility for trusteeships, the 1939 Act eliminated the most egregious conflicts for the trustee: being a trustee under another issue with conflicting rights, controlling the issuer, the issuer's owning more than 10% of the voting trustee's stock, etc. However, the most controversial area of alleged conflict was not forbidden: a trustee can also be a lender to the issuer. Trustees which are not lenders argue that the 1939 Act should be amended to eliminate this area of possible conflict. However, the practicalities are that some of the most vigorous and efficient trustees are also commercial banks, and it is doubtful that eliminating them from trusteeships will result in any public benefit. A preferable remedy may well be to articulate clearer and tougher standards about the performances of all trustees.

The 1939 Act also specifies the wording of certain provisions of indentures, particularly those dealing with events of default and the responsibilities of the trustee. Essentially, the way most indentures are structured, if there is an event of default known to a trustee, the trustee must generally notify the holders within 90 days. Once there has been a default, the trustee must act prudently, but the holders of not less than a majority of the securities may direct the trustee to conduct any remedy of proceeding or to waive defaults, if the trustee's costs are covered. However, without the consent of each individual holder, no right to principal may be waived, and a right to an interest payment may be waived, at most, for a period not exceeding 3 years from the date due, and, in fact, most indentures do not allow any waiver of interest.

Although the practicalities of the trustee's role will be considered later in connection with the description of bankruptcy proceedings, a natural question arises as to why a trustee is required for debt and not for equity securities. As a general proposition, debt securities are more complicated than stock. First, there is the payment of principal and interest, which is due rather than discretionary as with stock dividends, and the presence of various sinking funds and prepayments, which are, however, also often used in preferred stocks. Second, there are the various covenants in debt instruments, the restrictions on the issuer, to police. Third, there are generally no default provisions in equity securities, although sometimes preferred stockholders are entitled to additional directors based upon the occurrence of certain events. However, to the degree that the prime function of a trustee is to protect holders in bankruptcy proceedings and that function is recognized as useful, it should also be a good idea for other classes of publicly owned securities to be represented by trustees. As will be seen, however, in connection with bankruptcy situations, it is most unclear what existing indenture trustees should, in fact, be doing and how they should be compensated for their efforts. Any extension of the concept, therefore, is premature, although thought-provoking.

The certificates for debt securities come in two basic forms themselves: registered or bearer instruments. In the United States, most corporate debt instruments are registered; the name and address of the record holder appears on the face of the instrument, and payment of interest and principal is made at that locale. The more unusual bearer instruments, which are very popular in Europe, do not have any record holder. Interest on bearer securities is paid by detaching the coupons attached to the security and submitting them to a paying agent. Before the mid-1960s, registered instruments were also rare in the United States, but a number of corporate trustees and the American Bar Foundation Corporate Debt Financing Project pushed successfully for the popular adoption of the registered form because of its administrative simplicity.

Among the related projects of the Bar Foundation were model forms of debentures for financings. Although often not exactly identical, public debentures today generally conform to the model instruments as to their "boiler plate" administrative provisions, those sections required by the 1939 Act, and certain stylistic requirements of the stock exchanges. Despite the desire of the Bar Foundation Project to simplify indentures by having them selectively incorporate the Bar Foundation model, in fact, most indentures today are thick documents which contain all the standardized provisions. In a public issue, the terms of the indenture are summarized in the prospectus, and the indenture is, in theory, available upon request from the underwriters. However, they are usually reluctant to give indentures away because, customarily, few are printed, and they are quite expensive documents. Nevertheless, particularly if the prospectus indicates that there are unusual provisions in the indenture, it is worthwhile for an investor to examine the document.

Sometimes an indenture must be amended by the execution of a supplemental indenture. For example, there may have been an ambiguity in the original indenture; the issuer may have been merged, if merger is permitted under the indenture; or the issuer may wish to loosen a particularly restrictive covenant. If the amendment is mechanical or contemplated by the original indenture as amended, it can be done by the trustee and the issuer executing the supplemental indenture. If, however, the change is substantive, generally, the approval of the holders of two-thirds of the amount of the debt is required.

Conventionally, bond and debenture prices are quoted on the basis of $1,000 of principal amount, although, for example, a registered holder may have $8,000 in principal amount in a particular instrument, and even coupon instruments may be sold in other amounts—say $10,000 and $5,000 units—as well as $1,000 pieces. Generally, each denomination of bonds or debentures is numbered separately, with the numbers of $1,000 bearer pieces being prefixed with an *M* and the numbers of registered instruments being prefixed with an *R*.

In analyzing debt instruments, the following major items should be carefully analyzed:

Security The strongest position for a lender is to be a secured creditor. In the event of bankruptcy, a secured lender is entitled to satisfy itself from the value of the collateral before unsecured creditors. Also, a fully secured lender is entitled to postbankruptcy interest and expenses, and generally an unsecured creditor is not. Even if there seems to be no other debt outstanding, unsecured debt is not as well off as secured debt because in bankruptcy creditors other than lenders are considered on the same level as unsecured creditors and will share equally with them. And, if worse comes to worst and a lender is not fully secured, it is entitled to a preferred position to the extent of its security, and is treated as an unsecured lender for the rest of the claim. A brief note of caution is, however, appropriate. If the security is not sufficient, the value of being an unsecured obligation depends on what entity is the obligor. If, for example, an insolvent subsidiary was the obligor rather than the parent, the general creditor status may not be so helpful.

There is a wide variety of types of secured debt, including loans secured by equipment, securities, inventories, or accounts receivables, which will be discussed later, as well as the conventional mortgage on property and equipment of an issuer. If the bonds are senior in priority on the security, they are generally referred to as First Mortgage Bonds. However, it should be noted that even First Mortgage Bonds may be second in priority to tax liens and prior claims on segments of the property. General Mortgage Bonds or Second Mortgage Bonds, on the other hand, are bonds which are explicitly second in priority to other bonds. Their worth obviously depends on the extent to which the value of the security exceeds the claim of the First Mortgage Bonds.

With any bond, a lender must be careful to examine exactly what is the security. The property descriptions in a mortgage for a large industrial corporation may go on for pages, including property, equipment and even key contracts, as well as land and the plant. What is excluded explicitly or by omission is as important as what is included in the long description. Of course, reading all the other mortgages of the issuer is necessary to see whether all the documents fit together. In addition, care must be taken that the mortgage (for the real property) and the security agreement (for the other forms of security) are all filed in the right places and manner. Otherwise, the security may prove to be illusory.

Many blanket mortgages, mortgages covering all or nearly all the property of the issuer, are open ended—allowing future issuances of similar bonds to have the same property as security. Mechanically, the original indenture contemplates supplemental indentures for additional series of bonds which can be executed by the indenture trustee without the consent of the bondholders.

In theory, this future issuance of similar bonds sharing the same property as security dilutes the protection of the existing bonds. Two protective devices, however, exist. First, open-ended indentures frequently have after-acquired-property clauses, as do, sometimes, close-ended indentures, which subject future property owned by the issuer to the mortgage. Thus, even though the original security of the bondholder may be diluted, there will probably be additional security. Second, as will be discussed, the covenants in the mortgage often restrict in a number of ways, through a variety of tests, the amount of debt which can be issued.

Covenants A key section of an indenture deals with the covenants, or agreements, which an issuer makes regarding future actions. Covenants in indentures range from standardized general provisions (in effect, limited to the payment of interest and principal on the debt) to very specific negotiated restrictions, such as coverage tests. In addition, especially in private placements with powerful investors such as the major insurance companies, there are often additional covenants in the purchase agreement itself. This is particularly true if the security involved is one which will also be held by other investors, and the purchasing group or the company wants the added flexibility of the purchasing group's being able to waive terms on its own.

In most public debenture issues of major industrial companies, the covenants are quite limited. Simple affirmative covenants, those involving promises as to future acts, such as that principal and interest will be paid and paying agents will be maintained in certain cities, are included, and little else. These affirmative covenants are usually standardized and follow the American Bar Foundation model form. One reason for such few covenants is that these firms have the ability to borrow without restrictions on their financial flexibility. Another reason, however, is the practicalities of the situation. It is mechanically extremely difficult to get the necessary consents of public debtholders to any change in covenants, as contrasted to soliciting consents from a few institutional holders of privately placed debt. A restriction in a public issue may be potentially extremely dangerous to the issuer because the ability to negotiate a sensible modification of the provision is limited.

To the degree that the lack of covenants increases the risk, it should theoretically be reflected in the interest rate required by the market for the debt to sell. More practically, many indentures have cross-default provisions, as will be discussed. As a result, a default under other instruments becomes a default under an indenture with a cross-default provision. Thus, assuming other privately placed debt of the issuer has restrictive covenants, a simple public issue may get the advantage of those complicated provisions, anyway. The disadvantage is, however, that those other instruments can always be amended, and the holders relying on the cross-default provisions will have no voice in the modifications.

Negotiated covenants, mostly negative covenants prohibiting specified actions, are as varied as the fertile imagination of the counsel involved in the deal. Institutional lenders, particularly large insurance companies, will insist on a whole array of covenants, arguing that they are standard for their loans. The common temptation is to sign the loan agreement and worry about the covenants later, but this can be a serious mistake, which may severely hamper the future flexibility of the borrower. Whatever they may say in negotiating sessions, the lenders' representatives are sophisticated professionals who realize that deals need to be tailored to the specific situation. On the other hand, of course, the borrower doesn't want the lender to walk away from the transaction. The desire of both borrower and lender to have the company successful is the key to effective tactics: In fact, figures and analysis demonstrating the potential harm of over-restrictive provisions are often persuasive.

Among the more common negotiated covenants are the following:

Information requirements. Under the 1939 Act, the periodic filings of the issuer with the SEC must be furnished on a regular basis to the SEC. In a direct placement, especially for a company which is not public, the range of required reports can include not only quarterly and yearly financial statements but also periodic budgets and such additional information as may reasonably be requested. Often, when there are a number of holders of the privately placed debt, the request must be made by holders of a certain percentage of the debt. From the borrower's perspective, aside from the nuisance of sending a lot of reports to a number of lenders, there is the risk that confidential information too widely dispersed becomes, in effect, public. As a result, it is often the case that the larger the lending group the less the information provided.

Insurance. In many transactions, especially for smaller companies on secured transactions, it is common to require insurance on the assets of the borrower and, often, on the lives of key executives and against product liability. To the degree that these policies are above those the borrower would otherwise have, they would represent an additional indirect cost of the loan.

Pledge clauses. The trend in financings has been for large industrial companies other than utilities to attempt to avoid mortgages with their debt for a number of reasons. Not only are mortgages voluminous documents, but the filings and releases of property in the event of sale are quite cumbersome. For debentures to obtain security approximating that of an open-ended mortgage with an after-acquired property clause, various pledge clauses are used. An affirmative pledge is a covenant to give proportional security to the debenture holders if any secured debt is incurred. A variant on this is the conditional negative pledge, which states that no secured debt will be incurred unless proportional security is provided to the debenture holders. The strongest form of pledge clause is, of course, an absolute negative pledge which flatly bans the granting of security on debt. With any of these pledge clauses, the difficult negotiations are in regard to the exceptions to the covenant. Among the common negotiated exceptions are existing mortgages and purchase-money mortgages on newly acquired property. In drafting these provisions, a lender should be careful that the pledge covenants are comprehensive. For example, the borrower shouldn't be able to bypass the pedge covenants by selling assets and leasing them back or by spinning off assets to subsidiaries which then mortgage them.

Debt limitations. The total amount of debt which may incurred by a borrower is of great concern to a lender, particularly if the debt will be senior to, or will rank equally with, the investor. As more debt is incurred, the position of the existing holders is diluted. Therefore, it is quite common in open-ended mortgages and debentures issues to state through various tests the maximum amount of debt which can be issued by the borrower and its subsidiaries. These provisions tend to be more tightly tailored in privately placed deals than in public offerings because of the practical difficulty in modifying the terms of public debt, and the worse the credit rating of the borrower, the more restrictive the provisions.

There are many methods of limiting debt issuance, among which the following are the most common:
- a flat dollar limitation
- a maximum permitted ratio between long-term debt and tangible net worth, total capitalization, or net tangible assets
- a maximum permitted ratio between current debt and current assets
- coverage tests of the relationship between income and interest charges or interest and debt-amortization costs
- continuing "cleanup" provisions, which mandate that a borrower be free from current debt for, say, 90 days each fiscal year

These provisions are often used in combination, particularly those relating to short- and long-term debt. Borrowing by subsidiaries is either banned, except for intracompany transactions, or included within the coverage of the tests.

In thinking about which of these covenants, if any, make sense for a lender to require, it is useful to remember that the objective is protection of the lender without strangulation of the borrower by unnecessary restrictions. In addition, the number of lenders and their working relationship with the borrower constitute a key factor. If, in the past, institutional lenders have given their consent to reasonable changes in covenants without acrimony and extortionate demands, a borrower will feel freer agreeing to restrictive provisions. Further factors to consider are industry practice and, perhaps most important, the particular financial situation of the borrower.

For example, the flat dollar limitation is perhaps the simplest covenant, but, if the provision is applicable for a long term, the amount is very difficult to fix. If the amount is set appropriately for the borrower's current financial situation, it may be extremely restrictive 10 years later, especially if there is inflation and if the firm expands. On the other hand, an overoptimistic amount provides no near-term protection. By way of contrast, the various ratio and coverage formulas, although more cumbersome, do build in a mechanism for dealing with changes over a long period.

Each of the various alternative ratio tests has its own strengths and flaws in describing the balance sheet as of a given date. Mechanically, the tests generally read that the borrower will not incur long-term debt unless, after giving effect to the debt and the net proceeds from it, the required ratio will not be exceeded.

An important difference between the various ratio tests is the treatment of intangibles such as goodwill, start-up costs, patents, and franchises. Historically, tests net of intangibles have been used for industrial corporations on the theory that these are soft assets which could not be realized upon in the event of financial distress. However, utilities traditionally do not separate out intangibles on their balance sheets, so the ratios applicable to them use total capitalization rather than net tangible assets.

A fundamental flaw with all ratio tests, however, is that they are based on book values, and, of course, the book values are not necessarily indicative of the value of the assets. In addition, ratio tests are not necessarily sensitive to the flow of funds. For example, the proportion of debt may be small but the principal all may be due within eighteen months, or the interest burden may be very heavy because the rate was high.

One protective device is to have covenants directed at current debt in combination with the long-term ratio provisions. Among the most common provisions are a maximum ratio between current debt and current assets, a dollar limitation on current debt, and the application of a coverage test. Most of the analysis pertaining to similar covenants regarding long-term debt apply to these provisions. Coverage tests, however, are a different concept.

When added to ratio tests, coverage requirements give much more complete protection than ratio tests alone because they are oriented toward comparing cash needs to the flow of earnings. Mechanically, a covenant for interest coverage, for example, states that the borrower cannot incur additional debt unless the ratio test is satisfied and that income available for interest payments for the latest four financial quarters shall be at least a certain number of times the interest charges on the long-term debt. Similarly, a coverage covenant regarding debt amortization is based on the income available for debt servicing as compared to the interest and principal costs of repaying debt.

It must be remembered that these provisions are all tests to prevent the incurrence of new debt; they are not violated if a borrower does not meet the standards but does not seek new debt. However, there are sometimes additional covenants, usually found in the purchase agreements, which create a default if a specified debt ratio is exceeded, even if no new debt has been incurred. This default generally occurs when a company has experienced heavy losses. There are also additional provisions commonly found in indentures, which are related to the continuing financial health of the enterprise.

For example, the affirmative duty of a cleanup covenant mandating freedom from current debt for 90 days each fiscal year assures a lender that the borrower is not getting around long-term debt restrictions by simply rolling over current debt on a more or less permanent basis. Similarly, an affirmative covenant to maintain working capital (current assets less current liabilities) at a specified level is another way to prevent overloading on current debt, although the effect is quite different.

The cleanup provision does not prevent very high levels of current debt during most of the year as long as it can be wiped off the books for a relatively short period. With a highly seasonal business, this arrangement makes sense unless the current debt level goes so high that if the season doesn't go well, there is a chance of insolvency. On the other hand, the maintenance of a working-capital covenant lacks the flexibility for a highly seasonal business. Current assets and current liabilities do not rise together in neat proportions; raw materials are purchased on credit, building up current debt, and the incremental profits are shown only in the receivables which bulge later in the year.

With all these covenants, definitions and exceptions are crucial. What exactly "debt" and "income" encompass is crucial, and the exceptions built into the definitions are heavily negotiated. The ingenuity of modern finance is reflected in a bevy of vehicles designed to bypass conventional restrictions, and it is imperative that these devices—guarantees, take-or-say contracts, long-term leases—all be carefully considered.

Dividend and redemption restrictions. If a company could declare as dividends its cash and assets to its shareholders without limitation or could redeem their stock for cash, lenders might well find themselves as creditors of a shell. For these reasons, dividends, redemptions, and other distributions to shareholders are often restricted unless certain conditions are satisfied. Often, the key condition is that dividends be no more than a specified percentage of the accumulated earnings since the date of issuance of the debt. To allow dividend payments under a cumulation test in the first year of the debt, dividends in a set amount, usually equal to those of the prior years, are often permitted to be paid. An alternative to the cumulation test is to limit dividends in any particular year to a specified percentage of income in the previous year. This test is highly restrictive if, for example, in a cyclical company, there are large accumulated profits but last year the profits happened to be sour.

Similar provisions are applicable to redemptions, although if there is a sale of equity securities subsequent to the issuance of the debt, additional redemptions are often permitted.

Disposition of assets limitation. A standard covenant is a limitation on the borrower to sell, lease, or otherwise dispose of all or substantially all its assets. Some privately held debt, however, goes further by providing that divisions or major business units may not be sold without consent. Again, the problem is that the lender is left holding the bag if the assets are siphoned away. The necessity of consent gives the lender power to decide for itself whether a transaction is sensible. On the other hand, the borrower's flexibility is limited, and it may decide to fight any bolstering of the standard "all or substantially all" language.

Mergers. The most common covenant bans the borrower from being merged into, or consolidating with, any other corporation unless all the debt is assumed by the successor. This does not, however, prevent a merger with a heavily leveraged partner, and the debt-limitation covenants are directed to the incurrence of new debt, not the debt of a merger partner. To prevent this situation, sometimes there are test ratios similar to those applicable to the incurrence of new debt which must be satisfied before a merger is permissible.

Events of default   A key section in a debt instrument deals with events of default. If a covenant is not complied with or if principal or interest hasn't been paid on time, a trustee or a specified number of debtholders can declare that there has been a default. Some events of default—often the nonpayment of principal or interest—have a trigger action; they immediately take effect after certain specified events. Other events become defaults only with the passage of time, for example, after 30 days. Upon such default, all the debt and accrued interest may be accelerated and become immediately due.

Being able to demand back the principal invested is a key characteristic of debt, differentiating it from, for example, preferred stock, and giving its covenants extra power. Even in strong preferreds, the worst that happens if dividends aren't paid is that the preferred stockholders are entitled to elect additional directors—but rarely enough to control the board. A borrower must take care that events of default do not recklessly and unnecessarily endanger its financial standing. For example, it is quite common to have cross-default provisions, which in essence state that if a company defaults under another instrument, that default will be regarded as a default under the debt being negotiated. But what if the default problem is cured in the other document? A borrower should make sure that cross-default provisions aren't triggered, anyway.

Interest Generally, debt instruments have a fixed rate of interest, although occasionally income bonds (securities where interest must be paid only if earnings are above a certain level) are used by small companies or in bankruptcy reorganizations.

Repayment provisions All debt instruments are due at maturity, but most also have provisions regarding their repurchase during their life. Sinking funds and call provisions have been discussed in connection with preferred stocks, but in debt securities, the sinking funds are much more common and often more complex.

Sinking funds provide for the mandatory repurchase of a certain amount of the debt during a specified time period. From this schedule, an average life can be determined for a debt instrument. There is usually also an optional sinking-fund provision which allows a company to purchase, at its option, additional securities equal to the amount provided in the mandatory sinking fund on the same terms and conditions.

In addition, most debt securities have optional redemption provisions through which a company is entitled to "call" all or part of the debt at stated prices. Usually, there is protection against a call for a number of years. Naturally, if interest rates go down, it is in a firm's interest to exercise the call, and an investor will lose the benefit of a favorable interest rate. For this reason, the call price generally is higher in early years and decreases over time. Most companies also retain the flexibility to repurchase securities in the public market.

Subordination Debentures which are subordinated rank after both bonds and unsubordinated debentures in their claim on assets. The utility to a company of subordinated debentures is that they are a means to increase debt capacity. From the perspective of a senior lender, they provide an additional cushion in the event of bankruptcy. They have a claim against the borrower's assets only after the senior lender has been fully satisfied. However, it should be remembered that their issuance does create a fixed charge which can get a company into default problems. In theory, subordinated debt should provide a higher yield than senior debentures because the risk is greater. Often, however, these debentures are convertible into common stock, and because of that privilege, the interest rate is often lower than it would be on straight debt.

Perhaps the most important provision in a subordinated-debenture indenture is the one which specifies exactly what debt is senior to the issue. Often, the language will speak of the issue being subordinated to all senior indebtedness. Then the definition of senior indebtedness must be examined carefully. Although some subordinated debentures do limit senior indebtedness to be created in the future, most provisions are completely open-ended. The borrower has complete power to shovel additional debt above the subordinated-security positions for an investor, but perhaps it is worthwhile if the security has some glamour to it, such as a high rate or a conversion feature.

Convertible Securities

As discussed, preferred stock and subordinated debentures are often convertible into common stock. The conversion terms are stated either in a conversion ratio (the number of shares into which a particular security may be converted) or, more commonly, in a conversion price, which, divided into the face value of the security, indicates the number of shares obtainable.

Generally, the interest rate on a convertible is lower than on a nonconvertible security, and the conversion price or ratio reflects a premium over the existing market price for the security, usually in the range of 10 to 20%. Convertibles almost always have a call provision which allows a company to force conversion if the stock price is high. For example, if the conversion price is $20 and the stock is at $30, a call at $1,005 for a debenture will force investors to convert because they will be getting stock worth $1,500 instead of the price of $1,005.

Some academic critics have criticized the convertible debenture as being a most peculiar hybrid of the safest and the riskiest security. However, even if the stock's value falls, a convertible debenture's price will remain stable or rise if the borrower's basic credit is unchanged and interest rates are rising. Conversely, interest rates can fall, but an increase in the value of the issuer's stock will boost the price of the convertible debenture. From an investor's point of view, the convertible features also give potential voting rights equal to those of the common stock and a specified level of control, a characteristic particularly important in venture-capital deals. Companies appreciate the security because it represents cheaper or easier debt financing with the possibility of becoming a form of deferred equity-financing if things go well. On the other hand, the critics, most notably UCLA law professor William Klein, retort that the implicit cost to the issuer of selling equity at what may become a cheap price is being ignored by this perspective. Furthermore, Klein argues that the indentures for convertibles should protect the holders from excessive dividend payouts to common shareholders while the convertibles are still outstanding. At present, they generally do not.

One practical problem public companies do have with convertibles is that of overhanging securities. If the price of a security drops well below the conversion price, investors will not convert. Meanwhile, it is difficult to issue new convertibles or new equity, and a company consequently loses flexibility in future financing.

In evaluating the impact of convertibles, the accounting treatment should also be considered. Under Accounting Principles Bulletin 18, a convertible with an interest rate less than two-thirds of the prime rate at the time of issuance is considered a common stock equivalent and will be assumed to be converted for purposes of calculating primary earnings per share. Whatever the future interest rate patterns, only the relationship upon issuance counts. If upon issuance, the interest rate was higher than two-thirds of the prime rate, a convertible will not be amended to be converted in calculating primary earnings per share. It will, however, be considered to be converted in calculating fully diluted earnings. Thus, convertibles do have a positive leverage effect on primary earnings.

All convertible securities and warrants have provisions guarding against possible lessening in value through dilution or elimination of their conversion rights. For example, if a stock is split in two, the conversion price is automatically reduced in half, so that twice as many shares can be purchased. Or if assets are declared as a dividend, the convertible holders sometimes are entitled to a proportional share of the assets, as though a common stockholder or the conversion price is reduced by the value of the dividend. Similarly, if there is a merger or capital reorganization, the holders' rights will be preserved by entitling them to whatever securities the common stock becomes. To avoid dilution from the issuance of convertibles and options, these securities are treated as though they were converted or exercised at the time of issuance, although considerable negotiation goes into which contemplated future options are excluded from the formulas (usually a limited number of employee options are) and whether amendments of the prices on existing securities should trigger any adjustments.

One particularly difficult issue, which has generated a heated academic debate, is whether there should be an adjustment for the sale of stock below its then applicable conversion price or an adjustment for sales at a price below the existing market price. The supporters of having a provision for adjustment which is triggered only by a sale below market price assume that the real purpose of an antidilution provision should be the protection of the current market value of the right, which is determined by the current stock price, not the conversion price. On the other hand, those proponents of the conversion-price-dilution clause maintain that issuing shares below the conversion price dilutes the economic interests of holders, regardless of market price.

As a rough rule of thumb, it is in an investor's interest to get a conversion-price-antidilution provision and in the issuer's, to get a market-price provision. In fact, the most likely event to occur is that a stock price has dropped since the date of issuance, and the conversion price is relatively high. With a conversion-price-dilution formula, the additional issuance of common stock would result in a shaving of the conversion price. Under the market-price clause, no adjustment would occur. Indeed, a company rarely issues its stock below the market price; the directors would have a most difficult time showing they lived up to their fiduciary obligations if they did. Occasionally, there are options issued below market to key executives, and blocks are sometimes sold to investors at discount prices, but these sales are much less realistic concerns than sales below the conversion price.

Insurance companies often insist on a provision requiring an adjustment on a sale below either the conversion price or the market price. Whatever the intellectual inconsistencies in this approach, it is advantageous to the investor, especially if the market price is above the conversion price. Mechanically, the insurance company's double-barreled antidilution provision adjusts the conversion price to the lower of the following conversion price and market clauses:

1. The new conversion price is equal to the number of shares outstanding before the sale times the current conversion price, added to the new number of shares issued times their price, all divided by the number of shares existing after the sale.

2. The new conversion price is equal to the old conversion price times the following number of shares outstanding before the sale times the market price, added to the number of new shares issued times their price, all divided by the market price times the number of shares existing after the sale.

Both these clauses, which could be used as independent conversion-price and market-price provisions, weight the proportionate effect of the bargain price on the equity base as a whole—in effect, the amount of the discount is multiplied by the percent of the equity involved. Because adjustments are frequently quite small, there is often a provision that the conversion price will not be changed until the cumulated adjustments total some figure such as 10 cents.

Warrants

Warrants represent an option to buy shares of stock at a specified price. Like the conversion price in convertible securities, the exercise price is usually subject to adjustment provisions. Unlike convertible securities, warrants, if exercised, result in additional funds being paid to a company by the party exercising the purchase right. Warrants have an expiration date, and as it approaches, their value declines until, if not exercised they become worthless. Institutions often ask for warrants as "kickers" to sweeten a deal: essentially, they offer the maximum upside potential for the smallest investment. For example, assume a stock is selling at $20, and a warrant to purchase the stock at $20 is selling at $2; if the stock should go up to $30, the profit is $10. But if the $20 was invested in 10 warrants and the stock went to $30, the warrant holder could always purchase ten shares at $20 and immediately sell them at $30, giving an $80 profit, after deducting the $20 cost of the ten warrants. In fact, until their expiration date, warrants are rarely exercised because they trade at a price near their exercise value. Warrants are often an indispensable financing tool when one party or an employee is contributing know-how but not capital. Rather than allocating stock to that party, warrants can be given. The capital is then not diluted, but the party with know-how shares in the profit if things go well.

FIVE

Legal Requirements for Selling Securities

Before any attempt can be made to structure the capitalization of a company, answers are required to two distinct but related questions: Who are the likely investors, and who can they legally be? In starting a business, an entrepreneur has a fair idea of the sources of money: friends, relatives, savings, perhaps a professional associate, and maybe a corporation or institution familiar with the founder, all of whose needs must be meshed with those of the company.

The problem is that both state and federal law limit the manner in which securities may be sold and the persons to whom they may be offered. Under some procedures, investors are eligible who might not be eligible under another alternative, but the cost and bother of the former is invariably higher. In the end, a balance must be struck between the desired investors and the preferred procedure.

BLUE-SKY REGULATIONS

Nearly every state in the country has laws regulating the issuance of securities to its residents. These statutes are known as "blue-sky" laws because their original purpose was to prevent abuses by promoters of speculative ventures, whose promises had no more basis than so many feet of blue sky. The federal securities laws explicitly preserve the state blue-sky laws, although they are generally not applicable to securities of companies listed on a national stock exchange or of certain regulated companies, such as railroads, and to offerings made to institutional investors. Compliance with these statutes is usually quite inexpensive and simple, often requiring only the filing of the pertinent offering documents. However, failure to satisfy the local requirements may subject the violator to fines, criminal sanctions, and rescission claims.

The blue-sky laws differ state-by-state. Common approaches in these statutes, which frequently exist in various forms of combination, are fraud-penalty provisions, requirements for registration of brokers or dealers in securities, and requirements for the registration of the securities themselves with state authorities. Often, there are substantive tests before a security can be registered. For example, in California, a security offering must meet a "fair, just, and equitable" standard.

Inevitably, there are complicated conflict-of-law problems when a corporation incorporated in, say, Delaware, with mostly California shareholders, attempts to sell stock in New York. The difficulties are obviously exacerbated when there is an attempt to sell in more than one state at a time.

An attempt at clarification has been made by the Uniform Securities Act, which has been adopted by a substantial number of states. Blue-sky statutes, nevertheless, remain intricate and conflicting, and, furthermore, the state administrators have discretionary authority to promulgate rules and regulations under their state statutes.

The blue-sky statutes list a number of exemptions which can usually be relied on by a small corporation. Some statutes track the exemptions in the federal securities acts. Frequently, there is an exemption for an isolated buyer, so that only one purchaser in the state will not trigger a registration requirement. There often is also an exemption based on the total number of shareholders of the corporation residing in the state, but the number differs in each jurisdiction.

California's blue-sky procedure is among the most frequent sources of difficulty. Under the California law, a permit from the state Commissioner of Corporations is required before even a limited private placement can be made. The Commissioner's staff does review the underlying documentation and draws conclusions as to the fairness of the transaction. Although approvals are not difficult to obtain, there is a time lag between the application and the granting of a permit, which should be allowed for in any schedule.

Often, especially for a beginning corporation, an exemption can be found from the blue-sky statute. But as deals become more complicated and as more parties become involved, encounters with blue-sky laws become increasingly likely, and they should be carefully checked.

The prime focus of this book, however, will be on the regulatory policies of the SEC. Blue-sky laws will be discussed again, however, in connection with tender offers, where they have become an extremely important factor. Before exploring the SEC's position regarding small business financing, it will be useful to sketch briefly the evolution and key functions of the Commission.

THE ROLE OF THE SECURITIES AND EXCHANGE COMMISSION

Origins of the SEC

The stock market collapse of 1929 engendered outrage in the investing public. In reaction, the Senate authorized its Banking and Currency Committee to investigate the abuses on Wall Street. Under the guidance of Ferdinand Pecora, this committee's findings ultimately resulted in the key federal securities legislation.

Debate about the inevitable new securities laws focused around their technique: Should they be based on a system of disclosure, or, rather, should there be administrative findings as to the fairness of the particular deal?

In his message urging adoption of a disclosure statute, President Franklin Roosevelt said:

> Of course, the Federal Government cannot and should not take any action which might be construed as approving or guaranteeing that newly issued securities are sound in the sense that their value will be maintained or that the properties which they represent will earn profit. . . . There is, however, an obligation upon us to insist that every issue of new securities to be sold in interstate commerce shall be accompanied by full publicity and information, and that no essentially important element attending the issue shall be concealed from the buying public.

Louis D. Brandeis, then a Supreme Court Justice, was a formidable influence on the result. His famous 1914 dictum, "Sunlight is said to be the best of disinfectants," was ultimately persuasive. A statute premised on the utility of public disclosure was adopted, the Securities Act of 1933.

Critics found that concept superficial. Then Professor William O. Douglas (later an SEC Chairman and a Supreme Court Justice) complained about the "nineteenth century piece of legislation" with "the great reliance placed on truth about securities, as if the truth could be told to people who could understand it." But, today, the disclosure system still prevails, although the debate as to its effectiveness still goes on.

The Securities and Exchange Commission itself was created by the Securities Exchange Act of 1934. Until the Commission was established, the Securities Act of 1933 was administered by the Federal Trade Commission. Today, the SEC has a staff of more than 2,000, making it relatively quite a small federal agency, with a budget of about $58 million; some 60% of its budget is accounted for by fees it collects in connection with its operations. The SEC is composed of five members appointed for staggered 5-year terms by the President with the consent of the Senate. Not more than three of the commissioners can be members of the same political party. The Chairman of the Commission, selected by the President, is the dominant force. However, the staff, which, over the years, has built an unusual reputation for competence, has considerable independence.

Statutory Responsibilities and Organization

Although the Commission administers six key statutes, the focus in this book will be primarily on the Securities Act of 1933 and the Securities Exchange Act of 1934 and, to a lesser extent, the Trust Indenture Act of 1939 and Chapter X of the Bankruptcy Act. These statutes will be described in detail later, but their key characteristics can be briefly sketched.

The Securities Act of 1933   The 1933 Act focuses on the mass distribution of securities; it basically provides that securities which are offered to the public through interstate commerce must be registered with the SEC unless there is a specific exemption for the transaction, such as a private placement to a limited number of sophisticated wealthy investors, or for the security, such as U.S. government bonds. Assuming no exemption, a registration statement containing a prospectus must be filed giving specified information; the SEC does not judge the merits of the security but, at most, only reviews the completeness and accuracy of the filing. The prospectus must be given to potential buyers, and there are specific penalties for material misstatements.

The Securities Exchange Act of 1934   The 1934 Act is concerned with the trading of securities, the financing of purchases, and the election of corporate directors. Companies listed on stock exchanges or having more than 500 shareholders must file certain regular reports with the SEC, including a Form 10-K annually, a Form 10-Q quarterly, Annual Proxy Statements, and Form 8-K for special events, all containing financial and other information prescribed by the SEC. In addition, the 1934 Act contains a general fraud provision applicable to all securities sold in interstate commerce, even though they are exempt from registration.

The Trust Indenture Act of 1939   As previously discussed, the 1939 Act requires that publicly held debt be issued pursuant to contract, an indenture, containing specific provisions to protect the public. For each debt issue, there must be a trustee whose obligations in the event of a default on the debt is to protect the public debt holders as if the trustee were a "prudent man" acting on his own behalf.

Chapter X of the Bankruptcy Act (1939) In the event of a bankruptcy of a publicly held company, the company or its creditors may seek a reorganization under Chapter X. In contrast to Chapter XI reorganizations, which do not affect secured creditors, a Chapter X reorganization can involve all the creditors of a corporation. Unlike under Chapter XI, a trustee is usually appointed to replace present corporate management. The SEC's role is advisory but often definitive. It studies any proposed reorganization plan and issues a report on whether the proposal is fair, feasible, and equitable; in Chapter XI, the SEC has no role.

The SEC is divided into various divisions and offices. The five most relevant for the purposes of this book are the Division of Corporation Finance (perhaps the most important), the Office of the Chief Accountant, the Division of Market Regulation, the Division of Enforcement, and the Division of Corporate Regulation.

The Division of Corporation Finance is basically charged with implementing the disclosure function of the SEC under both the 1933 and the 1934 Acts. All registration statements, proxy statements, 10-K forms, and other reports are reviewed by members of this division's staff. In collaboration with the Division of Enforcement, this division also reviews tender-offer filings. The division itself is organized into branches which report to the different Assistant Directors of the Division, and it is customary for each branch chief to run his or her branch slightly differently. Because corporations usually have all their filings examined by the same branch chief, it is quite helpful to be familiar with the chief's views. The Office of Chief Accountant works with this division in determining the financial accounting standards applicable to disclosure documents.

Stock market activity is the focus of the Division of Market Regulation. Regulation of stock exchanges, brokers, and dealers is within its mandate. The Division of Enforcement is the litigating arm of the SEC. It institutes the enforcement proceedings for violations under all the Commission's statutes and serves a "tough cop" function. Most of the disclosure regarding corporate bribery is attributable to the efforts of the Division of Enforcement. The Division of Corporate Regulation is charged with the advisory function of the SEC under Chapter X. Until the 1970s, this division was relatively dormant. With the dramatic rise in Chapter X proceedings, however, it has recently become quite active.

All documents filed with the SEC are readily obtainable. Various services will provide fast photocopies, or copies can be ordered from the Commission. In addition, all documents may be inspected at the Commission's Washington library, and most documents can be inspected at the Commission's regional offices in New York and Chicago, as well as at the exchange on which a security is listed.

The SEC and Small Business

Under the 1933 Act, it is generally illegal to sell securities without register-ing them with the SEC. However, a series of exemptions from the registration requirements may be applicable to small issuers. The criteria for eligibility for these exemptions differ considerably; certain potential investors may be included under one test but must be excluded under another. Even though a particular transaction may be exempt from registration, the offering is still subject to the SEC's rule prohibiting fraud in securities sales.

Intrastate issues   Under Section 3(a)11 of the 1933 Act, securities offered and sold solely to persons residing within a single state by a corporation incorporated and doing business in that state are exempt from SEC registration, even if "publicly offered." In reaction to confusion about the scope of this exemption, the SEC adopted Rule 147, which states the guidelines for 3(a)11's applicability. In theory, Rule 147 is not an exclusive interpretation of the exemption, but as a practical matter, it is. Under Rule 147, a firm incorporated and doing 80% of its business within a state (or which has gross annual revenues of less than $5,000) may sell its securities without registering them if at least 80% of the proceeds from the offering must be used within the state and all offerees are residents of that state. Resales for 9 months must be offered only to state residents, and the stock certificates must bear a legend indicating these restrictions.

Rule 147 limitations are quite severe, especially for an ongoing business which may be locally based but have interstate sales. The most frequent problem faced by potential users of Rule 147, however, is that each and every purchaser must be a resident of the same state. In metropolitan areas such as New York, all the prospective buyers may work in the same city and live in three different states; so Rule 147 doesn't help, even though the transaction is local in nature. If Rule 147 is satisfied, the SEC doesn't require any paperwork in connection with the offering, a sizable advantage over many of the other exemptions.

Regulation A issues   Under Section 3B of the 1933 Act, the SEC has authority to exempt issues smaller than $500,000. Pursuant to Section 3B, the Commission has issued its Regulation A exemption rules, which cover these situations. Unless the offering is less than $50,000, a prospectus must be delivered conforming with the Regulation's requirements, which are considerable. Essentially, Regulation A, often referred to as "Reg. A," provides for a short-form registration. In fact, however, many Regulation

A prospectuses are as detailed as full-blown, standard registration statements.

Form 1-A states the information which must be filed with the SEC in a Regulation A offering. In addition to general background as to the issuer, its officers and directors, and its securities, the circular must include, roughly, the following information, conforming with the requirements of Regulation A's Rule 256:

• the name, address, and state of incorporation of the issuer
• the amount of securities offered, their price, and the commissions being paid
• the name and address of any underwriters and any relationship between the underwriter and the issuer
• a breakdown of the use of proceeds
• a description of the terms of the securities offered
• the nature of the business, including principal markets, facilities, patents, backgrounds of officers and directors, their pay as a group, and the pay of the three highest-paid officers
• the security holdings of the officers and directors and
• financial statements in accordance with generally accepted accounting principles, which need not be certified.

The difficulty with Regulation A is that the business description and the financials may require a great deal of effort, and yet Regulation A filings lack the marketing prestige of a fully registered offer. Regulation A's key advantage is that under it the statutory liability is more limited for officers and directors for a false or misleading statement than it is in connection with a standard prospectus. Section 11(a) of the 1933 Act is the basis for suits against persons deemed participants in the public offering registration process whether in fact they were involved (such as all directors), and it is inapplicable. Rather, in Regulation A deals, the offering company itself and actual participatns in the perpetration of a fraud are the only parties liable under Sections 12 and 17 of the 1933 Act, the general antifraud provisions, and Section 10b of the 1934 Act.

Regulation 240 For a small issuer, Regulation 240 may be the most practical method of issuing securities. Regulation 240, which was established pursuant to the power of the SEC under Section 3B to exempt certain small issues from registration, allows an issuer to sell to the public up to $100,000 in securities, provided, however, that the company's securities are not owned by 100 persons and no advertising commissions are used to sell the issue. Subsequently, up to $100,000 may be sold in any 12-month period, but a notification form must be filed with the SEC. Securities purchased pursuant to Regulation 240 have the same status as those acquired in a private placement; they may not be resold without being registered or being eligible for an exemption from registration.

Simplified registration In reaction to the needs of small businesses for easier access to the investing public's funds, the SEC has recently proposed that public offerings for less than $2 million be made through simplified registration procedures. Although the proposed requirements are very similar to Regulation A, the liability on directors will be similar to that in a normal public offering. At the moment, it is unclear how successful this approach will be. On the one hand, it would be a great advantage to be selling unrestricted, publicly registered securities to investors. On the other hand, the projections which are at the heart of a private placement to sophisticated investors are generally not included in registration statements which may be given to unsophisticated investors. Furthermore, it may well be that lawyers will feel that to protect against possible omissions, the same level of information as is contained in a full-blown registration statement is advisable. The key advantage as to format may well be the use of unaudited financials, but, this too, is a mixed blessing. When audited statements are used, directors and officers may rely on them unless they know them to be incorrect; unaudited figures would place a burden of investigation on these insiders. All in all, simplified registration is probably not a panacea for the problems of small businesses raising capital.

The private offering exemption Under Section 4(2) of the 1933 Act, a specific exemption exists for "nonpublic offerings," commonly known as private placements. Since a nonpublic offering is not defined in the 1933 Act, the SEC and the courts have struggled to come up with useful standards.

Prior to the landmark 1952 Supreme Court ruling in the *Ralston-Purina* case, the presumption was that an offering was private if there were not a "substantial" number of offerees involved. "Substantial" was interpreted in 1935 by the General Counsel of the Commission to mean 25 or fewer persons.

It is important to point out that this numerical standard was devised in terms of persons offered the securities, not actual buyers. The SEC and the courts have taken a very broad view of who is an offeree. Quite clearly, an offer is not limited to a formal proposal. For example, inquiries as to whether prospective purchasers would be interested in a formal offer are themselves regarded as offers.

In *Ralston-Purina,* the Supreme Court upset this numerical rule of thumb by holding that the number of offerees by itself was not determinative. Ralston-Purina, a food products manufacturer, periodically offered its stock to hundreds of its employees. Although the company claimed that only its key employees were involved, the SEC alleged that, on its face, the numbers guideline for a private placement was violated. However, according to the Court, the key question was whether the offerees needed the protection of the securities laws—the large numbers by themselves did not necessarily create an illegal offering. For example, the Court was interested in whether there was access to information similar to that in a registration statement and whether the investors could fend for themselves. The key employees, it turns out, included stenographers, a loading dock foreman, and a veterinarian. As the Court stated, "The Statute would seem to apply to a 'public offering' whether to few or many."

Cases since *Ralston-Purina* have tightened the definition of a permissible private placement. In fact, the decision in a 1972 appeals court case, *Continental Tobacco,* was so strict that, if taken literally, it would have almost eliminated the concept.

Continental Tobacco was a venture whose business was the manufacture and sale of low-tar and -nicotine cigarettes. After a reorganization under Chapter XI, the company's management tried to raise funds by a series of meetings in hotel rooms and homes, where movies were shown and information regarding the firm was distributed. The SEC, which, before Continental's reorganization, had won a case charging it with securities violations, again accused Continental of illegally peddling the stock. However, the lower court held that the SEC did not have a strong enough case to warrant a preliminary injunction. In reaction, the SEC staff wrote an extremely strong appeals brief taking a very narrow view of private placements, which, in essence, the appeals court adopted.

According to the appeals court, meeting number-of-offers or distribution-of-information tests was not sufficient; an investor had to be in a position to acquire knowledge equivalent to that of a corporate insider, with the power to ferret out any additional informational needs. The mere fact of receipt of information equivalent to a registration statement or of the giving of an investment representation was not sufficient.

Continental Tobacco threw the securities bar into a state of confusion. If its doctrine governed, private placements with noninsiders, no matter how well-informed or sophisticated, would be illegal. Clearly, most types of transactions then being effectuated were in jeopardy. The SEC gradually began to back away from its brief in *Continental Tobacco,* with some Commissioners admitting that the staff might have been overzealous. But the situation remained confused, and eventually the SEC attempted to clarify the standards for eligibility for a private placement exemption by promulgating Rule 146 in 1974.

Rule 146 is a safe-harbor rule, which sets forth one set of standards for a private offering; if you comply with it, the transaction will be exempt. If you do not, there is still the possibility of exemption under the judicially developed standards in existence before Rule 146. Rule 146 will be discussed in detail in the following section. For most beginning companies, it has proved impractical. The time, expense, and trouble of producing one essential requirement—a document strictly equivalent to a registration statement—are often not feasible for a small enterprise. Furthermore, the other technical aspects, such as who can act on behalf of rich but unsophisticated investors are quite restrictive, as will be seen.

Most small businesses, in fact, take advantage of the pre-146 private placement exemptions. There is often, however, an attempt to conform as much as practicable with Rule 146 without being in absolute compliance. What, then, about *Continental Tobacco?* Most practitioners have felt that the case went too far and, over the years, has lost some of its vitality. Finally, in a 1977 case, *Doran v. Petroleum Management Corp.,* the appeals court which decided *Continental Tobacco* itself said that its holding had been misconstrued. Insider-type status is required only if adequate information was not directly supplied to the purchasers, according to the court.

In thinking about eligibility for private placements, it is useful to remember the prime reasons for a rigid rule. First, the unknowing public should be protected from being bilked by hustlers. By requiring the registration of securities unless the investors are sophisticated and can fend for themselves, fair disclosure is more probable. The second basic consideration is the avoidance of an eventual distribution of securities to the general public through resales, even though the initial investors may have been sophisticated. For this reason, a long-term-investment intent and financial ability to retain the securities for a substantial period of time are required, as well as explicit restrictions on the transferability of the securities. Based on the cases and the Commission's views, some criteria become evident as rough guidelines for non-146 private placements:

Dollar amounts. The dollar amount of the offering is relatively insignificant. Small dollar amounts involving large numbers of unsophisticated investors are clearly illegal; the $1.75 billion Alaskan Pipeline financing with major insurance companies was clearly exempt.

Number of offerees. Although the number of offerees is not dispositive, it is an important factor to consider. As a rough rule of thumb, thirty-five offerees, unless they are corporation or institutional investors, should be the limit. Corporations have a tendency to soft-pedal the number of offerees by insisting that only formal solicitations count. Unfortunately, this is not the law. Negotiations, discussions, and inquiries all may be offers.

Sophistication. The offerees should all be financially sophisticated or represented by someone who is. A particularly important characteristic is past experience in similar private placement deals. To state the qualification another way, sophistication has been defined on the level of general financial acuity rather than familiarity with the particular product line. Thus, an investment banker qualifies more easily than a surgeon for stock purchases in a company making scalpels. The theory is that the surgeon may have no understanding of the financial structure and risk. It is generally felt, however, that an otherwise eligible, financially naive investor may be represented by a sophisticated agent.

Wealth. All investors should be able to bear the risk of the investment. The purpose of this test is twofold: To the extent a small or new company is involved, there is relatively high risk, which the investor should be financially able to take. Second, the risk of an eventual public distribution increases if an investor is financially pressed. Wealth in this context must, however, be a relative concept. For a $5,000 investment, a person with $50,000 in liquid assets may be wealthy; for a $25,000 investment, a real estate millionaire with liquid assets of $50,000 may be poor. Gross assets, size of investment, liquidity are all factors, but they can be more readily summarized by a simpler test: Can the prospective investor easily afford to walk away from a deal when it turns sour?

Investment intent. If investors in a private placement are contemplating resale, the chances of a distribution to the public are obviously high. Therefore, most private-placement purchase agreements require a representation as to investment intent. In addition, the securities purchased are themselves legended, as will be discussed, with language restricting their resale.

Information received. The quality of the information assembled about the offering concern is a key factor. On the face of it, a one-page advertising blurb raises serious questions about whether adequate information has been provided to investors. On the other hand, a detailed prospectus, which highlights risk factors, indicates an attempt to provide full disclosure. However, as the court cases indicate, an offering memorandum by itself is not sufficient. Access to additional information is imperative.

Relationship to the issuer. The closer the relationship between the issuer and the offerees, the better the chance for qualifying for the placement. Friends, relatives, employees, and existing stockholders are all more likely to have access to information than strangers. As the *Continental Tobacco* court indicated, the closer to insider status, the better.

Rule 146. After the *Continental Tobacco* decision, the law regarding private placements was completely confused. Rule 146, which was proposed in 1972 and adopted in 1974, was designed to be a toned-down incorporation of the *Continental Tobacco* tests: the standards for eligibility are high, but the zealous overkill position of the SEC staff was softened.

The rule is a safe-harbor provision. It defines what is clearly legal, but it is not exclusive; the pre-146 case law survives for those transactions which do not qualify under 146. Many of the rule's provisions are quite sensible. Unfortunately, it is structured as an all-or-nothing proposition. If a deal doesn't qualify for 146 completely, its provisions are theoretically totally irrelevant. As a practical matter, lawyers in the field now try to comply with 146 as much as possible, on the theory that a court may be influenced by its provisions, but legal opinions are based on general pre-146 private-placement criteria. Still, a transaction which purports to be fully in compliance with 146 is a rarity, and the old confusion about private placements is still very much present.

The provisions of Rule 146 can be summarized as follows:

1. *Limitation on purchasers.* Unlike the cases which, in effect, limit the number of *offerees,* Rule 146 limits the number of *purchasers* to a maximum of 35 in any offering. The figure is misleading, however, because certain purchasers are excluded from this computation, including relatives sharing the same house, certain trusts and corporations controlled by a purchasing party, and any person buying $150,000, or more, in securities through the offering.

2. *Manner of offering.* No general solicitation or advertising is permitted. Letters or invitations to meetings or seminars are allowed to be sent only to persons the issuer reasonably believes capable of evaluating the merits and risks of the proposed investment, which for convenience will be referred to as being "sophisticated," or able to bear the economic risk of the investment, which shall be referred to as being "rich." According to the SEC, the relevant criterion is that the offeree could hold unregistered securities for an indefinite period and could afford a complete loss.

3. *Background of offerees.* As pointed out, before any solicitation can be made, the offering company must believe that the offeree is either rich or sophisticated. However, before a sale can be made, reasonable inquiry must actually be made and the offeror must then reasonably believe that the prospective purchaser is either rich and sophisticated or represented by a sophisticated "offeree representative."

4. *The offeree representative.* If a prospective purchaser is rich but unsophisticated, Rule 146 requires an "offeree representative." Essentially, the offeree representative is expected to be a sophisticated investment counselor. The practical problem is that the qualifications for an offeree representative are so rigid that they block the usage of 146 for many typical private placements, particularly venture-capital transactions. Under Rule 146, the offeree representative cannot be an officer, a director, or a beneficial owner of 10% or more of any class of equity securities of the issuer. Assuming the offeree representative qualifies, the offeree must designate in writing the offeree representative to act. This designation must be specific to the transaction; appointing a representative for "all private placements" is not sufficient. Furthermore, disclosure must be made in writing of all relationships between the issuer and the offeree representative.

Unfortunately, these criteria pose a number of problems in a typical venture-capital deal. Normally, a venture-capital firm has a number of rich but unsophisticated clients who ask its advice on private-placement transactions. Many of these accounts are discretionary; the venture-capital firm is charged with investing the funds to the best of its abilities. The net result is that it is inconvenient to get deal-by-deal authorizations.

Furthermore, when the venture firm does make investments in small businesses, it usually ends up with a substantial proportion of the equity, and, often, an officer of the concern is elected to the board of directors of the issuer. Therefore, it is often impossible for a venture firm to qualify as an offeree representative for its own clients.

Of course, the SEC is trying to avoid blatant conflicts, but disclosure may be more appropriate, especially for larger investors, than blanket prohibition. Not surprisingly, venture firms, in the meantime, rely on the general private-placement exemption rather than Rule 146.

5. *Required information.* Unless there is particularly strong access to information, by virtue of employment, a relationship, or economic bargaining power, a memorandum equivalent to a registration statement must be provided, except that under certain limited circumstances, the financial statements need not be audited. Prior to the sale, an opportunity must be given the purchaser to ask questions and receive further information from the issuer. Although the rule has been amended to state that information may be condensed or omitted if not material, the SEC included a warning that the burden of proof to show that such editing was appropriate is on the issuer. Many lawyers seem to believe that the SEC is still contemplating a full-blown registration statement and that this requirement may be too burdensome to small businesses.

6. *Transfer restrictions.* Reasonable inquiry is required as to whether the purchasers are buying for their own account, and the purchasers must sign an agreement stating that they know they are purchasing securities which cannot be resold without registration or an exemption. In addition, the issuer is required to place a restrictive legend on the securities and to issue stop-transfer instructions to the stock transfer agent, if any.

In summary, Rule 146 is often thought about but rarely explicitly followed. At this stage, it is overdrafted and mechanically cumbersome. Indeed, the SEC has recently recognized this fact itself by asking the investing community for comments regarding the possible revocation or the major revision of the rule. Unfortunately, the SEC discovered that the rule was being abused in the field of oil and gas partnerships, and has proposed revisions to clamp down on those abuses. Basically, under the SEC proposals, there will be reporting forms to give the SEC notification about a pending 146 offer and its characteristics above a certain dollar limit and a follow-up form to get information about the results of the offer. The result may well be an even heavier burden in venture-capital situations. Assuming the rule is not eventually revoked, it may, as amended over the years, evolve into a more functional role. Meanwhile, parts of it are seeping into legal practice as broad guidelines rather than as technical mandates.

Resale of Restricted Securities

Having acquired securities in a private placement, when and how can an investor resell? If the securities could be immediately resold, the purpose of the private-offering exemption could obviously be defeated. Under the 1933 Act, control persons are treated as if they are the issuer, and are subject to the same limitations on securities sales. Normally a noncontrol person is not restricted on resales because the 1933 Act specifically exempts transactions by sellers other than issuers (including control persons), underwriters, or dealers. However, a buyer in a private placement who resells, even if not a control person, is acting as an underwriter, as defined by the 1933 Act, by facilitating the distribution of the securities. Underwriters under the 1933 Act may not sell securities without registering them or finding an exemption. Although it may seem at first surprising, one does not have to be a securities firm to be an underwriter within the 1933 Act definition. Anyone who acts in the chain of transactions through which securities move from an issuer to the public is acting as a statutory underwriter.

To prevent resales, the SEC and the courts have insisted that certificates for privately placed securities, including those sold under Rule 146, state on their faces that they were purchased in a private placement and may not be resold unless the securities are either registered or sold in a transaction exempt under the 1933 Act. These legended certificates, known frequently as "letter stock" or "restricted stock," are virtually impossible to sell except through another private placement.

In the boom years of the 1960s, many investors bought letter stock, only to find that they couldn't dispose of it. As a result, lawyers were constantly besieging the SEC with requests to let their clients sell their stock because the clients had originally purchased with an investment intent and circumstances had changed. They were divorced, sick, poor, etc. You name the sob story, and some lawyer presented it in the form of a petition for a no-action letter. In addition, control persons were allowed to dribble out small amounts of stock. This sytem was imprecise and took a great deal of SEC staff effort.

In 1969, a study headed by former SEC Commissioner Francis Wheat examined the situation and recommended major revisions in the SEC's approach.

Rule 144 Based on the Wheat Report recommendations, the SEC adopted Rule 144 in 1972. Rule 144 is the only way control persons are permitted to resell their securities to the public without registration. For investors other than control persons, Rule 144 does not purport to be exclusive, but the SEC has made it quite clear that it does not encourage alternatives to the rule. For example, it announced it would issue no more no-action letters regarding restricted stock and that the whole change-of-circumstances concept was no longer a factor in determining eligibility for sale. So the pre-144 case law is reduced to a very simple proposition: Hold the securities for a long, long time and you're probably not involved in a distribution and are, therefore, not an underwriter. Thus, unlike Rule 146, Rule 144 is in frequent use today. The alternatives, Rule 237, as will be discussed, and the pre-existing case law are impractical. Essentially then, for noncontrol persons, Rule 144 states the conditions under which a purchaser of letter stock may eventually resell the securities to the public without being considered an underwriter under Section 2(11) of the 1933 Act. The key terms of Rule 144 may be outlined as follows:

Holding period. No securities purchased through a private placement may be sold pursuant to Rule 144 for a period of at least two years from the date of purchase. Shares acquired upon the conversion of securities are regarded as having been purchased at the time the convertible security was bought, but shares acquired as the result of a default under a pledge agreement are deemed to be held from the time of forfeiture. This holding-period restriction does not apply to control persons who acquired securities in other than private placements.

Amount limitations. During any six-month period, a person can sell the following amounts of securities: If the securities are traded on a national securities exchange, the lesser of 1% of the pertinent securities outstanding or the average trading volume within the four weeks preceding the sale. If the securities are not listed, 1% of the pertinent securities outstanding may be sold.

Manner of sale and information requirements. Under 144, securities may be sold only in brokers' transactions—there can be no solicitation of a buy order nor payments of unusually high commissions. In addition, there must be adequate information about the issuer publicly available. For this reason, it is common in venture-capital deals for investors, at their option, to be able to insist that an issuer comply with the information requirements of Rule 144 beginning at a date nearly two years from the closing. In effect, these information requirements mean that a company has to have gone public. Notices of proposed 144 sales must be filed with the SEC and the pertinent stock exchange if sales for a six-month period exceed $10,000 or 500 units or shares.

Rule 237 In addition to Rule 144, Rule 237 gives some additional flexibility to holders of privately placed securities. Five years after full payment for the purchase, the lesser of $50,000 of securities or 1% of the securities outstanding in a particular class may be sold within a 1-year period. No restrictions on brokers' transactions or publicly available information is included in this rule. However, by the time 5 years have passed, the argument that an investor had an investment intent is solid under any standard, so Rule 237 may well be moot. The likelihood of investors being attacked as statutory underwriters because they resold in 4½ years or exceeded a $50,000 test is limited. So Rule 237 really represents an absolute safe harbor to protect against a nonexistent storm.

Venture Capital
and Private Placements

If a small company has the potential for substantial growth, it often turns to the investing institutions that specialize in nurturing new concerns into major corporations—the venture capitalists.

INTRODUCTION TO VENTURE CAPITAL

Venture capital is a glamorous industry. Suddenly, a small investment doubles, triples, even quadruples. But there may be constant heartache because many investments are simply duds or require a great deal of effort before they turn around. In the early 1970s, nothing a venture-capital firm could do could go right. Lately, however, the situation has been improving.

The key assumption of venture capitalism is that the profits from the investments in the select companies that prosper will more than offset the devastating losses from those that don't. Indeed, venture capitalists feel that a lack of some dramatic losses indicates that an investor hasn't taken enough risks.

The difficulty is that when the public market dries up, as happened in the early 1970s, the venture capitalist loses the "out" that makes the high return possible. For example, in 1969, 649 issues with a preoffering net worth under $5 million went public, raising $1.4 billion. During 1975, only three such issues went public, selling a total of $13.4 million in securities. If the companies invested in can't go public and don't want to merge, the venture capital firm's portfolio of letter stocks is extremely illiquid. Furthermore, the companies invested in have their future clouded by a lack of liquidity because they can't raise funds for their needs from the public. Ironically, the more successful the concept, the more the new firm has a need for capital which it can't obtain on reasonable terms, thereby jeopardizing the venture capitalist's investment. To compensate for investing in venture situations under these circumstances instead of in IBM or Exxon or Disney, the promise of a truly golden future is required.

Exacerbating the difficulty is the fact that although venture deals involve less money than public financing, they are as complicated, if not more so. Inexorably, there are an infinity of complicated variations on the securities sold, designed to appeal to the maximum number of eligible investors. Furthermore, since the venture capitalists are usually investing a large sum in proportion to the founder's equity, there are always control problems. Needless to say, negotiations are complicated and expensive.

What exactly is a venture-capital firm? There is no precise description applicable to all, but as the expression goes, you would know one if you saw one. Some are investment divisions of major corporations who want to invest on the frontiers of industrial technology. Others are, in essence, private mutual funds in which wealthy investors and major institutions invest. Such funds are managed by professionals in the venture-capital field who have been trained in the analysis, development, and rescue of small companies. Others, as will be discussed later, are small-business investment companies which receive certain financial benefits from the federal Small Business Administration and are restricted by federal law in their investment policy. All have one common characteristic: the twinkle in the eye when they dream about the future. Not surprisingly, however, there are now a decreasing number of firms with this gleam. It has been estimated that more than 25% of the concerns in the business stopped investing in venture situations during the early 1970s.

The venture capitalists don't think of themselves as dreamers. By experience, they have classified companies into different stages of development and have an approach appropriate to each level. If something goes wrong, they have troubleshooting experts on their staffs to fill the breach. Interestingly, venture capitalists seem to agree that the key to success in small business is the quality of management. Many sound technical ideas do not come of age commercially because of the inability of the officers of a company to manage. Indeed, one of the most helpful things a venture-capital firm can do is, in effect, to offer management consultant advice.

Conventionally, venture capitalists analyze companies as having four growth stages:

Stage 1 is the start-up of a new venture; the entrepreneur has probably put a great deal of thought into the project already, but the venture is only beginning to be formalized. At this stage, most of the money comes from the entrepreneur and friends. Unless it had a previous acquaintance with the entrepreneur, a venture-capital investor might not get involved until the late part of Stage 1, after the initial round of financing from closer backers.

Stage 2 is the period during which the company already has some sort of performance record, and conventional sources of financing, such as banks, begin to provide for its financial needs.

Stage 3 occurs when a company has prospered but needs additional funds, often from the public, in order to continue its expansion.

Stage 4 brings the mature company, with full access to conventional financing.

In theory, venture capital is invested late in Stage 1 and early in Stage 2 to keep good companies going. Although the risk is great, the anticipated rewards are high: venture capitalists used to target for a return of some 40% on their money. Unfortunately, the realities of the 1970s have made these theories mostly academic. The fact is that Stage 3 is now very hard to attain for a young company, because the public market for new stocks has dried up. As a result, venture capitalists are investing more in Stage 3 companies than in Stage 1 and 2, and because of the costs in following an investment, are looking for situations where relatively large chunks of more than $100,000 are required.

Structuring a venture-capital deal necessarily involves arduous negotiations between the investors and the company. At this point, it is useful to get an overview of the deal-negotiating process generally before returning to its specific application in the context of a venture investment.

NEGOTIATION STRATEGY

Successful negotiation tactics are partly instinctual, but largely rely on accumulated insight and interpersonal skills. The fundamental fact a negotiator must recognize is that, unlike litigation, where one side wins and the other one loses, negotiated deals necessarily involve working together with the other party to a mutually satisfactory resolution of the issues. Experts on the strategy of negotiations stress the need for a cooperative approach. In a truly successful bargaining session, everybody can feel some satisfaction.

How much difference does a good negotiator make? In a routine transaction or one in which the terms are fairly standardized, the answer is, probably very little. In complicated deals such as mergers, joint ventures, and venture-capital investments, the ability of the negotiator is fundamental in two respects: First, the terms negotiated can substantially alter the economics of a transaction—in an assets acquisition, some 20%, as a rough estimate, of the agreed-upon basic purchase price. Second, however, and more importantly, the negotiator may be the determining factor in whether the deal survives. Unless skillfully handled, a myriad of small issues sometimes builds into mutual antagonisms. Unfortunately, out of this accumulation of irritation, the building up of lethargy, disorganization, and lack of creative problem-solving ability, many a deal that should have lived has died.

Objectives

Before entering into any bargaining session, some preliminary reflection is necessary. The first, and perhaps the hardest task, is determining your own side's objectives. One reason for the difficulty is that the differing representatives of a party often will not share the same perspective or, even worse, will not have thought in depth about the main issues. A key challenge is, therefore, dealing with one's own side and helping to focus their energies, To consider techniques independent of a clear set of objectives makes little sense. Two polar examples illustrate this point: On one hand, a buyer is willing to buy a house only if it can be bought for $100,000 even though its fair market value is $150,000; a maximum of $100,000 is simply the limit of the buyer's resources. On the other hand, the seller needs to sell the house immediately in order to obtain the down payment for another house being purchased in another city. The seller is naturally impatient but very reasonable; the objective is to sell at all costs. The buyer, however, is extremely fussy as to terms; it makes no sense to be reasonable in the conventional manner because the buyer then could not afford to buy the house. Necessarily, the strategy in both cases is dictated by the objectives.

Preparation

Extensive preparation is the key to giving an edge to a negotiator. Not only is it desirable to research the issues involved, but possession of as much data as possible about the other side's representatives and its current position and techniques is imperative. Determining as early as possible in a particular transaction the needs of the other side, both in personal and economic terms, is fundamental to successful negotiation. But just as important is an understanding of your own nature and mannerisms, and the personalities and reactions of your side's representatives.

Despite conventional wisdom, it is often quite helpful if the other party is being represented by a sophisticated advocate. When the other side at the bargaining table does not have a knowledgeable team, an atmosphere of suspicion and delay often arises. Knowledge gives the confidence to be flexible, to recommend reasonable compromises. When it makes sense, the strong can afford to be weak. On the other hand, the natural reaction of people in over their heads is to be recalcitrant. To take a typical situation, if a buy-out of a small company has complicated tax implications, it is extremely difficult to persuade someone who does not understand the tax laws to devise a structure which uses those laws to maximum advantage.

Techniques

Techniques are mechanisms to obtain objectives. Obviously, the appropriate technique depends on the particular objective. There are, however, some universal guides used by lawyers and other negotiators:

Control A key element in negotiation is retaining control. For example, the basic maxim many young lawyers learn is to keep the master document and do the drafting, When parties are making comments around the table, the copy which will be sent to the typist is the one the negotiator controls. Naturally, this gives the negotiator a good bit of added leverage. First, the negotiator usually has the choice of redrafting a comment later to reflect his or her own input or of inserting the actual language now. Second, if the negotiator feels the debate on any point should continue, he or she can keep the issue open simply by not writing anything down yet.

Pace is a related point. Good negotiators never let a deal get away from them; if substantive issues are being discussed too rapidly without careful thought, haste may haunt them later. One ideal way in which to control pace is to be the host for the meeting. The negotiator controls when the documents are distributed, when breaks are taken, and often what the time pressures are. It is very important, however, to be cordial and accommodating so that the adversaries will want to return. Just as in sports, when the home team usually performs better in its own stadium, a negotiator often obtains improved results by bargaining in friendly territory.

On the other hand, it is also the responsibility of the negotiator to make sure the pace of issue resolution is such that the deal survives. Long hours, lists of key issues, and constant prodding may be necessary, but a deal is like a soufflé; timing is of the essence.

Credibility It is very important to establish credibility early in a negotiation. Credibility is accorded some negotiators because of their reputation, and unless they demonstrate otherwise, they have no need to establish that stature. For example, a senior partner in a major law firm is assumed to be skilled. However, his young associate or the local counsel for a corporation may not be assumed to have that credibility. Here is where preparation comes in very handy. If, for example, the associate can demonstrate an awesome familiarity with the documents and can make a few obviously salient points early, respect and credibility may be earned.

A related problem is that of firmness. Although negotiating is a cooperative process, most parties are prepared to pick the other's pockets if the opportunity presents itself. If one side thinks that the other is an easy mark, the negotiations will inevitably degenerate. Usually, the tendency of inexperienced negotiators is to be too belligerent and inflexible. When these negotiators realize that the goal is to close on reasonable terms rather than to bulldoze the other side, this youthful overindulgence is soon toned down. But the art of not being too pliant is a more delicate one, depending in large part on the situation. Bright-line rules are much easier to use than case-by-case calls based on judgment, but the latter are required. One way to handle overbearing advocates is to take one issue as a test case and spend extra time resolving it. Hopefully, the other side will realize that, if necessary, bullying will be firmly resisted and will desist. Sometimes, the other side will be represented by someone who is obstinate for obstinacy's sake. If all else fails, try to make sure that the clients on both sides watch a performance in person. Often, a rebuke will follow, and behavior will change with surprising rapidity.

Sensitivity Because negotiation is necessarily a cooperative process, the other side has to be reasonably happy for the deal to work. It is therefore important to be reasonable, although not obsequious, and, ideally, to give the other side enough so that its advocates do not feel resentful. A little psychology is required. All those involved in a deal like to feel that they made a positive contribution and that they obtained some concessions from the other side. After all, otherwise, their presence wasn't required. It's not that all parties need be equally happy with the results of a deal; it's just that everyone should have some limited solace. Courtesies, such as specifically marking changes, providing extra copies of documents, and giving personal assistance may also bear important dividends, especially if the parties are to have an ongoing relationship, such as in a joint venture. When a side has bargaining strength, it sometimes becomes giddy with power. Retention of perspective is important; one day, the tables may turn, and a loss of dignity is seldom forgiven or forgotten.

In addition to these universal techniques, other strategies are very much dependent on the situation:

Confusion versus clarity Generally, it is advisable to articulate a clear, concise position. Sometimes, however, there is great advantage to confusion, especially if time is running against the other side. For example, in buying a company with a tax-loss carry-forward, the excuse can be used that operating managers refuse to allow that element to be significantly reflected in the purchase price because they really don't understand or care about after-tax impacts, since incentive compensation is based on pretax results. Such an excuse is frustrating but much less bothersome than the sheer exploitation of stating that those rights are valuable and then refusing to pay for them. Similarly, confusion often simplifies bargaining by limiting flexibility. For example, an advocate may assert that though there is great merit in the 20 modifications sought by the other side, the client is a large organization with standard policies and it would require months of delay and myriad committee decisions to alter the documents as suggested. Confusion, whether just apparent or, all too often, real, gives the other side a rational reason for accepting proposals which are irrationally unfair. Even if one does not care to use this confusion gambit, as a matter of principle, it should be recognized in the techniques of others.

Emotions The Russians have developed a reputation among executives as negotiators who kick and scream over every comma. Pretty soon, the other side becomes immune to the dramatic effect. But there are negotiators who can skillfully turn on righteous indignation at precisely the right point and be extremely effective. Certainly, control over feelings is useful and histrionics are seldom persuasive, but all anger need not be repressed. Especially if one has been cooperative and reasonable, a show of anger may well be justified by the situation, particularly if you feel the other side has begun to try to take advantage of your flexibility.

Support As a general rule, it is useful to have at least as many representatives of your side at a meeting as the other side has. Otherwise, there is an element of feeling overpowered, especially to the inexperienced negotiator. There are, however, some caveats. First, if you overwhelm the other side with numbers, the reaction may well be obstinacy instead of willingness to make reasonable concessions. Second, the lack of full representation gives a negotiator more personal control and more chance to ferret out information from the other side without a quid pro quo. The more people from the negotiator's side present, the more likely that strategic planning will be upset. For example, in a large conference, it is common for two business people to begin talking directly to each other instead of going through the negotiators about issues that one negotiator would rather have brought up later. What usually makes sense is the development of a small team with the negotiator as the authorized spokesperson who can turn to the others on the team as appropriate. Some coordination is required, or the team will act as a jumble of individuals with contradictory ideas and techniques which cannot help weakening a side's bargaining position.

Agents versus principals For sessions to be productive, the negotiators must have the bargaining authority, subject to their principals' comments, to compromise the less material issues. A more fundamental question is whether a principal should always be present to make the major decisions. Without doubt, proceedings are expedited if disputes can be immediately resolved, but there are serious drawbacks—most important, the loss of time for reflection and an opportunity to keep the various outstanding points in balance. Furthermore, principals often get impatient with discussions of details which may be cumulatively important. It frequently helps to have the principals present at early meetings to discuss fundamental terms and then let their staffs attempt to implement the agreed-upon principles. If, as usual, there is a list of major items which cannot be agreed upon by the staffs, the principals can meet again to resolve them.

One common tactic is for the negotiator to try to elicit concessions from the other side and then refuse to make corresponding compromises because of a lack of authority. If this technique is allowed to succeed, the result is a one-way give-up. Either insist on principals being present or agree that both sides can in good faith revise their positions, but that the concessions are points the negotiators will, respectively, recommend.

Term sheets In structuring a deal, the fundamental principles are first informally agreed upon. Then the issue is whether a letter of understanding or a term sheet should be drawn up to highlight these major points or whether the parties should begin working on the definitive papers. Usually, letters of intent are not legally binding—they are subject to the approval of the respective boards of directors and the drafting of an acceptable definitive contract. However, these letters do have the advantage of limiting the scope of debate in the negotiations, morally if not legally. After all, if a term sheet says a debt instrument will have a stated sinking fund, it's rather difficult to raise the point as a fresh issue in negotiations. The problem is that as letters of intent become more detailed, they consume energy which could better have been spent working on the definitive contract, and, on the other hand, if they are not detailed enough, allegations may be made that some point was waived. As a general rule, letters of intent are useful if they have been thought through; quickie documents often backfire. The risk is worthwhile, however, if there is a desire to pin down the other side on the fundamentals before extensive bargaining begins.

Approach Some negotiators like to slug through the documents, correcting a typo here, a comma there, and then focusing on a substantive point. At some time, this must be done. The danger in doing it prematurely is that it submerges key principles, bores the important executives present who are not interested in grammatical debates and treats related problems in isolation. Another, and generally preferable, approach is to treat issues like a story in a newspaper, with important issues first, followed by more minor disputes. The recurrent difficulty is that problems are never fully explored until there is an attempt to resolve them on paper. It often, therefore, makes sense for the parties at the beginning and the end of sessions to agree on a list of major unresolved issues and attempt to get clarification from their principals. Many executives understandably get bored by the legal byplay on drafting provisions. In the end, however, the wisdom of the conference room discussions is unimportant; it is the wording of the contract which counts.

Good cop/bad cop   One common negotiating tactic is the good cop/bad cop routine. Essentially, one member of the negotiating team makes unreasonable demands and exhibits an excitable temper. The other negotiator says that although he is understanding of his colleague's viewpoint, compromises should be obtained. The temptation is to like the "good cop" and make concessions to keep the "bad cop" out of the bargaining. Often, of course, the whole routine is a ruse and should not unduly influence decisions.

The salami slice   Any negotiation has a host of issues. Instead of treating them together as a whole, the salami technique is to slice off one issue at a time and dispose of it. This approach has great advantages in complex deals; if one doesn't find an arbitrary starting point, the task seems impossible. Strangely, however, your bargaining strength may lie in this very complexity rather than in any one issue. When piece after piece of salami is sliced, you may be left with nothing but the casing.

SELLING THE DEAL

Investors and other would-be titans of industry often have the mistaken impression that venture-capital firms are philanthropists—ready, willing, and able to sponsor a needy idea. In fact, successful venture-capital firms must blend being hard-nosed investors and dreamers; they can possibly support only one out of every hundred ideas presented, so the concept had better be enticing.

What sort of idea is supported? A high potential for growth is mandatory, since the expected returns must be considerable to justify the risks. Traditionally, high technology fields such as computers and lasers have dominated venture-capital portfolios, but, over time, the realization set in that fast foods, small-package-express distribution, or merchandising can have as strong potential if the concept is right.

A key ingredient is credibility. An inventor with a preeminent reputation and skilled managers with experience in an industry have a head start on getting backing. Perhaps most important are a detailed business plan and the apparent ability to implement it. Nobody believes pie in the sky figures. Thorough projections, with assumptions highlighted and supported, are necessary. Although any proposed offering memorandum will be thoroughly revised by the venture-capital firm, it is advisable to submit with a proposal a draft booklet outlining the facts regarding the company and the proposed financing.

If a venture firm is interested in the company, decisions must be made as to how to structure the deal. Usually, the venture firm, after committing its own resources, is anxious to get other substantial investors interested in a transaction. Sometimes, there is a fee negotiated in connection with a placement; otherwise, the motivation is to spread the risk and to demonstrate, if it manages a mutual venture fund, that the firm has been acting in a prudent manner. Naturally, the structure of the deal reflects the interests of the likely investors. Often, convertible preferred stock is used to give the venture investors a senior position over the original stockholders. Sometimes, investors will be offered units of securities with each unit containing, for example, one debenture and 100 shares of common stock in order to give a desired mix to the capitalization.

Other than price, the most recurrent basic issue in venture transactions is control. Many venture investors not only demand positions on the Board but also insist on control. Most entrepreneurs vigorously fight loss of control, and the wisdom of the newcomers demanding it is dubious. In new ventures, morale is everything, and sudden loss of power over one's own company breeds antagonism—not cooperation.

The realities of venture capital are that investments, even if ultimately successful, are rarely instant bonanzas. One of the key functions of the sophisticated venture firm is to handhold the infant company as it is buffeted by the forces of the commercial world and to give advice from experience when needed. Much grief and agony and many successive financings and restructurings are required. Stamina is more useful than sheer greed.

The example of a major venture firm's recent investments illustrates the point. One investment was in a medical instruments company in the forefront of technology. In the lab, everything went fine, but translating the concept into production at a reasonable price was another matter. Mundane engineering, despite bold scientific insight, could make or break the firm. Meanwhile, it has had to go through three financings to keep the money flowing. Eight years after the first investors backed the project, widespread commercial use has yet to occur. The backers, however, are still optimistic.

The venture firm's second investment was a company with a new device for detecting uranium. It was a gusher—the rare but possible success story that brings many investors who don't belong there into venture capital.

The third investment was in a firm manufacturing new printing devices. In the end, it was a bust. The idea was good, but the implementation was poor. Once money started to be lost, the venture capitalists muscled control away from the founder, who allegedly proceeded to loot the company by feeding out assets through low-priced contracts with a friend acting through a dummy corporation. Over the years, as the company gasped for breath, there were successive recapitalizations. In fact, the company did not go under because a key customer decided to buy the remains in order to retain access to the process. The proceeds were enough to compensate the preferred stockholders, who were mostly venture-capital firms, with very little left for the original individual investors who held common stock—an illustration of the utility of senior securities.

Even assuming that the venture firm has no desire to be overbearing, there are inevitably some clean-up steps that it may require. Often, a young company has a complicated capital structure to reflect the varying interests of the original investors, and sometimes the terms of previously issued securities, especially their rights to registration may conflict. The venture-capital firm may well insist that the structure be simplified and the potential dilution to its own position presented by warrants, options, and convertible securities be limited.

Once a basic proposal is structured, the venture firm tries to locate lead investors. The theory is that in, say, a $2 million deal, if the venture firm purchases $750,000 of securities and a lead investor, such as a major corporation or insurance company, purchases another $500,000, the rest of the package will be easy to sell. Often, potential lead investors will suggest major modifications in the terms, which may or may not be acceptable to the venture firm and the company. Most commonly, for example, the lead investor may want an understanding that it will be entitled to designate a director.

One related problem is that the venture firm's interests may differ from the other potential investors in the company. For example, the commission for doing the placement may be so lush that, even though the venture firm is investing, it may not be as sensitive about terms as the other investors. More commonly, the venture firm may already have a significant stake in the company and is therefore not as interested in hard bargaining against the position of existing security holders.

VENTURE DEAL DOCUMENTS

Assuming a lead investor has been found, an additional limited number of potential investors are contacted. This more generalized solicitation must be done in a very careful manner in order to satisfy the requirements of the 1933 Act under Rule 146 or the pre-Rule 146 standards which have been discussed. The number of solicitations made is limited and recorded, and, before any party is contacted, there should be reason to believe that the investor is either sophisticated in venture capital matters or is rich and is represented by a sophisticated agent.

The Offering Memorandum

Each of these potential investors is supplied with an Offering Memorandum. The Memorandum has a blend of purposes; it is both a marketing tool and a protective disclosure device. One of the key requirements under both Rule 146 and the case law is adequate information in a private placement. Although a thorough Memorandum is not dispositive, it is certainly helpful in establishing legal defenses. To this extent, the function and wording of the Memorandum is very similar to that of a standard public-offering prospectus for a young venture, replete with risk factors and disclaimers and stating clearly the material facts which, if not disclosed, might be the basis of liability if the deal sours. One critical difference, however, is that to the degree projections are included, the wording of the disclaimers must be particularly carefully drafted. Even when, technically, a Memorandum may not be required, such as an offering to present major stockholders or senior employees under the pre-146 standards, it is advisable to highlight material negative developments simply as a protective device.

Generally, however, the Memorandum also serves a marketing function unless the investors, such as key employees, are already presold. After all, just knowing a lot of negative facts and risk factors is hardly an incentive to buy. Investors want to know the potential of the business. In this respect, the Memorandum sharply differs from a standard prospectus and comes much closer to being a stock analyst's report. Projections, industry trends, key assumptions, production plans are usually all outlined. Indeed, it can be strongly argued that this form of Memorandum makes much more economic sense than a standard prospectus, which generally does not contain any projections. Of course, a Memorandum is devised for a more sophisticated audience, which presumably is accustomed to the frailties of projections, and there are analysts' reports and other data available about public companies, which displace to some degree the need for projections. Nevertheless, the fundamental question of whether the contents of prospectuses should be reformed is well worth careful consideration, and will be discussed in the context of public offerings.

Often the figures in Memoranda are fanciful, but sophisticated venture capitalists know that a crucial element in a successful Memorandum is establishing credibility, and this doesn't happen when squishy soft numbers are used. The firmer and more detailed the analysis and the documentation, the more the concept seems realistic rather than visionary. In analyzing a Memorandum, a perceptive investor will want to have a good feeling for when the company needs more cash and what its record will look like at that time. Too many people are mesmerized by mere projections of gross profit without realizing that the inevitable next financing will dilute their interest. Therefore, it is critical that a company have enough financing to reach a point in its development where it can raise additional funds on favorable terms. Of course, no matter how plausible the numbers seem, an experienced investor will take them with a tablespoon of salt. Somehow, inevitably, the numbers don't work out, but if the assumptions are sensible enough, an investor may conclude the upside potential is worth the obvious risks.

The Purchase Contract

The investors buy their securities through a purchase contract with the corporation. In this book's discussion of asset-acquisition contracts, the standard provisions of purchase agreements will be discussed in detail. At this point, however, it is worthwhile, to focus on some of the unique problems of venture deals.

Representations As is customary with most purchase agreements, the beginning of the contract is replete with representations. The key representations are that the information contained in the financial statements and in the Offering Memorandum are correct and have no material omissions. In addition, there are usually detailed representations about patents licensed or owned by the company, its major real estate and equipment, key leases and contracts, etc. In theory, all representations other than those about the Offering Memorandum and the financials should be irrelevant because if they are about material facts, they should be reflected in the Memorandum. If a client insists on a thin purchase contract, it can include adequate protection by leaving in the key representation. However, it is generally preferable from a purchaser's point of view to go through the litany of more detailed representations for two reasons. First, the detailed representations, in effect, define what the concept of materiality means for the agreement. For example, if the company represents that all employee contracts for salary over $30,000 a year are listed in Exhibit X, presumably that is the cutoff level of materiality. Second, and more important, the specificity increases the probability of effective due diligence by the company in ferreting out material facts. Generalizations are easier to ignore than specifics, and if a company has to list all loans to officers, it may well stumble over some which should have been described in the draft of Memorandum but weren't. In addition, specific lists give the purchasers a comprehensive idea of the documents they or their representatives should examine before investing.

One should not, however, be under any illusion about the efficacy of representations in venture deals. Once the deal has closed, it is highly unlikely that any suit will be brought for untrue or misleading representations for a very simple reason: It is doubtful that any money would be left in the company to pay for any recovery. When young companies go under, they sink fast and leave no traces.

Following the representations of the company are the representations of the purchasers regarding their investment intent in order to satisfy the requirements of the 1933 Act. In addition, the company supplies a list of prospective purchasers contacted and a description of their background, including their financial status and sophistication, in order to meet private-placement standards.

Covenants   Covenants (or promises) of the company follow the representations. Of course, if the securities involved are debt or preferred stock, any number of covenants described in discussing those instruments may be used. In addition, common covenants include the company's maintaining life insurance policies on the key executives; complying, at the option of the investors, with the information requirements of Rule 144; supplying regular financial reports and periodic projections to major investors; and management's using its best efforts to nominate persons designated by the investors to the board.

Closing conditions   The next section of the purchase agreement usually deals with the closing of the transaction. One fundamental question is whether all the money should be transferred to the company at once or whether it should be dribbled out over time. Once money is absorbed by a new company, it is almost impossible to get it back out, even though representations were false or the company's prospects have dramatically worsened. The dribble-out is an attempt to give the investor more control over the flow of funds in order to decrease the risks while assuring the company of financing if no materially adverse events occur.

There are two basic approaches to the dribble-out. The most complicated is to require that a certain percentage of the cash proceeds from the sale of the securities be kept in an interest-bearing escrow account for a period of time. Then, if no litigation arises, the company would be able to draw gradually on the escrow fund for its financing needs. Thus, for example, if a new venture raised $2 million, it might need $500,000 immediately and the balance over the next 6 months. So $1.5 million would be placed in escrow and could be drawn down at a rate of $250,000 per month. Meantime, however, if there were a rescission right, the cash would be available.

The easier dribble-out is simply to have multiple closings. Thus, the purchase contract might commit the investors to purchase at three closings as long as the conditions to the closings, including the accuracy of the representations, were fulfilled. Of course, of these two approaches, companies prefer the escrow technique because the cash has already been committed, and as a practical matter it is harder for an investor to prevent a drawing down of funds from an escrow account than to merely refuse to go through with a closing. Furthermore, the company gets the benefit of the interest.

These dribble-out concepts are sometimes useful, but all too often they are impractical because the company needs all the money for current expenses. Only where a gradual capital expenditure program is involved does it make sense.

Aside from any provisions relating to a dribble-out, the purchase contract will contain a number of standard conditions to the obligations of the purchasers—that the representations were true on the closing, receipt of certain certificates from officers of the company, and a legal opinion from the counsel to the company as to the valid and binding effect of the pertinent agreements and their enforceability and that the 1933 Act was not violated.

There are, however, important negotiated aspects to the closing conditions. First, the opinion of the counsel to the company can be expanded to be more comprehensive. Counsel will resist any expansion fiercely—after all, lawyers sensibly don't want added risks if they can avoid it. But as with all legal opinions, the attempt is not to sue the lawyers in case they are in error; rather, it is hoped that the responsibility of an opinion will goad the lawyers into doing a more thorough job of diligence. The concept is that investors should be aware of the problems before they go into the deal. In addition to requiring a paragraph stating that no agreement of the company known to them is violated by the deal, investors should also get a statement that, to their knowledge, company's counsel is not aware of any material misstatements or omissions on the Memorandum. This sort of assurance is contained in public-offering opinions, and, assuming the counsel's familiarity with the company, should also be required in private placements, despite the howls of learned counsel who speciously insist that they give opinions only on law rather than on fact.

The closing conditions section also states any cleanup, reorganization, or performance standards required by the investors. For example, as conditions to the closing, investors may wish outstanding options canceled, the bylaws amended to eliminate certain class votes, the existing convertible preferred stock to be converted into common, and the key product to have passed a laboratory test.

Registration provisions   Inevitably, the provisions of the purchase agreement which take the longest to negotiate are those relating to registration rights. These sections are critical to investors, for without these rights, they could well be boxed in for a considerable period of time in an illiquid investment they don't control. As previously discussed, in the absence of registration, securities purchased in a private placement cannot be resold to the public unless under Rule 144 or Rule 237 or unless the passage of a long period of time makes it clear that the investor was not a statutory underwriter. Furthermore, the value of the securities is higher to investors because of their increased potential marketability. Once the company is eligible to register its securities, the investors have the option to sell publicly or privately, thereby enhancing their flexibility.

From the company's perspective, the granting of registration rights is an extremely expensive decision. First, the costs of registration are staggering. In addition to filing fees, the legal, accounting, and printing expenses in preparing a prospectus are a heavy burden, easily totaling more than $50,000 for a small offering. Second, management time and effort spent on the registration statement detract from the company's other efforts. Third, the sale of blocks of stock by existing shareholders limits the ability of the company to raise new capital by public sales; there is a glut of securities on the market, which may, in the end, hurt everyone.

All too often the company is in no position to bargain with its investors about registration rights, and grants them what they want. Unfortunately, however, the next group of purchasers are given similar rights. By the time the normal gestation period for a new venture is completed, there are often so many conflicting registration rights that they would, if literally enforced, bankrupt the company and make it impossible for it to ever have a public offering for its own benefit. What in fact happens is that if the company ever goes public, bitter negotiations take place about which investors can sell their shares when.

Demand rights. In examining these registration provisions, two forms of rights should be distinguished: demand rights and piggyback rights. Demand rights essentially state that if so requested, the company will use its best efforts to register the number of securities desired by the investors. From an investor's point of view, ideally, the company will pay all the expenses related to the demand offering—printing costs, legal expenses, and filing fees. Underwriting commissions are almost universally paid by the selling party. Sometimes, elements of these costs are not picked up by the company or are excluded after a certain number of demand registrations.

Obviously, if every investor were given unlimited demand rights, the company would produce registration statements and not much more. Limits are necessary. The first, most obvious, limit is the number of demands granted. More than a total of three demands is quite unusual, and a total of one or two is more common. Of course, a company's and an investor's analysis of these issues differ.

From the company's perspective, an investor having at least one demand right has the option to sell all the securities owned; so an out is present, and any additional demand rights harm the company more than they help the investor. If the investor decides to retain some securities, the company can argue that less drastic remedies than a demand right, such as piggyback rights and Rule 144, can be relied upon to dribble out securities to the public. Furthermore, the key problem for an investor is whether the company has gone public at all, since if it has not, Rule 144 would be inapplicable. Once the demand right is present, the investor has the ability to make the company go public.

From the investor's point of view, however, one demand right may seem totally inadequate. If the holdings are sufficiently large, Rule 144 allows only a dribble-out of immaterial amounts of securities, and it may well be impossible for the market to absorb all the investor's securities at one time. Furthermore, the investor may well wish to retain a healthy block of stock even if a substantial number of securities are sold, and, as will be discussed, there is no guarantee that piggyback rights will ever result in the effective registration of an investor's securities.

An added complication enters the picture when, as is frequently the case, groups of investors are involved rather than a single purchaser. From the company's point of view, it is best if investors in similar positions can be grouped into classes, with each class having certain specified rights for a certain period of time. For example, all the original investors in the company may be grouped together and collectively have one demand right for 4 years, which may be triggered by the request of, say, the holders of 60% of the securities in that class, and, subsequently, all later investors may be grouped together and have one demand right. This sort of system has many advantages, particularly if the rights of the differing classes are reconciled in a single document which is periodically amended and restated, with the consent by a class vote of, say, the holders of 67% of the securities in each class, to reflect new investors and changing circumstances. At least the rights of each group of investors would be clear and formulated with a set relationship to existing holders rather than in flat contradiction to them, as is often the case.

The difficulty with this class system is that the minority members of any class, even though their holdings may be substantial, can be victimized. For example, assume a class with two demand rights triggered by the action of 60% of the holders in the class and a venture firm with 25% of the class. Even though the venture firm's holdings are substantial, it will have no effective control over the timing of the demand if 60% of the class has different ideas. Thus, for example, if the venture firm wished to continue to hold all its securities, all the demands could be used up before it sold a single share. One solution is to set a higher quorum for triggering demands, but this tactic has its own problems because a small minority could then block a large majority from getting a registration. For these reasons, substantial investors attempt to have separate demand rights for themselves and their affiliates.

As a result of all of these conflicting needs, the negotiation of registration rights is a lengthy process. The necessary starting point must be, however, something which is all too infrequently done: the careful reading of existing contracts relating to registration rights. It is sensible to make a condition of the purchase commitment the rationalization of the registration right structure by requiring cancellation of existing agreements and replacement of them by new provisions.

In addition to the issue of allocation of demand rights, additional technical issues arise. Frequently a provision allows a company to reply to a demand request by stating that it was planning to make a public offering within, say, the next 3 months. In effect, the company's plans take precedence, and the demand request is canceled. Sometimes these provisions apply only to the initial public offering by the company. Similarly, there are often restrictions stating that demands can't be made for a certain period after the last public offering of the company in order not to hurt the after-market for that issue. Demand provisions should be carefully drafted so that a right is not exhausted until a registration statement based on the demand request becomes effective.

Piggyback rights. Piggyback rights entitle investors to have their securities registered if the company was already registering other securities. Generally, piggyback rights are applicable whether the securities being registered originally were being sold for the account of the company or pursuant to other demand provisions. Sometimes, there are no limitations on the number of piggybacks, the theory being that the company is not really harmed if it is preparing a prospectus, anyway, and the unlimited piggybacks compensate for a limited number of demands. In fact, however, there is a real burden to the company in constantly registering investors' securities when it intends to sell for its own account, and many agreements attempt to limit both the number of piggybacks and the amount of time the right to them lasts.

The most serious problem with piggybacks is that if all investors have them, it is conceivable that when the company attempts to have an offering, all the investors will jump aboard with all their securities, making a successful deal impossible. Most agreements, therefore, contain cutback provisions under which the managing underwriter can inform the company whether too many securities are being offered for sale, and the excess number will be eliminated from the deal. The vital question is whose securities will be "cut back" and not be registered at the time of the offering. One common way to handle the problem is to have a pro rata clause so that each piggyback requestor is cut back equally in proportion to the number of securities requested to be registered. Frequently, however, investors with strong bargaining power get a provision mandating the cut-back of every other piggybacker pro rata and before their own cutback. This preference system would work, except that often many groups of investors have similar provisions guaranteeing that everyone else will be cut back first. Again, an overall reconciliation of these registration provisions makes great sense.

THE ROLE OF THE SMALL BUSINESS ADMINISTRATION

Any discussion of venture capital would be incomplete without a brief summary of the role of the Small Business Administration. One difficulty with any analysis of the role of the SBA is that its role shifts dramatically based on its funding. Sometimes it is freely making loans; at other times, there is simply no cash available. For example, in 1976, it announced that it had no funds for direct new loans but could issue guarantees. Although the SBA may directly make loans to some eligible small businesses, the aspect of its actions most relevant to venture capital are the activities of Small Business Investment Corporations (SBIC).

An SBIC is a privately owned and operated venture-capital firm licensed by the SBA to provide financing to small companies. Although most SBIC's are closely held by small groups of investors, more than 20 SBIC's are publicly traded and more than 70 commercial banks have at least partial ownership of SBIC subsidiaries.

Investors in an SBIC get a number of advantages. First, there is a sizable tax advantage: SBIC shareholders may treat losses on the sale of an SBIC's stock as an ordinary loss, but gains are treated as capital gains. In addition, the SBIC itself is allowed to receive 100% of the dividends from its investments tax free as opposed to the 85% nontaxable standard applicable to most corporations. Second, and most important, the SBA will also purchase or guarantee the debt of the SBIC's in an amount equal to four times the equity in venture-capital oriented SBIC's so that they can be highly leveraged at a low interest cost. SBIC's which invest in enterprises owned by minority groups (MESBICS) are entitled to similar support. The chief drawback to SBIC's are the hosts of investment restrictions, including not lending on a debt maturity shorter than 5 years and when there are fifty or more investors, not owning 20% or more of any company. In addition, SBIC's must file myriad reports with the government. Finally, in recent years, they have had a generally disappointing performance record, but this is also true of the venture industry as a whole.

During 1975, SBIC's provided 1,655 financings to some 1,233 small businesses with financings totaling $122.7 million. Of this dollar total, 52% was represented by straight debt deals, and 33% was convertible debt. One reason debt is so prevalent is that, unlike many other venture investors, SBIC's need the cash flow to pay off their own considerable debt obligations. Therefore, whatever the shortcomings of SBA programs, SBIC's do represent an important potential source of capital for small business, especially for debt financing.

SEVEN

Alternative Means of Financing

In addition to the issuance of equity and long-term debt, a corporation has available a series of alternative means of financing its activities. Whether one technique or another is appropriate depends on the particular circumstances. Furthermore, it should be understood that increased reliance on vehicles such as inventory financing or assignment of accounts receivable often limits the ability to finance through conventional debt. Therefore, it is important to remember that any choice of alternatives must be put in the context of the firm's overall financial strategy.

SHORT-TERM FINANCING

In order to provide for seasonal fluctuations and working-capital needs, firms rely on a variety of short-term financing devices. There are a number of reasons why short-term financing may be preferable to the alternative of using intermediate- or long-term funds for short-term needs. First, the interest rates may be lower than the long-term rates. Second, a drop in long-term rates may be anticipated, so that it is cheaper for a firm to finance for the time being with short-term money and, later, to use longer-term funds when interest rates have fallen. Third, if seasonal needs are the cause for the financing, the money is not needed year round, and it is cheaper to borrow only for the period the funds are required. Fourth, short-term money may be more readily available than long-term funds because the lender's risk of unforeseen events is more limited. Fifth, using short-term borrowings may stretch debt capacity and create a healthier looking balance sheet than incurring a similar amount of long-term debt when a significant amount of long-term debt already exists.

Trade Credit

Trade credit is perhaps the simplest form of short-term financing. Usually, a purchaser of goods is extended credit by the seller on open account, without any specific debt instrument. Terms can vary, and often optional terms, such as 3/15, net 30, are used, which means there will be a 3% discount if the shipment is paid for in 15 days; otherwise, the full price is due within 30 days. Frequently, payments are stretched beyond even their net payment date in order to provide a source of financing. Such tactics may boomerang in the form of a bad credit rating. On the other hand, if discounts are sizable enough, financing early payments may make sense.

Commercial Paper

Large companies in the 1960s used the commercial paper market (particularly finance companies) as a prime vehicle for their short-term debt placement. The paper ranged in maturity from 1 month to slightly less than 9 months, was usually sold in denominations exceeding $25,000, and was unsecured. Under the 1933 Act, debt securities with a maturity of less than 9 months and used to finance current activities are exempt from registration, and, therefore, no filings with the SEC are necessary. Another advantage of the paper was that it often was priced at an interest rate below that which banks charged for short-term loans. With the collapse of the Penn Central, commercial paper got a bad name, both because unwary buyers were purchasing it without the benefit of a prospectus and because it was unsecured and, therefore, often relatively junior debt. It is inevitable, however, that the market in commercial paper will continue to resurge as an alternative to bank loans for well-known companies.

Lines of Credit

The most informal short-term arrangement with a bank is a line of credit. Essentially, a bank annually reviews the financial statements of the borrower and establishes the line limit, say $1 million, and the rate, say one-half of one percent over the prime rate for the bank's most credit-worthy customers. Generally, as part of the short-letter agreement, the company agrees to be out of short-term bank debt for some "cleanup" period, say 90 days, during the fiscal year and generally to maintain its financial condition. When the loans are drawn down, they are usually for a 90-day period, but can be turned over, subject to the cleanup period. The main advantage to a company is the flexibility the line offers to meet its short-term needs. Unlike a revolving credit agreement, which is more formal and has a longer term, however, the line may not be renewed after a year, and as conditions change, a bank can, although it is highly unusual, limit the borrower's flexibility during the year.

Secured Loans

Many loans, both short- and long-term, are made on a secured basis, like a bond. Under Article 9 of the Uniform Commercial Code, there are specified procedures for implementing a secured transaction other than real estate, for which mortgages are used. The basic contract for a secured financing is the security agreement which states what articles, inventory, equipment, accounts receivable, etc. are being pledged as collateral. In order to "perfect" (protect) a security interest against other parties, a lender must file a financing statement at the proper state offices. The financing statement itself is a short standardized form, UCC Form 1, which briefly describes the collateral.

For example, the broadest financing statement might contain the following response to the question of what types of property are covered by it: all property, real, personal, or mixed, tangible or intangible (wherever located and whether now owned or hereafter acquired), including, without limitation, all accounts, contract rights, equipment, furniture and fixtures, chattel paper, documents, instruments and general intangibles and inventory, and all proceeds and products thereof.

A lender must be careful to file the financing statement in the right places. In some states, filings are required in both the offices of the secretary of state and the local counties where the property is located. If a business has numerous locations, the filing procedure can become quite complicated. The idea behind these cumbersome mechanics, which, incidentally, represent a considerable improvement over prior systems, is that if everything is filed in the right location, there will be public notice as to who has the prior lien to a property. Therefore, the system does allow a lender to conduct a lien search before a transaction is closed.

In addition to securing specified property, a UCC lien can also "float" over a category of property such as inventory or receivables over time; as the current assets shift from cash to inventory, to receivables, to cash, the lien still applies.

Assignments and factoring of accounts receivable   One of the most common forms of secured loans is the assignment of the right to collect accounts receivable to a bank or finance company as security. If specific receivables which are quality rated are assigned, a lender might advance between 50%

and 75% of the face value of the receivables. Of course, if all the receivables are from major corporations, a higher rate of financing would be possible. For example, a parts supplier to General Motors would probably be able to get advances on 100% of the receivables. The interest rates can run very high, especially for a finance company loan, where they can range up to 18%. Bulk receivable assignments, the borrowing on all credit sales, even though not quality rated, are even more expensive, and loans may be made on as little as 50% of the face value.

Sometimes, although sellers object to it strenuously, loans are made on a notification basis: Customers are informed that their checks should be made out to the lender. If a loan is, however, made on a nonnotification basis, there is often a provision in the loan agreement allowing the lender to convert to a notification system. If the lender should suspect that not all the receivables are being passed on to it, a switch to a notification basis is a useful protective device.

In contrast to the assignment of accounts receivable for security, a factor actually purchases a firm's receivables on a nonrecourse basis; for bearing the risk of collection, the factor pays a price less than the face amount of the receivables, the amount of the discount depending on the apparent quality of the receivables. In addition, a factor usually advances money for the purchased receivables before they are collected and charges a hefty interest rate.

The key advantage of using receivables as a financing vehicle is flexibility. As sales increase, receivables and the capacity for financing based on them increase. To a growing business with otherwise limited debt capacity, this built-in flexibility can be invaluable.

Inventory financing   Inventories can also be used as a vehicle for financing. Of course, the value of the collateral in the event of a foreclosure determines the extent to which money can be borrowed against it. Commodities such as metal ores, grains, and coal may finance a loan of, for example, 80% of book value; a specialized piece of equipment may be used, on the other hand, on the basis of its scrap value because of the lack of marketability.

In addition to a floating lien, there are other methods of securing an inventory loan. Loans can be made against receipts issued by a warehouse company that segregates the inventory being borrowed on at the company's plant. These field warehouse receipts assume that, even though the inventory is on the borrower's premises, the warehouse company will keep control and make sure the inventory is there in the event of a foreclosure. Alternatively, the inventory can be placed in a public, or terminal, warehouse, and receipts can be issued. Both field and terminal warehouse receipts can be negotiable or registered in the name of the lender.

The difficulty with warehouse loans is that the system depends on the effectiveness of the warehouse. Particularly in the case of field warehousing, there is the real possibility of fraud or error. Indeed, one of the great financial scandals of the 1960s was the nonexistence of some $100 million in salad oil, which had been used as a basis for financing field warehouse receipts.

Equipment financing   Like receivables and inventory, equipment can be used as the basis to receive a secured loan. Of course, to the degree the resale value of equipment is limited, its value as collateral diminishes. On the other hand, a seller is often willing to arrange highly advantageous financing, even on specialized equipment. Sometimes the seller, as an alternative to having a UCC mortgage on the equipment, will keep the title in its name under a conditional sales contract: if the purchaser defaults, the seller can repossess the equipment.

INTERMEDIATE FINANCING

Bank Loans

Banks are a prime source for intermediate financing, roughly 1 to 7 years to maturity, for a company. As opposed to insurance companies which normally prefer longer-term obligations, banks generally dislike maturities longer than 5 years.

Among the leading types of bank loan agreements are revolving credits and term loans.

Revolving credit agreements   A "revolver" is a legal commitment to lend money up to the maximum amount of the credit line. Usually, there is a commitment fee, for example, 0.4% annually, based on the entire line, even if only a portion or none of the money in the line has actually been borrowed. The advantages of a revolver over a line of credit are its longer term, its formality, and, usually, the lack of a cleanup period. Many an executive can sleep better at night knowing that in need, it is possible to draw down more money under the revolver.

Term loans   A term loan is a commitment to lend a fixed amount of money for a specified period of time, and is, therefore, less flexible than a revolver. Usually, bank loans have a maturity of less than 5 years and represent shorter-term financing than public debt or insurance company loans.

The actual terms of these bank loans can range from unsecured obligations with few limitations on a company's activities to secured loans with myriad restrictions, such as the covenants discussed in detail in connection with the description of debt securities. Bank loans, however, have some characteristics not yet discussed:

Banking relationship. A loan agreement is only a part of an overall banking relationship, many aspects of which are not reflected in formal legal documents. As a result, the negotiating process is somewhat different than a one-shot, arm's-length deal. Both the bank and the borrower have good reasons for maintaining harmony and good will.

Standardization. On the other hand, some banks often have a tendency to standardize their forms of loan agreements with overreaching provisions. In some states, where it is legal, for example, banks often have provisions in their loan documents allowing them to foreclose without notice on collateral.

Compensating balances. In addition to explicit interest costs, banks often require borrowers to keep compensating balances in checking accounts. These balances, which can range up to as high as 25% of the loan, create an implicit interest charge in the event the balance is larger than the firm would ordinarily keep at the bank. An additional advantage to the bank is that the cash provides a ready target in the event of a default.

Interest computation. Banks generally compute accrued interest on the basis of the actual number of days elapsed in an assumed 360-day year. This technique has the effect of slightly boosting the effective interest rates charged on bank loans, as contrasted to using a 365-day year or the commonly used 360-day year composed of twelve 30-day months. One has to be careful with the 360-day year, however. When state usury laws are applicable (they generally do not apply to corporate loans, but do apply to partnerships and individuals), the interest rate is often pegged at just below the usury limit. The difference between using a 360-day year and a 365-day year may be sufficient to inadvertently bump the interest rate above the usury level.

Margin problems. For standard commercial loans, banks will usually ask for a representation that no part of the loan is being used to purchase any margin securities in order to clearly establish that the federal margin rules, which will be discussed in detail in connection with the financing of tender offers, are inapplicable to the transaction. If the loan is being made for the purpose of purchasing margin securities, but is unsecured, the margin rules are inapplicable to the bank. The situation is, however, quite tricky. For example, a negative covenant may be construed as an indirect form of security and trigger the applicability of the margin standards.

Funds used. Banks, as managers of money, are particularly sensitive to which type of funds are used in a transaction. Immediately available funds (usually federal funds) can earn interest the day they are received. Clearinghouse funds, on the other hand, are generally not available for use until a day after deposit. Of course, it makes sense for sums to be repaid in the same type of funds as used for the original loan of the money, but sometimes, they differ.

OTHER MEANS OF FINANCING

In addition to the vehicles discussed, there are a variety of alternative mechanisms for financing transactions whose features will be briefly highlighted:

Lease Financing

Lease financing has been one of the burgeoning areas of corporate finance. The simplest lease is one under which an asset, such as a building, is rented for a portion of its economic life. This is generally called a "true" or an "operating" lease. If investors buy the asset partially with borrowed funds and then rent it out on a true lease, the transaction is called a "leveraged lease." Under a leveraged lease, which must comply with exacting tax regulation requirements, the equity owners are able to increase the tax advantages of the deal by taking depreciation and investment tax credits against the cost of the equipment as a whole, rather than merely the proportion supplied by their equity contribution. Leveraged leases will be discussed in more detail later. The most common lease for major equipment is really not a lease at all but a device for financing the purchase price of an asset. These leases, known as "capital" or "financing" leases, are for the economic life of the asset, or they give the person leasing the asset the option to buy it at a relatively low price at the end of the lease.

A lease transaction may arise in a variety of ways and for differing reasons. For example, in a sale and leaseback deal, a firm needing financing sells an asset it already owns to a financing firm, and then leases it back from the financing firm on a capital lease. In another common situation, a corporation may set up a dummy subsidiary which purchases assets and leases them to the parent in order to avoid covenants applicable to the parent or complicating its security structure.

In addition to these general forms of leasing arrangements, there are specialized leases to meet certain unique needs. Equipment trusts are certainly one of the most prevalent forms, especially in the railroad industry. Investors buy equipment trust certificates in a trust. With their money, the trustee, usually a major bank, purchases from a manufacturer equipment, often railroad rolling stock, and then leases the equipment to the railroad which gave the specifications to the manufacturer. The lease payments fully pay off the obligations under the trust certificates if a capital lease or a leveraged lease will cover only part of the economic life of the rolling stock.

Equipment trust certificates are considered a high quality investment because the railroad rolling stock usually retains its resale value. Even if the railroad goes bankrupt, payments on equipment obligations have traditionally received first priority. The Penn-Central bankruptcy has raised some questions in this area because the government would periodically ask that it be allowed to pay the equipment obligations rather than the railroad. Some lenders feel that, therefore, equipment obligations are no longer inviolate, but this is a minority view.

The Attractions of Leasing

Accounting   One of the principal attractions of leasing has traditionally been that the lease did not appear on the balance sheet as a liability but was rather disclosed as a footnote, even though the lease was the economic equivalent of ownership. Those days are now over.

Under prodding from the SEC, the Financial Accounting Standards Board, the rule-making body for the public accounting profession, in December of 1976, finally issued its controversial standards for the accounting treatment of leases. Under the new Financial Accounting Standard No. 13, leases are classified into categories, with the most important being a capital lease.

A capital lease is essentially a lease which has the same economic effect as an installment sale. Under Standard No. 13, a new lease with any of the following four elements will be regarded as a capital lease, and must be capitalized by the lessee on its balance sheet as an asset with the lease payments reflected as a liability:

- Title transfers before the end of the lease term from the lessor to the lessee.
- The lessee may at its option buy the property at a bargain price.
- The lease term is 75% or more of the estimated economic life of the property.
- The discounted present value of the lease payments is equal to 90% or more of the fair value of the property.

If none of these criteria is applicable, the lease is deemed to be an operating lease and needn't be capitalized. Essentially then, an operating lease is one through which the lessor has some significant risk of ownership.

It has been estimated that about two-thirds of the $15 billion in new equipment leased each year will have to be capitalized under these standards. In certain industries such as the airlines, where the bulk of equipment is leased, the impact on the balance sheet will be tremendous.

If a lease is not treated as a liability, the entire financial picture of a corporation changes, including the principal ratios. The lease industry will, however, continue to grow, basically because it offers an alternative to the immediate commitment of capital.

Tax factors   Through a lease, the tax attributes of owning a property, such as taxes paid and investment tax credits, can be shifted from a company to other firms and, to some degree, to individuals with higher tax brackets, thus building in a higher after-tax economic value in the transaction. An additional advantage of leasing generally is that the cost of any land is deductible by the corporation in its lease payments, while if the firm owned the land, there would not be any deduction because land is not a depreciable asset.

A leveraged lease, in particular, has traditionally yielded additional benefits to the transaction as a whole because the company leasing the assets often cannot utilize the tax advantages as effectively as the investors. For example, its tax bracket might be lower than the investors' or it might already have utilized fully its investment tax credit. In essence, the property acquisition is financed by a mixture of equity and debt; the equity holders get all the income tax advantages of depreciation and investment tax credits on all the equipment rather than just on their equity. Under the Tax Reform Act of 1976, there was a general tightening of standards regarding tax shelters such as leveraged leases. Currently, individuals can get the tax advantages only in proportion to their equity contribution unless they are personally liable on the debt used to purchase the assets. These "at risk" provisions of the 1976 Act have substantially replaced the attractiveness of leveraged lease deals to individual investors. Nevertheless, investments in leveraged leases are still popular for institutions and other corporations.

The Internal Revenue Service has also toughened its position on what constitutes a "true" leveraged lease eligible for tax advantages. Under the IRS guidelines issued in May 1975, among other determining factors, an investment of at least 20% of the property must be made by the equity investors and must remain at risk throughout the term of the lease. In addition, it must be shown that at the end of the lease, the reasonable estimate of the property's fair value is not less than 20% of the original cost, and that the property will have a remaining useful life, the longer of 1 year or 20% of the estimated useful life of the property. To guard against tax shelter transactions where all the benefit comes from tax factors, the IRS requires that there be a showing of an expected pretax profit, which can be as low as $1, on the deal.

Financial flexibility The terms of leasing arrangements are often more flexible than comparable borrowings. First, the provisions of other debt instruments may not pick up leases in their covenants. Second, the leases themselves often do not restrict the company's financial activities. Third, and perhaps most important, the firm can use its cash for other purposes which may yield higher returns.

The Disadvantages of Leasing

Costs The interest costs of leasing may often be higher than borrowing.

Residual value The residual value of property at the end of the lease may well be higher than anticipated, raising the effective interest cost if replacement equipment has to be bought or leased. Since buyout provisions for less than fair market value are not permitted under the IRS Guidelines for leveraged lease transactions, the actual costs of these transactions are always uncertain.

Advantages may be exaggerated Sophisticated analysts can presumably back in lease data disclosed in footnotes. So the cosmetic effect leasing has on balance sheets may be more illusory than real.

ESOP's

Perhaps the hottest recent development in corporate finance has been the rise of employee stock ownership plans (ESOP's). Although ESOP's have been in existence since the 1930s, a series of statutes passed in the mid-seventies, particularly the Employee Retirement Income Security Act of 1974, gave ESOP's new luster. It has been estimated that several hundred ESOP's have been restructured or established to take advantage of this legislation.

Essentially, an ESOP is a retirement plan whose assets are the employer's stock. The stock is owned by an employee stock ownership trust (ESOT) which administers individual retirement accounts for the employees. Each year the employer may contribute up to 15% of covered payroll in the form of stock or cash and receive a tax deduction for the contribution. While the stock is held in trust, voting may be administered by a committee appointed by the company. The key to the financing vehicle's flexibility is that stock may be purchased from any source by the trust through a loan (which one should be careful to see complies with the applicable margin requirements) repaid through the periodic corporate contributions. It is important to remember, however, that the purpose of any of these transactions must be the employees' benefit in order for it to be eligible for the favorable tax treatment. Indeed, getting a tax ruling on the structure of an ESOP is currently a necessity. Among the corporate finance areas in which ESOP's have important implications for are the following:

1. *Divestitures.* When a company has a division it wants to sell and can't get the right price, an ESOT is a new alternative buyer. For example, a company can sell a subsidiary to the ESOT for the sub, which borrows the purchase money. This borrowing is in turn guaranteed by the subsidiary, which by periodic contributions to the ESOP will, in effect, pay back the loan and get a tax deduction at the same time.

2. *Going public.* When a principal shareholder in a closely held business wants to sell a block of stock, the ESOT can purchase it with borrowed money. Again the loan is usually guaranteed by the company, contributions are used to fund the debt, and the company receives a tax deduction for its contributions. The most important function of ESOP's may be

making it possible for boxed-in owners, in effect, to go public when there is no public market available. In using this going public route, an owner should be careful to make sure that there will not be ordinary income tax imposed on the sale of the shares.

3. *Going private.* Conversely, a company desiring to limit its public shareholders can purchase directly in the open market shares to be given the company ESOT, claiming a tax deduction, or the trust can purchase a block of shares, using the company contributions as the basis for loan repayment.

4. *Conventional financing alternative.* When a corporation borrows money, it must earn approximately 2 dollars for every dollar it repays in principal. But if money is borrowed by an ESOT to purchase stock from an issuer, the company gets its financing, but ends by repaying the principal on the basis of a dollar of principal repaid for every dollar earned. To fund the debt of the trust, the company guarantees the obligation and makes the standard deductible, periodic contributions. The same economic effect is produced by a company borrowing on its own and, in result, using the cash generated by the loan to fund the ESOP, although at present, it is not as desirable an approach because the loan is clearly a liability on the balance sheet. On the face of it, these methods allow bank financing at considerable after-tax savings. However, the fact remains that additional stock has been issued, diluting the equity interest of existing holders. Furthermore, although currently ESOP guarantees are generally reflected in footnotes to financial statements, there have been proposals to require the guarantee to be included as a liability in the balance sheet itself. For these reasons, some financing experts have concluded that in the final analysis, ESOP financing is no bargain. Arguably, however, there is the offsetting factor of increased employee motivation.

Of course, these tactics work only if the company has enough cash flow to service the debt and be eligible for the loan. For a financially weak company, these creative devices simply don't work.

Critics have pointed out that the recent popularity of ESOP's is largely due to a tax windfall in recent legislation, which allows a firm through 1980 to deduct an extra 1% investment tax credit on capital spending if the savings are put into an employee stock plan. This could amount to big money for capital-intensive businesses, such as the oil companies. For example, a corporation with $200 million in capital spending could have its taxes reduced by $2 million. Once the tax credit ceases, it is possible, according to the critics, that the ESOP boomlet will subside.

One important question regarding ESOP's is whether they really benefit the employees. Peter Drucker, among others, has charged that ESOP's may be unsound and reckless as an alternative to conventional pensions. If a company's fortunes decline, the employees could well be left holding the bag.

Pollution Bonds

Another special situation is the financing of pollution facilities. Under Section 103 of the Internal Revenue Code, a municipality can use its tax-exempt status to help finance the construction of pollution facilities by a private company. These facilities are leased (or sometimes purchased under a conditional sales agreement) from the municipality by the company at a rate equal to the servicing of the debt the municipality issues to pay for the facility. The key to the transaction is that the issuing municipality is not liable on the debt; the credit is wholly that of the issuing corporation. However, because a municipality is the formal issuer, interest on this pollution facility debt is tax exempt, and the company pays a much lower interest rate than if it issued the debt itself. To an investor, the key to the deal is the strength of the commitment of the corporation. Is a subsidiary or the parent behind the obligation? Are there any outs? To answer these questions, a close examination of the pertinent papers is required.

Naturally, corporations have been quite enthusiastic about pollution bonds and have attempted to use them as frequently as possible. The Internal Revenue Service, however, has become increasingly tough about the technical requirements for tax-exempt status. Technically, Section 103(a) states that interest on obligations of a state or a subdivision of a state are generally tax exempt, but Section 103(c) provides that interest on an "industrial development bond," an issue where the proceeds are being used by a private party, are not tax exempt. Since private parties are using the proceeds from the pollution bonds, they are deemed to be industrial development bonds. However, Section 103(c) (4) (F) goes on to say that even the interest on industrial development bonds will be tax exempt if "substantially all" the proceeds are used to provide air- or water-pollution control facilities. But the IRS keeps tightening its interpretation of what "substantially all" means so that today elaborate legal work, often including a tax ruling, is required before it is clear that a proposed project qualifies for tax-exempt treatment.

If the pollution bonds are being sold to the public, an official statement is prepared by the issuer and the underwriters describing the transaction. Although the content of an official statement is virtually identical to a 1933 Act prospectus, the official statement is not covered by the 1933 Act because it relates to a municipal financing, and municipal securities are exempt from the SEC registration process. However, full and complete disclosure is still advisable because the 1934 Act's antifraud provision, Rule 10b-5, is applicable to municipal securities.

One peculiarity of any municipal deal is the role of bond counsel. In addition to the bevy of counsel normally involved in any financing, a specialist in municipal bonds and their legal status and consequences receives a healthy fee essentially for rendering the opinion that the bonds are exempt from taxation. Incidentally, it was as a bond counsel that former Attorney General John Mitchell began his rise to dubious distinction.

Project Financing

Project financing has also been a popular financing tool in the 1970s. This phrase covers such a wide variety of transactions that the contours of each deal must be examined with care. The ideal vision is that a project such as a mine or an oil refinery should finance itself rather than having the parent company use its limited debt capacity. In fact, project financing is often not a pure form; there are generally parent company guarantees or absolute commitments to buy the production of a project. However, even in these cases, the basic aim of stretching the debt capacity of the parent is attained because guarantees or purchase commitments are reflected only in footnotes.

To examine project financing, it is useful to take an example of the concept in its ideal form. A diversified natural resources firm is thinking of building a coal mine. It signs up some local utilities to long-term, take-or-pay contracts. These contracts state that the utilities have an obligation to pay certain amounts to the subsidiary of the natural resources firm operating the coal mine, whether or not they need the coal or, indeed, whether or not any coal is produced. The obligation is fixed, clear, and absolute. With these take-or-pay contracts in hand, the natural resources firm goes to its friendly institutional lender, usually a large insurance company, and says it would like to borrow some money, or more precisely, its new subsidiaries would like to borrow the money. The lender agrees, giving a good rate because of the credit of the utilities. Essentially, from a lending point of view, if the contracts are drawn tightly enough, the loan is equivalent to an unsecured loan to the utilities, probably with the bonus of a mortgage on the venture's property. Indeed, the rate on the loan to the subsidiary may be lower than on that to the parent because the credit of the utilities may be stronger than that of the parent. The parent then decides to bring in a joint-venture partner to own 50% of the subsidiary. A subsidiary is consolidated only when ownership is above 50%. Therefore, the investment, including increases in net worth, is shown on the parent's balance sheets, but no debt at all is indicated, even on its consolidated statement—a very attractive deal.

Of course, this ideal vision is often not the reality. For example, the supply contracts may not be unconditional. For any hole in them, the lenders demand additional security. Frequently, the parent ends by guaranteeing the debt obligation of the subsidiary. But guarantees are still "off-balance sheet" financing, and, therefore, preferred to direct borrowings.

What are possible holes in the supply agreement? First, what if costs escalate? Well-drafted supply contracts contemplate increases in costs, as well as the costs for servicing the debt used to build the facility. To the extent the purchasers balk at full-cost escalation provisions, there is a risk for the lender. Second, what happens if production ceases? For example, a strike or a natural disaster could terminate production. In order for the loans to be fully covered, payments must be made by the utilities during these periods.

Obviously, bringing together a package which works is a complex business. Often, the skills of a sophisticated investment banker are required. The trick is to juggle the credit objectives of the parents, the accounting treatment of techniques such as leases, long-term contracts, guarantees and joint ventures, tax factors, and impact of alternative structures.

The potential array of financing devices is numerous, and not limited to a loan being paid off through proceeds from a supply contract to a third party. For example, the sponsors of the facility themselves may be individual parties to take-or-pay contracts. With its flexibility, it is inevitable that in the next decade project financing will become even more prevalent.

Joint Ventures

"Joint venture" is another magic term encompassing a wide variety of differing financial activities. Often the joint venture will take the form of project financing with each of the joint ventures agreeing to finance a joint mining facility by setting up a new company and entering take-or-pay contracts with it. Another frequent example of a joint venture is the case of two parties who wish to develop a new product when one has technical know-how and the other, marketing expertise. The respective joint venturers then enter into license and know-how agreements and service contracts with the new company to pool their resources.

Joint ventures carry the potential for one party to either exploit the other or block progress for the new company. Bylaws of these firms are replete with detailed provisions as to what actions require whose consent, and the purchase agreements will require specific financial commitments. It is often said that joint ventures are like marriages; but like wedded bliss, the relationship can sometimes be tempestuous. Although all problems can't be anticipated, some elementary precautions are making sure that the service contracts don't build in the opportunity for overcharging the venture and that any license or know-how agreements are sufficiently broad to allow the licensing of improvements and related products and the fast, free flow of knowledge about recent developments by the licensor.

One recurrent problem in a joint venture is the difficulty of one of the venturers in selling its interest. Often, there are restrictions on sale, coupled with cross-rights of first refusal in the event either party tries to sell its share to another company. As a practical matter, it may well be impossible to market shares in a joint venture without at least the tacit approval of the other venturer because of the complicated and "incestuous" relationship between the parties.

Joint ventures inherently raise serious antitrust problems. First, the combining of two firms on a common project is judged by merger law standards, which will be discussed. Second, however, misguided working agreements and license contracts may contain language which might be interpreted as a concerted attempt to restrain competition. Arrangements for joint ventures must be conceived and prepared with great care.

Guarantees

Instead of directly borrowing funds, a firm will often have a subsidiary (many times, a special purpose finance subsidiary) do the borrowing, which it will guarantee. To be worthwhile, a guarantee must be unconditional. Although reflected in the footnotes to the parent's financial statements, the guarantee is not reflected as a liability, even on the consolidated statements of the parent, because finance subsidiaries usually are not consolidated under generally accepted accounting principles. The device of setting up a financing company is particularly popular among companies selling equipment, such as cars, which require financing the parent does not want on its own balance sheet.

EIGHT

Bringing the Deal Together

Knowing about the host of factors that should go into planning the financing of a new venture is necessary, but hardly sufficient. The pros and cons of one form of business organization or another, the alternative means of allocating control, the various methods of offering securities, and the multiplicity of financing possibilities, are all interesting, but the hardest part of any deal is integrating all these considerations into a coherent package.

What makes the task so difficult is that the factors will inevitably conflict. Subchapter S sounds great until one investor wants preferred stock. Complex voting allocations may seem to resolve important problems until it is realized that complexity breeds its own difficulties, including distrust. For a simple business to incorporate as a Delaware close corporation under Subchapter S with special dissolution, buyout, and arbitration procedures , as well as a Section 1244 declaration, may appear to be wise but may realistically be foolish. And the legal bills can be devastating. Unfortunately, the structure of all but the very simplest deals necessarily involves compromise.

One useful way to get a rough overview is to project a financial profile of the company, the assets required, its riskiness, and likely pattern of earnings. Then go through the names of potential investors and analyze the likely investment amount, the type of business organization, and if a corporation, the type of security the investor would probably be interested in, the degree of control desired, and the basis of legal eligibility for the purchase. With this perspective, the problems begin to clearly emerge.

The following story of Jerry Ambitious' entrepreneurial efforts illustrates the typical financing problems a start-up business faces and some of the possible resolutions.

Jerry Ambitious has a great idea: He wants to go into the growth industry of lawn servicing as a sideline investment. To start the business, Ambitious estimates that he will need $200,000, but he has only $40,000 in cash available himself. Jerry anticipates that Jane Friendly, a competent professional sales manager, is going to do most of the work, but Friendly wants a "piece of the action," as well as a customary salary, even though she has only $2,000 in savings. The local bank has informed Ambitious that his proposed venture is not a good credit risk even for a secured loan because the equipment is too specialized, and Ambitious' rich mother-in-law, Sally Puller, a dentist whose investments currently consist of government bonds, is skeptical about the scheme. Ambitious hopes, however, to interest in the deal Puller, some of his fellow teachers, or his friend Fred Fetish, a shoe salesman who periodically plunges into speculative ventures.

The first vital question faced by Ambitious is which form of business organization the new venture should take. Among the pertinent questions is whether the venture anticipates high cash needs or will pay out its earnings in dividends, and what the income tax situation of the investors is. In fact, Ambitious expects at least some earnings from the beginning, which will be kept in the company, and the corporation's tax bracket is relatively low compared to that of Puller, a likely major investor. Therefore, the flow-through attribute of partnership makes little sense, nor is Subchapter S status desirable. On the other hand, if early losses are to be anticipated, a partnership or Subchapter S corporation may initially be more attractive, especially for Puller with her high tax bracket.

The next issue for Ambitious is who is eligible to invest. Rule 240, which exempts small deals from registration, doesn't work because, although quite convenient, it is limited to a $100,000 offering. If all investors live in the same state and the venture will be incorporated and do its business there, Rule 147 is the simplest alternative because the investors do not require sophisticated financial backgrounds. By contrast, Rule 146 and the general private placement rules would probably make most of these investors ineligible for their lack of sophistication, except Jane, who is, more or less, an insider; however, her lack of wealth may be a problem under general private placement standards because of a possible inability to hold the securities indefinitely. Puller, even though a relative of an insider, and Fetish, if his past speculations have made him rich, probably require a formal offeree representative under Rule 146 or an informal investment counselor under pre-146 standards.

If the potential investors are located in different states and are ineligible for private placement treatment, and the offering is in excess of $100,000, Regulation A is a viable but cumbersome and relatively expensive alternative. In the end, the deal may well be cut back to $100,000 or the investors who clearly are not eligible under private placement standards, such as the school teachers, may be eliminated from the transaction, and all the other investors except Jane may get sophisticated representatives. Of course, care must also be taken to comply with the blue-sky laws.

Since Ambitious wishes to retain control, a simple system of voting allocation might be to have two classes of stock, Class A and Class B, all of whose rights would be identical except that Class A stock, to be owned by Jerry, would elect three directors and Class B, owned by the other investors, two directors. Puller may well insist on convertible preferred stock or subordinated convertible debt, but Ambitious should resist her desire for secured debt because it would limit the financial flexibility of the new company. If the preferred is issued to Puller, Puller will probably insist that it have voting rights equivalent to the number of Class B shares into which it is convertible as well as the specific right to elect an additional director in the event of the nonpayment of accrued dividends for six consecutive quarters. One possibility is for all the investors other than Puller to receive securities proportionate to their investment to avoid tax problems, but Jerry and Jane, as incentives, would get options to purchase additional shares of common stock for 4 years at the initial issue price. It should be remembered, of course, that if Subchapter S were used, this multilayered capital structure would not be possible.

Meanwhile Jerry may want an option to buy Puller's shares at a healthy price if the business booms, and Puller may want a right to "put," require the purchase of, the preferred stock to Jerry for a 2-year period beginning 2 years after incorporation at the original issue price. Although it may be premature to specify registration rights, Puller's representative will probably want an agreement that no right to registration will be given to other investors without stockholder approval.

Many alternative approaches are, of course, possible. The challenge is to bring all the factors into account and devise a system that seems to work. With time, as new venture capital investors are brought in, as sophisticated financing tools such as leasing are used, and as preparations are made for a public offering, the venture will inevitably be reorganized. But having a sensible capital structure from the beginning will save a lot of grief later.

Public Financings

Publicity is justly commended as a remedy for social and industrial diseases. Sunlight is said to be the best of disinfectants.

—LOUIS BRANDEIS, *Other People's Money & How the Bankers Use It,*
(1913)

Customers in 1968 and 1969 often sat watching the tape . . . chanting "Go, go, go."

—JOHN BROOKS, *The Go-Go Years* Weybright & Talley (1973)

NINE

Preliminary Considerations in Going Public

Public financings involve a special set of problems because they must be executed in conformity with myriad detailed SEC rules and regulations as well as the customs of the legal and investment banking fraternities. First, the unique problems of a small company having an initial offering of common stock will be explored. Then questions relating to both initial offerings and public financings of more mature companies will be discussed.

DECIDING ON AN INITIAL OFFERING

Going public used to be considered the thing to do if one had a successful business or one with glamorous possibilities. The experiences of the 1970s, however, have made the virtues of being a public company rather debatable. Long-term effects and personal factors must be weighed as heavily as immediate financial impact. Being a public company today is not all recognition, glory, and gold; it is a heavy and constant burden on management, which may limit future flexibility and can not easily be cast off.

The Advantages of Going Public

The vision, though, is glorious: Pick up a newspaper, and there is your stock. Quoted. Of course, the price makes you rich; so if you need a little money for your daughter's wedding, no problem; a few shares in the market can easily be sold. And with all the money received from the public, the investment opportunities are mind boggling. Furthermore, those acquisition targets will sell for stock, and at a cheaper price because the securities will be marketable. And if, Lord forbid, a key shareholder should die, the estate can much more easily determine the value of the stock and pay the estate taxes. Although somewhat overstated, this euphoric vision does reflect the benefits of going public when it works well. Specifically, the following factors are commonly considered the advantages of making a public stock offering:

Access to public funds   A growing young enterprise is always hungry for cash and a public offering provides it. In most cases, the resources of the founder are limited, the original investors wish to risk only so much in any one venture, and other potential private investors may insist on stiffer terms than the public. Additional equity also has a multiplier effect because based on it, if necessary, additional debt can usually be raised.

Personal enrichment   Often in an initial public offering, most of the stock is being sold by the company itself rather than its principal stockholders. However, even if an offering is for the company, stockholders can usually join in through piggyback registration-rights provisions such as those described in connection with the discussion of venture capital. The ideal of controlling shareholders is that they can obtain a healthy chunk of cash, retain control, and still have the possibility of further appreciation by keeping a large block of stock.

Care should be taken not to slay the proverbial golden goose. As was discussed, an underwriter generally has the theoretical power to force cutbacks on piggyback registration provisions, but, as a practical matter, may be reluctant to do so when the largest piggybacker is the company's chief executive officer. In any event, though, the public and the underwriters may get a little nervous when key personnel are selling large chunks of their holdings.

Even if no stock is sold by them in a public offering, there are economic benefits to the existing stockholders. First, there is the possibility of some liquidity through a dribble-out under Rule 144 after the offering. Second, a public offering provides an easy way to determine the market value of the stock. Once that value is known, borrowing against the stock is much easier, which means there is more cash available to insiders for spending. Third, if there should ever be an emergency situation such as an estate sale, both valuation and disposition become easier.

Perhaps the crucial expectation, however, is that the valuation placed on the stock will be quite high, and this pricing itself will eventually work to the advantage of the holder through the sale of a block, dribble-outs, credit loans, or general perceptions of affluence. This price expectation is predicated on the notion that the market will give a high price-earnings ratio to a stock in a dramatically growing company. Certainly, this was true in the 1960s when small computer firms could show explosive growth and sell at multiples exceeding 30 times earnings.

Acquisition opportunities   A young company seeking acquisitions may well wish to use its stock instead of cash. A firm with a stock selling at a high multiple of earnings can increase its earnings growth record by purchasing with its stock companies whose stock is selling at a low multiple. In addition, stockholders of potential acquisitions will probably be more willing to accept securities of a public than a private concern because of the increased marketability. Therefore, going public may open new acquisition vistas.

The Disadvantages of Going Public

No return   In theory, going private, once a company has gone public, is simple enough. If the number of shareholders falls below 300, a company can elect to be no longer a reporting company under the 1934 Act. As long as it doesn't then sell any securities under the 1933 Act, it has become again a private company. The theory is quite difficult to implement in practice without a great deal of anguish. Minority stockholders will inevitably complain that going private deprives them of a valuable asset and will allege that management is exploiting the public shareholders for personal advantage, an argument some courts have listened to recently with great sympathy.

The reporting burden   Under the 1934 Act, a company must file the following reports during the course of a year:
- Annually, a report must be sent to all shareholders.
- Annually, a Form 10-K must be filed, with a description of the business and detailed financial statements, including breakdowns by major profit lines. Major contracts and agreements often have to be filed as an exhibit to the 10-K.
- Annually, a proxy statement describing the background, stock holdings, and payments made to directors and key officers must be sent to all stockholders.
- Quarterly, financial statements on Form 10-Q must be filed with the SEC.
- Form 8-K's must be filed with the SEC whenever there have been material events which should be disclosed.

Furthermore, the individuals who are major stockholders or are directors or officers have their own paper work burden. Any officer or director or major stockholder must have his or her personal financial affairs open to the public's scrutiny. Any person acquiring 5% or more of a company's shares must file a Form 13D explaining how the shares were purchased and describing any future plans that may have been formulated regarding the company's securities. If the number of shares owned should materially change, an amendment to the 13D must be filed. If an individual owns more than 10% of any class of securities, or if the individual is an officer or director of the company, a Form 3 must be filed indicating the ownership of securities of the company, if any, and any subsequent changes in holdings or status must be reflected in a Form 4 filing indicating the change.

All this paper work is not only burdensome on the people filing, but it is also expensive. The additional printing, accounting, and legal fees alone, forgetting about the time cost for a company's own executives, may total more than $50,000 a year, even for a relatively small public company.

Limitations on action Management of even a nonpublic company has fiduciary obligations mandated by state law, but the executives and directors of a public company are governed by an even stricter standard. In addition to acting in a prescribed manner, they must also fully disclose their actions as required by the federal securities laws. The dilemma of deciding how to act in gray situations is compounded by the quandary of disclosure. Small companies usually abound with such problems. Is the office building the company rents owned by the founder? Is the company's lawyer also the owner's sister-in-law, and are her opinions objective? Is there major purchasing from companies controlled by large stockholders and is the pricing system fair? The more entangled the web of interpersonal relations in the insider group, the greater the problems of dealing effectively with them in a public company. Doing business under a glass dome is a nice concept but, as a practical matter, is quite disturbing to inside management.

The magnification of short-term objectives Everyone likes to be a hero, and chief executive officers are no exception. So when the stock that was sold to the public at twenty times earnings begins to dip, the pressures on the company president increase. Deals are made, accounting practices are changed, techniques altered, all to resume or maintain the growth record. But short-term results may be quite different from long-term impact. All too often, companies become mesmerized by their stock price, trying to retain the luster of the go-go years while neglecting fundamental business considerations.

A low market price   If a company should encounter the disfavor of the market, the situation becomes even worse. When a company is private, the major investors find it difficult to dispose of their stock rapidly. But with a public company out of favor, the dumping process has its own momentum. A sharp decline in price is quite visible and leads many new investors to get itchy. The result is an overhang of willing sellers' securities in the market that dampens the price for some time in the future, defeating many of the benefits of going public in the first place. Indeed, as a result of this overhang, the public market price is sometimes lower than what otherwise would have been the perceived private-placement value of a security. Unfortunately for the seller, the public price will be the base against which even private purchases will be negotiated; it is presumptively the fair market value.

Control   A related problem is that of control. In a privately held company, controversial decisions are easier to make. If necessary, a consensus can be obtained among the key shareholders. In a public company, as had been discussed, freedom of action is more limited. The added risk, however, is that management may find itself booted out of its own company. Of course, this risk depends on the share of the company the public owns, but after a few years, many of the original insiders may, one way or another, have dribbled out, and other stockholders may be disillusioned and willing to sell to an outside raider.

Striking the Balance

In the end, the decision whether to go public depends on the nature of the company and the individuals involved. Unusual firms whose stories are hard to sell to the public in conventional terms may well be better off as private concerns. For example, a real estate business may be doing well even when earnings are low; cash flow may be high, and the assumed depreciation may be, in fact, an unrealistic figure in economic terms. The fact that so many firms that have gone public have recently attempted to return to being private raises substantial questions about the going-public imperative. Much, of course, depends on personality. An autocrat with an eccentric management style is better off in a private company; being the chief executive of a public concern is a task of some delicacy. Inevitably, however, when times are booming, the public route seems paved with gold, and many companies who shouldn't will go that route to their subsequent regret.

The real difficulty is that for a small firm there are very few routes for management or early investors to sell even part of their investment so that they can realize on some of the appreciation in value. Internal development may have limited possibilities because the venture-capital firms and investors financing the small business will want a structured opportunity to realize on their investment. The only realistic alternative is acquisition by another company, but this generally means even more limitations on the freedom of action of the old management than being a public company.

THE ROLE OF THE INVESTMENT BANKER

Once a company has decided to go public, it must find an investment banker willing and able to underwrite the deal. Essentially, as an underwriter, an investment banker acts as a wholesaler aiding an issuer to distribute securities to the public. Before describing the specific role of investment bankers in public offerings, it it useful to describe briefly some of the background of the investment banking industry.

Investment Banking Background

Leading firms   In 1976, according to *Corporate Financing Week*, the ten largest investment banking houses and the amounts of public securities for which they were lead managing underwriter (ran the books for the deal) were as follows:

	Billions of Dollars
Morgan Stanley	$9.6
First Boston	5.1
Merrill Lynch	5.0
Salomon Bros.	4.8
Blyth Eastman Dillon	2.6
Goldman Sachs	2.6
Kuhn, Loeb (now merged with Lehman)	1.6
Lehman Bros.	1.5
Kidder, Peabody	1.4
White, Weld	1.4

These statistics, however, can be misleading. For example, certain houses have specialties in terms of both client corporations and purchasing customers. Some smaller firms, such as Lazard Frères, have a good capability in specialized fields such as mergers, and a regional food chain seeking area investors may be better off dealing with a distinguished local investment banking firm, such as Alex. Brown of Baltimore. Similarly, there are firms, such as New Court Securities Corporation and Heizer

Corporation, with expertise in venture capital situations. Others, such as First Boston and Goldman Sachs, are known for their broad competence in the full range of investment banking activities.

In addition, standings are constantly in flux. First, a merger wave has hit the industry over the last several years in reaction to competitive commission rates and the general state of the stock market. Inevitably, there will be additional mergers in the future. Second, firms shift their orientation. For example, Morgan Stanley has traditionally had many AAA major industrial companies as clients, and its distribution has been oriented to institutions. Merrill Lynch, Pierce, Fenner & Smith, on the other hand, has had a very strong retail operation and could be quite powerful in selling an issue to small investors. Merrill Lynch used its small investor leverage and started to be included in more and more offerings. Then it began hiring a research and sales staff to appeal to institutional clients. In fact, Merrill Lynch reportedly went out to hire as many of the leading analysts as it could, jumping it from eleventh place in 1975 to first place in 1976 in the *Institutional Investor* magazine survey of research capabilities. Soon, Merrill Lynch became a leading underwriter. In the first half of 1976 (analyzing all public securities offerings by issues for which the investment banker was one of the managing underwriters rather than the lead underwriter), Merrill Lynch was, by far, managing underwriter of the greatest dollar amount of securities of all investment bankers. Morgan Stanley, however, began itself to affiliate with a series of strong regional firms to improve its retail distribution and beefed up its own research staff. Meanwhile, E. F. Hutton and Bache Halsey Stuart have begun to revitalize their investment banking operations and, with their retail distribution power, are expected to become major factors in the industry.

In the investment banking field, prestige, reputation, and distinction are precious assets. Perhaps the best example of the battle for prestige was the great 1976 alphabet war. Underwriters in the same bracket, or category, are listed together on the tombstone for a deal in alphabetical order. Bache's investment banking subsidiary, Halsey Stuart, was naturally listed under the H's. Someone at Bache got the wonderful idea that if Bache and Halsey Stuart merged, the resulting name, Bache Halsey Stuart, would move up in the alphabetical order in the major bracket, the category reserved for the leading underwriters. Many of the other members of the major bracket reacted with sound and fury, but when the howling was all over, Bache's gambit worked. At first impression, this may all seem petty, but such tactics are useful both in preserving a certain mystique and in signaling to the investment community that these firms care about long-term perceptions.

Indeed, in pricing terms and rigor of examination, a traditional investment banker may be more overbearing toward a young company than a one-shot operator looking for a killing. The traditional underwriter knows that months from now, the investment community will be looking at the price of the security to see how well a stock had held up. If in too many cases, the price in this after-market is lower than at the time of the transaction, the underwriter's reputation declines and selling a deal becomes harder.

History Today's investment firms grew out of the post-Civil War need to finance America's industrial expansion. Many firms acquired experience peddling U.S. government bonds during the Civil War, and later made handsome profits selling railroad bonds. Much of the capital was provided from abroad, and firms such as J. P. Morgan (the forerunner of Morgan Stanley) and Kuhn Loeb developed excellent European connections.

Around the turn of the century, the idea of selling securities in general industrial corporations began to gain currency. For example, the 1906 sale of $10 million in Sears, Roebuck & Co. securities by Goldman, Sachs was an important landmark, for it indicated that with considerable effort, securities in enterprises other than railroads and heavy industry such as steel production could be sold to the public.

With the massive floating of "Liberty Loans" to the government during World War I, investment banking became increasingly complex and sophisticated, setting up the system of syndication which was used through the great crash of 1929. But the crash brought about cries for reforms. The investment banking houses like Morgan's, who could both lend money to firms and underwrite their public offering of securities, seemed too powerful. In reaction, Congress passed the Glass Steagall Act of 1933, which, in addition to the federal securities laws, prohibits commercial banks from underwriting securities. As a result, J. P. Morgan, the First Bank of Boston, and others were forced to spin off their investment banking operations. In the case of these two firms, the spin-offs became the leading concerns of Morgan Stanley and The First Boston Corporation.

To illustrate a leading investment banker's activity, First Boston managed or comanaged in the 15-year period from 1961 through 1976 negotiated domestic public offerings of $25.2 billion of debt securities for 180 corporations and $115.1 billion of equity securities for 141 corporations, in addition to arranging billions of dollars in private placements and managing some $39 billion of securities issues won on a sealed-bid basis. Additionally, the firm is active in giving financial advice, arranging mergers and acquisitions, and trading securities. First Boston has about 1000 employees and capital of about $90 million.

Hot issues underwriters The history of the more eminent of the invest-ment banking firms, however, only tells a fraction of the story, especially for the offerings of companies first going public. In the early 1960s, the SEC found that some 60% of the securities registered with it were from companies who had never before filed a registration statement. The SEC's study of these deals gives some insight into the new issues market when it gets hot.

In most of the offerings, the motivation for going public was to obtain more funds for the business, although there was some piggyback registra-tion of insider shares. One important factor was the desire to have stock option plans covering marketable securities to attract new managerial talent. About half the deals were underwritten by securities firms formed within the previous 6 years, and one-fourth were formed within 1 year of the date of the offering. Of the concerns younger than 6 years old, 35% had net capital of less than $10,000. However, the deals underwritten by these firms tended to be much smaller than those underwritten by tradi-tional investment bankers. Many of the newer houses used a "best efforts" form of transaction, in which there is no firm commitment by the under-writer to purchase the company's securities. Often the underwriters received stock or warrants in the company as part of their fee.

The SEC found that the price-earnings ratios for 22 new issues, which it used as a sample, ranged from 6.9 to 125 times earnings. Within 2 days after issuance, all these stocks were trading at premiums on the offering price of from 5 to 150%; after about 18 months, 10 were below the offering price by more than 50%, and the rest had varied performances, with only 7 still above the offering price.

Since the early 1960s, Wall Street has gone through dramatic upheav-als. With the collapse of the market, the money to be made from mergers and new equity issues dried up. Meanwhile, the fixed commission struc-ture with its lucrative profits and by-products, such as the payment of soft dollars for research through commission orders, was phased out. As a result, many smaller investment bankers were merged or closed. Further-more, the increasing attempt by companies to bypass underwriters in placements and the broader corporate financing role played by banks, despite the Glass Steagall Act, raise fundamental problems for the future. However, the larger firms have survived and prospered, and the profits announced by firms when things are going well are stunning. For exam-ple, Salomon Brothers' profits in fiscal 1976 were $70 million, on the average more than $1 million per partner.

Choosing an Investment Banker

If possible, it is generally in a company's long-term best interest to get an investment banker with an established reputation. This does not necessarily mean a large firm. A prominent regional firm or one specializing in certain industries will often do a better job or offer better terms. Sometimes, there is little choice. A company which wants to go public but can't get leading firms to underwrite its securities may feel that it has to use less reliable concerns. In most cases, the reality is probably that the business is not yet ready for the public market. Not that investment bankers are infallible, but companies tend to lack appreciation for their own situation.

The decision to go public should not be made in a short time. Planning should start within the company at least a year in advance for an initial offering. Forgetting any other considerations, financial statements must be in the form prescribed by the SEC, and preparing them often takes considerable adjustment. Indeed, auditors are often hired with the requisite SEC accounting background that prior accountants, skilled as they may have been in auditing the books of a small, nonpublic concern, may have lacked.

Generally, if a company is growing, solicitations from aggressive investment bankers seem to sprout like weeds. A firm should not, however, limit its search to those soliciting it. Recommendations from directors, attorneys, and bankers can often be of particular value. Having narrowed the search to a few firms, a company should begin to test their performance. For example, it can quite legitimately ask a number of firms for general advice about capital structure and compare the analyses. In addition, a company can get generalized thoughts on pricing, commission spreads, and other requirements for a public offering from the bankers and can also examine the bankers' recent deals. The point is that a company's initial investment banker usually is with it for a long time, and frequent changes might seriously harm a corporation's reputation in the investment community. Aside from efficiency in placing the initial deal, an investment banker is useful in many other contexts: in making or warding off tender offers and acquisitions, in negotiating private placements, and in planning financial strategy.

Having had general discussions with a number of firms, it is often helpful for the corporation to prepare a memo outlining a proposal for an offering. Among the items which should be included are a description of the business, the company's view on what the appeal to investors might be, and an outline of the securities the firm is thinking of offering. As discussions end and negotiations begin, a company should think carefully about seeming to be carrying on bargaining with other investment bankers simultaneously. Some of the better banks are so sensitive about their reputation, they will often steer away from the potential embarrassment of losing an account, while others welcome the competition.

After a company selects its investment bankers, the next step is to consult with them as to the nature, prerequisites, and timing of a public offering. Among the key preliminary considerations are the following:

Corporate cleanup As discussed, the accounting records of a company must conform with SEC requirements before an offering can be made. However, many other items may require attention before a company is ready to go public. For example, there is the question of clear legal records. Have the corporate minutes been kept up to date? Are the company's main commitments evidenced by executed contracts? Then there are the more substantive questions. Do the certificate and the bylaws reflect the needs of a small close corporation or those of a public company? For example, restrictions on the powers of the board of directors and other control-allocation provisions must be specifically disclosed in any registration statement and may hurt the marketing of an issue. Similarly, there may be "sweetheart" contracts with various insiders which one might want to amend before selling securities to the public.

Restructuring In some cases, a private firm's entire capital structure should be reformed before its securities are offered to the public. For example, the rights of a preferred stock issue may be so strong that they limit the potential of the common stock, or the covenants in existing debt may be so restrictive as to restrict the future growth potential of the firm.

The situation is even more complicated when the entity that wishes to go public is really part of a web of interrelated concerns. For example, the owners of a ribbon manufacturer may wish to have their cutting operations, which use laser beams, go public because they believe there is great growth potential and glamour. But the cutting operations may be supplied from a textile plant in which the owners also have a sizable interest. Sometimes, the contractual relations in such situations have to be reformed to limit the possibilities of flagrant abuse. Other times, reorganizations and mergers of these interrelated concerns are prerequisites to going public. Generally, the cleaner the package, the more comprehensible and marketable. In any restructuring, care should be taken to avoid unintended tax consequences.

The letter of intent When an investment banker and the issuer have reached preliminary agreement as to terms, a brief letter of intent is often drawn up. The letter outlines some of the major negotiated terms, including the type of underwriting arrangement, the important conditions to the underwriting, such as required earnings levels, any contemplated reorganization of the company, the expected date of sale, whether there will be any piggyback sales by insider holders, and the general level of compensation to be paid the underwriters. All these descriptions are in the nature of a term sheet; usually, they are not binding and are only descriptive. However, they do limit the scope of negotiation when the definitive underwriting agreement is being written. Also, the one term of the letter of intent which is generally binding relates to the expenses of the underwriter in the event no public offering takes place—a very useful provision for the investment banker to minimize downside risk.

THE ROLE OF THE SECURITIES LAWYER

Having decided to go public, a company must resign itself to the inevitability of lawyers, for the massive paper shuffling involved is an attorney's delight. A small company may well find that its regular lawyers do not have the requisite expertise in securities matters to perform effectively on a public offering, and may well engage additional special counsel. In any event, the underwriters usually will be represented by attorneys specializing in the securities field. Although the issuer can rely on the technical advice given by the underwriter's counsel, it is likely to bargain more effectively, and put together a better prospectus faster, if its own lawyers are knowledgeable.

Although there are securities specialists throughout the country, including some excellent large firms, the "green goods" legal business, with the specialists in securities, is centered in New York to service the financial industry there. Among the largest securities firms are Brown, Wood, Fuller, Caldwell & Ivey; Cravath, Swaine & Moore; Davis Polk & Wardwell; Debevoise, Plimpton, Lyons & Gates; Dewey, Ballantine, Bushby, Palmer & Wood; Milbank Tweed, Hadley & McCloy; Shearman & Sterling; Sullivan & Cromwell and White & Case. Each of these firms has major clients among investment bankers, banks, institutional investors, and large corporations so that they repeatedly are involved in deals and have developed an expertise in the area. For example, over the years, Sullivan & Cromwell has represented First Boston, Davis Polk, Morgan Stanley; Brown Wood and Rodgers & Wells, Merrill Lynch; Cravath, often, Blyth Eastman Dillon, Salomon Brothers and Lehman, Kuhn Loeb.

Many of these firms now have about 200 lawyers, usually with two or three associates to every partner. The *Martindale Hubbel Legal Directory* gives some guidance as to the background of these lawyers. At Sullivan & Cromwell, for example, approximately half of the fifty-six partners graduated from Harvard and over two-thirds from Harvard, Yale, or Columbia. Although these firms are extremely close-mouthed about their fees, recent affidavits filed in connection with compensation petitions in corporate reorganization proceedings give a rough idea of the charges: associates seem to be charged for at an average rate of about $60 an hour, partners an average of about $110, with senior partners rising above $150 per hour at some firms. Of course, the charges differ from firm to firm, and on financial transactions, many firms charge by the deal, with time being only one factor. Among the other considerations involved are the complexity of the work, the money involved, the skill used, and the results achieved.

Surprisingly, a large securities law firm may charge less for a transaction than a smaller, nonspecialist firm. First, the specialists have often worked on similar deals, so that less time is spent on background; research and, many times, existing precedents in the office can be used as models. Second, associates are often doing most of the legwork, and their time is cheaper than even nonspecialist partner time. On the other hand, a modest deal may get more senior staff attention at a small firm.

One of the unusual features of securities law is that lawyers have a mixed role. Although the lawyers are representing the interest of their clients, the SEC and the courts, by increasing the lawyers' burden of diligence, have attempted also to appoint them as the guardians of the securities law, almost legal auditors of public offerings. Naturally, the concept is very unpopular with the securities bar, which even now is extremely reluctant to give legal opinions about much of anything.

The SEC suit against the prominent firm of White & Case regarding its role in the allegedly false and misleading actions taken by National Student Marketing has exacerbated the worries of these Wall Street lawyers. The complaint, as amended by the SEC, alleged that White & Case did not prevent the closing of a series of mergers by its client, National Student Marketing, when it had information from its client's accountants indicating that National Student Marketing's financial statements were misleading. White & Case was allegedly told on the day of closing of one acquisition that its client's financial statements contained errors which would result in net income being a slight loss instead of the $700,000 profit shown. The SEC claimed that White & Case showed the acquired company's lawyers only an incomplete draft of a letter from National Student Marketing's auditors, which did not state as clearly the effect of these errors as did the final version sent to the acquired company's lawyers after the closing. According to the SEC the acquired company's lawyers should have realized that shareholder approval of the deal had been obtained on the basis of misleading information when they received a draft rather than a definitive letter from the auditors at the closing. At that point, according to the SEC, the attorneys should have insisted upon the resolicitation of the shareholders, and, if the parties involved did not agree, bring the matter to the attention of the Commission.

The National Student Marketing complaint was settled in May 1977, with the White & Case partner involved suspended from SEC practice for 6 months and White & Case itself agreeing to enforce its internal quality control procedures. No violations of law, however, were admitted by

White & Case or any of its partners. Reaction to the settlement has varied widely, but, at least, the bar is now on clear notice as to its due-diligence burden.

Of course, the fear of the bar now is that if a firm like White & Case could be named in a suit, even though it was finally settled, no one is safe in the future. From the SEC's point of view, however, the only way violations of the securities laws are going to be prevented is by the vigorous action of the private bar, and adding to their potential liabilities is an effective prod. This situation explains why securities lawyers may well feel they have to disagree with a client and insist on disclosure. As much as the lawyers moan about their increased responsibilities, the current state of the law does give them the leverage to take an independent stance with their clients when required.

Public Offerings
under the 1933 Act

The manner of conducting a public offering is dictated by the 1933 Act. In analyzing that statute, it must be remembered that its function is to create a self-enforcing disclosure mechanism. Rather than the SEC deciding what is fair or not, the 1933 Act is a system designed to require the ferreting out and exposure of the pertinent facts by the preparers of the registration statement themselves. The issuer, its officers and directors, the lawyers, the accountants, and the underwriters all are under a heavy statutory burden to assure themselves that there are no material errors or omissions, or face severe sanctions.

THE BASIC PROHIBITION

In analyzing the 1933 Act, one must begin with the broad double prohibition of Section 5: First, it is unlawful under Section 5 for any person *to offer to sell* a security unless a registration statement has been *filed* with the SEC. Second, it is unlawful to *sell* a security unless a registration statement is *effective*. This standard, in effect, means that only when a preliminary prospectus has been filed is it permissible for securities to be offered to the public, but no sales can take place until the prospectus has become effective. The preliminary prospectus bears a legend in red ink which indicates it is subject to amendment and that the securities described may not be sold nor may offers to buy be accepted prior to the time the registration statement becomes effective. Because of the red ink, a preliminary prospectus is often referred to as a "red herring."

The time between the preliminary filing and the effective date is known as the waiting period, and it is during these days that the public can familiarize itself with the offering. Management must be careful during this period to avoid seeming to initiate publicity, especially any projections or estimates of the value of the company's securities, other than customary announcements. Although the SEC in Release 5180 urged companies to respond factually to unsolicited inquiries from financial analysts and security holders, most firms, on the advice of their counsel, attempt to limit communication while "in registration." The risk of an inadvertent violation of the 1933 Act by a loquacious executive is perceived to outweigh the benefits of responding to questions, a position which infuriates financial reporters and others interested in disclosure.

To grasp the scope of Section 5, it is necessary to turn to the definitional provision of the 1933 Act, Section 2. Under Section 2, the definitions of both "security" and "sale" are quite broad. "Security" as defined in Section 2(1) not only includes, among other specifics, any note, stock, treasury stock, investment contract, guarantee, and warrant but also any interest or instrument commonly known as a security. Although there are a great many cases on whether various obscure financial instruments are securities, in general, if you thought enough about it to ask the question, it is a security. Similarly, "sale" is defined in Section 2(3) to include every "contract of sale or disposition of a security or interest in a security, for value." An offer to sell includes "every attempt or offer to dispose of, or solicitation of an offer to buy, a security or interest in a security, for value." It should be noted, however, that preliminary negotiations or agreements with underwriters are specifically excluded from the definition of sale, so that investment bankers can bargain with the issuer prior to the filing of a prospectus. Of course, the 1933 Act is applicable only to transactions involving interstate commerce, but the cases have so broadly defined this concept as to make it basically irrelevant except to Rule 147 intrastate transactions.

EXEMPTIONS

Taken by itself, Section 5 prohibits the sale of any security without an effective registration statement; even the partners in a corner drugstore cannot sell securities to themselves when they set up a corporation. However, Section 3 exempts certain securities, and Section 4 exempts certain transactions from the registration requirements.

Exempt Securities

Among the securities exempt from the registration requirements of the 1933 Act are commercial paper, securities of governments, banks, charitable organizations, savings and loan associations and common carriers, insurance policies, annuity contracts, and securities issued in bankruptcy reorganizations. In addition, intrastate offerings conforming with Rule 147 and securities which are exchanged by an issuer with its existing holders if there are no commissions involved, such as stock for bond restructurings, are exempt. The 1933 Act also gives the SEC authority to exempt securities if the amount of the issue is not greater than $500,000, which is the basis of Regulation A.

Exempt Transactions

Section 4 provides that Section 5 shall be inapplicable to

(1) transactions by any person other than an issuer, underwriter or dealer;
(2) transactions by an issuer not involving any public offering; and
(3) dealer transactions except those which are part of a pattern of distribution of a security.

These exemptions are narrower than they may seem on first impression. To understand their scope, it is necessary to turn again to the definitions in Section 2.

Brokerage transactions   The first exemption under Section 4, transactions not involving an issuer, underwriter, or dealer, is the basis upon which normal brokerage transactions are made. Both the terms "issuer" and "underwriter" are, however, broadly defined so the exemption is relatively limited. For example, an "underwriter" is defined in Section 2 to include anyone who has purchased from an issuer with a view to, or who offers or sells for an issuer in connection with, a distribution of securities. So the term "underwriter" under the 1933 Act doesn't include just investment banking firms. Purchasers in a private placement, for example, who resell to the public are deemed to be statutory underwriters because they are part of a chain of distribution.

Similarly, the term "issuer" is defined broadly in Section 2(11) to include "any person directly or indirectly controlling or controlled by the issuer, or any person under direct or indirect common control with the issuer." Of course, the term "control" is ambiguous by itself, and there is no specific definition of it under the 1933 Act, although Rule 405 states that "'control'. . . means the possession, direct or indirect, of the power to direct or cause the direction of the management and policies of a person, whether through the ownership of voting securities, by contract or otherwise." As a rough rule of thumb, an individual or a member of a group of people owning 10% of the voting shares of a corporation is deemed to be a control person. Circumstances can, however, differ. A minority holding of 20% might not make a stockholder a control person if an antagonistic block has 51% of the stock. On the other hand, a holder of 1% of the stock may be deemed a control person if relatives together own about 10%.

To give an example of the impact of these definitions, a holder of 20% of the stock of a company who sells shares through a broker to the public might well be acting illegally, even though the shares had already been registered. The seller, under the broad definition in the 1933 Act, is an issuer. An issuer cannot sell a security unless there is an exemption, and there is no exemption for a public distribution by an issuer. Indeed, the broker in the deal is an underwriter because under the statutory definition, an underwriter is anyone who purchases from or sells securities for an issuer in connection with a distribution.

Given these definitions, sales by a control person to the public must be made through the registration of the securities; this process is known as a secondary distribution, as opposed to a company's direct, primary distribution. The alternative is to sell in a private placement or under Rule 144. Rule 144, in effect, defines what will not be considered a distribution to the public by both control persons and persons who purchased directly from an issuer in a private placement and who may be deemed to be statutory underwriters.

Private offerings   The second exempt transaction under Section 4, private offerings, has already been discussed in detail. Because the statute does not define a transaction not involving any public offering, the precise contours of what is permissible are most unclear. Rule 146 is the safe-harbor rule, which sets criteria for determining what is a private offering, but is not exclusive and, as noted, is not frequently used. The ambiguity of the pre-rule 146 case law seems to be preferred to the harsh certainties of the new rule.

Dealer transactions   The dealer transaction exemption under Section 4 allows dealers to trade for their own account or as brokers for customers without registering the securities. However, during the 40-day period following a public offering (or 90 days following an initial public offering), the exemption is not applicable, and the delivery of a registration statement is necessary. Thus, after a syndicate has disbanded, an underwriter can sell shares without registration if, in essence, the underwriter is acting as a dealer and the 40- or 90-day test is inapplicable. In addition, there is a fourth exemption for unsolicited brokerage transactions, which formerly was the basis of an SEC rule that has been rescinded and now has little practical effect.

LIABILITIES FOR ILLEGAL SALES OF SECURITIES

If Section 5 should be violated by the illegal distribution of securities without a registration statement, the 1933 Act provides a number of sanctions. First, the SEC can enjoin the distribution of the securities under Section 20(b). Second, Section 24 provides for a $5,000 fine and up to 5 years' imprisonment for violations of the 1933 Act. It should be remembered, though, that Section 16 states that all remedies imposed by the 1933 Act are in addition to any others which may be available.

Private parties also have the right to litigate securities cases under the 1933 Act. Under Section 12(1), purchasers of securities may directly sue for rescission or damages any person who violated Section 5 by selling the securities to them without the required registration. In addition, Section 12(2) imposes liability for material misstatements or omissions whether or not the transactions or the securities are exempt from registration, other than certain bank and government securities. Liability is also imposed under Section 12(2) for any representation to purchasers at variance with the prospectus. Thus, oral sales pitches can create liability even though an accurate prospectus has been filed. Under Section 12, there is no need to show any reliance by the purchaser on the misrepresentation. However, there is a requirement of "privity"—purchasers may sue only their immediate sellers and persons who control them, not any other party. Thus, for example, in an underwritten public offering, a purchaser from a brokerage house which acted as a dealer could not sue the issuer under Section 12(2) for an error in the prospectus, since there is no privity.

If a registration statement was filed but contained a material misstatement or omission, Section 11 entitles any person acquiring the security not knowing of the misstatement or omission to sue *every* person who signed the registration statement, including the issuer, as well as all directors, whether or not they signed the registration statement, and the underwriters. *A director not signing the registration statement is not relieved of liability.* In contrast to Section 12, no privity is required under Section 11. Buyers can sue the issuer even though they bought stock in the open market, but, like Section 12, there is no need to show reliance on the faulty prospectus.

Major stockholders may also be liable even though they haven't signed the registration statement. Section 15 states that any person who controls any person liable under Sections 11 or 12 is also liable under those provisions, unless the person in control can show that there was no knowledge or reasonable grounds to believe that the facts existed which gave rise to the liability.

The threat of suit does not, however, forever hang over the heads of all these parties. A built-in statute of limitations on damage actions is contained in the 1933 Act. Under Section 13, no action may be brought under Section 12(1) unless filed within a year of the offering of the securities without the required registration. Similarly, no action may be brought under Section 11 or Section 12(2) for errors or omissions in security offerings unless brought within 1 year of the date of discovery (or the date that, with reasonable diligence, there should have been discovery) of the error or omission, and in no event can any action be brought more than 3 years after the public offering.

Also contained in the 1933 Act is its own general antifraud provision, Section 17(a), which prohibits fraudulent transactions, whether or not there is an exemption. Because the statute is silent on the subject, the court decisions are split as to whether a private damages action is permissible under Section 17(a) and whether privity is required. Usually a reference to Section 17(a) is put in the complaint, but, to date, reliance in suits has been placed on the general fraud provisions under the 1934 Act, Section 10b, which is recognized as the prime basis for a private damages action.

Section 10b under the 1934 Act prohibits the use of deceptive devices in connection with the purchase or sale of any security. Although the statute and the general fraud rule promulgated under it by the SEC, Rule 10b-5, are both vague, the courts have developed through a long series of cases a federal common-law of securities fraud. Because 10(b) covers all sales, it is often the basis for insider information and manipulative trading cases, but it can also be used in distribution of securities situations, even if the securities or the transactions are exempt under the 1933 Act. Although 10(b) duplicates in some degree the coverage of Sections 11 and 12 of the 1933 Act in a distribution situation, it has the advantage of being governed by the applicable state statute of limitations, as is Section 17, rather than the short statute of limitations built into Section 13 of the 1933 Act. Recently, the Supreme Court has applied strict standards for the usage of Section 10(b), making it less attractive than reliance on Section 11 in suits regarding the public offering of securities.

DEFENSES

There are, however, substantive defenses to a suit regarding a public offering, as well as procedural ones, such as the statute of limitations. If the action is brought under Section 10(b) of the 1934 Act, a defense can now be established by a lack of evil intent, as will be discussed. Under Section 11, the basic provision in the 1933 Act regarding liability in connection with public offerings, the defenses are more limited and are built right into the statute. Indeed, the structure of these defenses in Section 11 determines much of the procedure used in preparing registration statements because each party is interested in complying with the statutory requirements for exoneration.

Section 11 provides that no person, other than the issuer, shall be liable if that person can meet one of the following defense criteria:

1. The person has resigned and informed the SEC and the company of the resignation and has asserted a lack of responsibility for the registration statement before its effective date.

2. The person gave notice to the SEC and the public that the registration statement had become effective without his or her knowledge and that he or she would not be responsible for it.

3. (a) If the statements were not made on the authority of an expert or were based on the person's own statements as an expert, the person had reasonable grounds to believe and did believe at the time registration statement became effective *after reasonable investigation* that the statements were true and there were no material omissions.

(b) If the statements were purportedly made on the authority of an expert or governmental officials or documents, the defense is the same except that no reasonable investigation is required.

The statute specifies that the applicable standard in determining what constitutes reasonable investigation and reasonable belief shall be that of a prudent man in the management of his own property. As a practical matter, the exceptions for resignations and notices to the SEC and the public are seldom used. The exceptions based on reasonable investigations and reasonable belief, however, form the basis for much of the activity of experts, underwriters, and directors in connection with the preparation of a registration statement.

In analyzing these defenses, attention should be drawn to the difference between statements which have been "expertised" and those that have not. For an underwriter or director, the duty changes depending on whether a statement has been expertised: If a statement has been made on the authority of an expert, reasonable belief is a defense; no reasonable investigation is required. However, if the statement is not based on the authority of an expert, a reasonable investigation is required. Remembering that the burden is on a defendant to document any of these defenses, it is obviously helpful to not have to show that a reasonable investigation took place. For this reason, it is extremely desirable to get as much material as possible expertised.

What exactly is expertised information? Obviously, purported copies of reports or valuations of an expert or of the government fit this category. In addition, the statements of experts based on their studies are also expertised; the experts have to sign a consent indicating their willingness to have statements attributed to them in the registration statement and file it with the SEC. Other than accountants and lawyers, experts can be mining engineers, surveyors, and other professionals who sign consents.

Most information in a registration statement is, however, not expertised. Even, for example, material covered in the standard letter from accountants to the underwriters as to certain facts in the prospectus, which will be discussed later, is not expertised as such, although receipt of the letter is certainly helpful, but not dispositive, in showing a reasonable investigation.

For statements in a prospectus which are not expertised (the vast bulk of the document other than the financial statements) an underwriter, for example, must show both a reasonable belief and a reasonable investigation in order to establish a defense. This reasonable investigation is commonly known as "due diligence," and much of the activity of an underwriter and its counsel in the registration process is determined by it. Documents must be read, officials interviewed, questions asked, sites inspected—all to establish this defense.

THE CASE LAW ON DUE DILIGENCE

The BarChris Decision

In order to get a more practical idea of the scope of potential liability and the effectiveness of defenses in securities litigation, it is useful to turn to the cases. Perhaps the leading decision in the field is a 1968 district court opinion regarding the BarChris Construction Corporation. Both the thoroughness of the opinion by the judge and the timing of the decision, at the height of the stock market frenzy of the 1960s, account for its preeminence.

BarChris constructed and sold bowling centers during the bowling boom of the 1950s and early 1960s. BarChris normally required only a small down payment from customers or arranged for a factor to finance the bowling centers, but remained liable itself for 25% of the lease payments due. To raise additional capital, BarChris sold $3.5 million of convertible subordinated debentures in May of 1961 through a public offering. By the early 1960s, the bowling fad tapered off sharply, resulting in a vast overcapacity of bowling centers. Soon, BarChris began experiencing difficulties in collecting amounts due from customers. Finally, in October of 1962, it filed for a reorganization under the federal Bankruptcy Act, and defaulted the next month on interest due on the debentures.

The plaintiffs in the case were purchasers of debentures who alleged, under Section 11 of the 1933 Act, that the registration statement contained material errors and had material omissions. In reviewing the prospectus, the judge found that sales, income, and assets had been overstated and contingent liabilities understated. Each of the defendants who were so entitled attempted to raise a due-diligence defense, but the judge held that none of them had fulfilled the test of having a reasonable belief after having conducted a reasonable investigation.

The directors and insiders First, the judge turned to the signers of the registration statement. The treasurer of BarChris claimed that he answered all questions asked, but because this was the first registration statement he had ever worked on, he relied on BarChris' accountants and lawyers as to what information was required. The court rejected this argument, stating that he didn't have a reasonable ground to believe the statements in the registration statement were true, given his familiarity with the company. Next, the court dealt with the young house counsel, who was on the board. Although it was likely that the house counsel did not know of many of the inaccuracies, he did not make a reasonable investigation, and therefore could not establish a defense.

Perhaps the most important aspect of the decision was its treatment of Mr. Auslander, an outside director of BarChris who joined the board after the preliminary prospectus had already been filed. Three weeks after he joined the board, Mr. Auslander, the chairman of the local bank, was asked to sign a signature page for an amendment to the registration statement. No document was attached. Although he vaguely understood that the page was for some filing with the SEC, he did not know it was for a registration statement. Later he signed a similar sheet for a second amendment and briefly skimmed the prospectus. Essentially, he relied on the representation of management that everything was in order. The judge found that as to the expertized sections of the registration state-ment, Mr. Auslander reasonably believed in the figures as audited by the accountants, Peat, Marwick, Mitchell & Co., because he trusted that firm and therefore had no duty of investigation. This aspect of the holding has been criticized by some commentators, who have argued that reasonable belief requires more than general reliance on reputation. However, as to the unexpertized portions, the facts that Auslander was a new director and that he relied on management were not a sufficient defense.

One of the directors was also outside counsel to the company. Although the court felt that he truly believed the prospectus to be correct, it held that a director who is also counsel to a company has a special burden to conduct a reasonable investigation. The court felt that the registration statement was largely a "scissors and paste-pot job" and that the counsel relied too much on the company officers, with too little attempt to verify information independently.

The underwriters The underwriters asked a series of questions of manage-ment at meetings and received satisfactory replies. No attempt was made to verify independently any of the information. Although the attorneys for the underwriters had a very junior associate read minutes, he read those of only a few subsidiaries and did not read the major contracts because he was told that there was no file of them. The court held the scope of investigation was not adequate and that the underwriters and Mr. Coleman, a representative of one of the underwriters who was on the board, were liable.

The liability of Coleman illustrates the difference between Section 11 of the 1933 Act and Section 10(b) of the 1934 Act as seen by the courts. In a sequel to *BarChris* decided in 1973, *Lanza v. Drexel & Co.,* Coleman, among others, was again sued for his role in the preparation of a BarChris prospectus. In this case, however, the prospectus was used in an exchange of BarChris stock for the stock of a company BarChris was acquiring, and the action was brought under Section 10b. The appeals court held that in the absence of willfulness or recklessness, Coleman would not be held liable under Section 10b even though the previous *BarChris* decision had held him liable under Section 11 for, in essence, a lack of diligence.

The accountants   The court found that Peat, Marwick, Mitchell & Co., the accountants, had not spent enough time in their review of the registration statement to establish that they had made a reasonable investigation of whether the 1960 year-end figures were not misleading as of the date of the prospectus, as required by Section 11. Indeed, the accountants failed to read the prospectus thoroughly. Furthermore, during the time they did spend, they had not made an attempt to verify independently the information given to them by management. For example, the accountant did not check to see that, in fact, certain of the alleys supposedly sold by BarChris were still being operated by it.

Accountants play a singular role under the federal securities laws. Although the standard applicable to them as experts is no different from that applicable to a mining engineer or an attorney, their exposure is broader because they certify the very heart of a prospectus, the financial statements.

The financial accounting profession is highly concentrated, with the "big eight" firms auditing the books of companies responsible for more than 85% of the sales of all publicly held companies. Ranked by order of the percentage of sales of public companies audited, the eight largest accounting firms are Price Waterhouse (20%), Arthur Andersen & Co. (15%), Peat, Marwick, Mitchell (12%), Haskins & Sells (11%), Coopers & Lybrand (11%), Ernst & Ernst (8%), Arthur Young & Co. (8%) and Touche Ross & Co. (under 8%). Over the years, these firms in particular have recognized the sizable risks involved in their profession and have attempted to limit them. For example, the scope of letters from accountants to underwriters regarding offerings has narrowed considerably. Although the recent cases, as will be discussed, have reduced to some degree the potential risk to accountants, *BarChris* is still good law as regards Section 11, and the exposure is, therefore, still substantial.

Recent Developments

Recently the Supreme Court has been cutting back the standards for establishing a civil damages case under Section 10b. Although not directly affecting suits based on other statutory provisions, such as Section 11 of the 1933 Act, these cases do indicate a more restrictive climate toward securities litigation. Of course, however, Supreme Court justices chosen by President Carter may well bring a resurgence of the expansionist trend to liability.

The first major case to herald the recent restrictive tendencies was *Blue Chip Stamps.* In that 1975 case, the Supreme Court held that to have standing to sue, a plaintiff must have been a purchaser or a seller of securities rather than a nonparticipating bystander who may indirectly have been harmed. The accounting profession breathed a heavy sigh of relief when, in 1976, the Supreme Court decided in *Ernst & Ernst v. Hochfelder,* that a finding of *scienter,* an intent to deceive, was necessary to establish civil liability under Section 10b. Thus, in the case of an underwritten public offering, mere negligence would not establish a case under Section 10b, although there may well be liability under Section 11 of the 1933 Act if the statute of limitations hasn't already run and a due diligence defense can't be effectively asserted.

In *TSC Industries v. Northway,* which involved a proxy statement, the Supreme Court indicated in 1976 that standards of materiality in 10(b) cases should be raised to a higher level so that minor errors would not be the basis for legal sanctions. According to the Court in *Northway,* "an omitted fact is material if there is a *substantial likelihood* that a reasonable shareholder would consider it important in deciding how to vote." In contrast, the Court of Appeals had used as a standard any fact the shareholder *might* consider important, which the Supreme Court felt was too suggestive of mere possibility. The implications of this decision may be quite broad, extending beyond 10b to the definition of material errors or omissions generally under the federal securities laws.

Finally, in March of 1977, in *Green v. Santa Fe Industries,* the Supreme Court reversed an appeals court's holding that a merger eliminating minority shareholders with no corporate purpose violates 10(b), despite full disclosure and compliance with state law. According to the Supreme Court, it did not want to give an expansive interpretation to 10(b) where there was a pattern of state regulation. The *Green* case will be discussed in detail in connection with tender offers, as will be the 1977 Supreme Court decision in the Chris Craft tender offer litigation, in which the Court also narrowly interpreted another antifraud provision of the 1934 Act relating to tender offers.

Despite these recent developments, the need for care is as great as ever. Even if the basis for liability is somewhat narrower, the parties interested in asserting it, such as disgruntled shareholders and skilled securities litigation attorneys, have grown in numbers. Having examined the statutory provisions regarding the preparation of prospectuses, we shall now turn first to the documents involved in a public offering and then go step by step through the registration process.

ELEVEN

Public Offering Documents and Expenses

In a public offering there are two groups of documents: those defining the relationship between the underwriters and those offering the securities to the public. Of course, over time, the contents of these instruments will change, but a review of these papers gives a better understanding of the public-offering process than any theoretical abstractions about disclosure policy. Ideally, the discussion in this book should be supplemented by a perusal of some prospectuses, which can be obtained readily from any broker.

THE UNDERWRITING AGREEMENTS

Underwriters are investment bankers who arrange the distribution of securities to the public. The firms that arrange the deal with the selling corporation or individual stockholder are called the managing underwriters. If there is more than one managing underwriter, the underwriter that dominates the deal by, for example, selecting the counsel to the underwriters, "running the books," and determining the allocation to the other underwriters in the syndicate is called the lead underwriter.

In order to sell the securities being offered to the public, the managing underwriters form a syndicate of investment banking firms. Each bank in the syndicate in a conventional underwriting agrees to buy a specified number of securities being offered. Syndication both increases the distribution powers of the managing underwriters and limits their risk by committing other concerns to purchasing the securities.

In addition, syndication allows the managing underwriters to meet the requirements of the SEC as to the "net capital" an underwriter must have to conduct a public offering. Rule 15c3-1 under the 1934 Act specifies that no underwriter can incur a liability, including a commitment to purchase securities, in excess of 1,500% of its net capital. For example, if a firm has $100,000 in net capital, it cannot commit itself to an underwriting in excess of $1.5 million, and this computation assumes that the firm does not have any other obligations. By arranging a syndicate of a group of underwriters to sell the offering, the burden of the net capital rule is lifted because each firm in the syndicate is responsible only for having adequate capital for its proportionate share of the deal.

The terms for the purchase of the securities by the syndicate from the seller and the rights and obligations of members of the syndicate are set forth in the three basic underwriting agreements: the Agreement Among Underwriters, the Purchase Agreement, and the Selected Dealer Agreement (sometimes called the Selling Group Agreement). In the discussion in the next two chapters, unless otherwise indicated, it will be assumed that a company, rather than a stockholder, is selling the securities and that the securities being sold are common stock. Generally, similar considerations are applicable to other deals, but unique features applicable to the varying types of transactions will be highlighted.

The Agreement Among Underwriters

Often referred to as the "Agreement Among," this Agreement governs the relationship between members of the syndicate. The Purchase Agreement and Selected Dealer Agreement are exhibits to the Agreement Among, and by signing the Agreement Among, the underwriters agree to the forms of the Purchase Agreement and Selected Dealer Agreement as well. The prime purposes of the Agreement Among are twofold: to designate the firm (or firms) which originated the deal as the syndicate manager (the managing underwriter) and Representative of the other underwriters, to establish its compensation, and to commit each member of the syndicate to purchasing a specified number of shares. If there is more than one managing underwriter, the lead underwriter is also specified.

In examining public offerings, it is important to focus on the structure of underwriter compensation. Underwriters make their money from the "spread," the difference between the price underwriters pay the issuer and the price paid by the public for the securities. The actual size of the spread in recent transactions will be discussed in connection with the analysis of the Purchase Agreement. For its efforts, the Representative is paid a management fee by the other underwriters, usually 20 to 30% of the spread. The remainder of the spread can be thought of as compensation for two functions of the underwriters: putting their capital at risk and making sales. As will be further discussed, the sales function is sometimes subcontracted to dealers in securities. The most important provisions in the typical Agreement Among are the following:

General authorization and compensation   The Representative is authorized to act on behalf of the underwriters, including the right to determine the form and manner of advertisement of the issue, to waive any conditions in the Purchase Agreement, and to sell directly to retail buyers a proportionate share of each underwriter's interest in the securities offered. In addition, the Representative is authorized to borrow funds to purchase the securities being offered in the market in order to facilitate a plan of distribution, to pay expenses, and to defend any lawsuits.

Trading and stabilization   The Representative is authorized to take independently certain market actions on behalf of the entire underwriting group, including trading in and stabilizing the price of the stock. Generally, manipulating the market to peg a price is illegal. However, stabilization (the placing of bids and the making of purchases to establish a price) is permitted under limited circumstances by Rule 10b-7 under the 1934 Act to aid a distribution if the objective is to prevent a decline in market price. Detailed reports are required regarding the stabilizing activity, and disclosure must be made in the prospectus of the possibility of stabilization in a standard form of legend.

Allocation of liability   The underwriters agree to pay their proportionate share of the expenses and liabilities relating to any suit against the Representative regarding the underwriting.

Confirmation   The underwriters acknowledge that they have received and read all the pertinent documents in the transaction and (unless the securities will be offered outside the United States) that they are members of the National Association of Securities Dealers, an industry self-regulatory body which promulgates rules as to appropriate practices.

Selected Dealer Agreement

In addition to the underwriters, distribution is made through certain dealers selected by the Representative pursuant to terms of the Selected Dealer Agreement. Essentially, the underwriters are willing to give up part of their fee to assure the placement of the issue; they are subcontracting the sales function, so the Representative arranges for resale of part of the deal. The harder the deal to place, the more the underwriters will rely on the selected dealers. In order to induce members of the selling group to commit themselves to help peddle difficult-to-sell securities, the Representative makes sure that a good relationship is built with a number of dealers by including them in deals that are easier to sell.

The Selected Dealer Agreement is in the form of a brief letter in which the terms of the offering are specified and the selected dealers agree to comply with all legal requirements. A provision in the agreement specifies a selling concession to the dealers taken from the underwriters' spread. The selected dealers themselves may resell the stock to other dealers to facilitate the distribution, giving these purchasers a concession known as a reallowance, which is taken from the selected dealers' concession. Thus, for example, in one offering the underwriters received a discount of $1.68 per share on a stock being sold to the public at $28 a share, with the Representative receiving a management fee of 45 cents per share from the underwriters. In turn, the selected dealers got a concession of $1 out of the $1.68 underwriters' discount; other dealers purchasing from selected dealers received a reallowance of 50 cents out of the selected dealers' concession of $1. Therefore, out of the total $1.68 spread, a share sold through a selected dealer would net an underwriter 23 cents after taking into account the 45 cent management fee and the $1 dealers' concession.

The Purchase Agreement

The key underwriting agreement is the Purchase Agreement in which the Representative on behalf of the underwriters agrees as to the terms of the offering with the company. A Purchase Agreement's particular provisions depend on the nature of the underwriting commitment and the particular style of the underwriter, each of whom develops its own model form.

There are, however, two basic forms of underwritings, "firm commitment" and "best efforts" transactions. Most commonly used, especially by the larger investment banking firms, are "firm commitment" underwritings. In the discussions in this book, it is assumed that underwritings are of the firm-commitment type unless otherwise specified. Under this arrangement, underwriters agree that they will purchase the securities being offered by the company for resale to the public; if other purchasers cannot be found, the underwriters are stuck with the stock. Even a contemplated firm commitment underwriting may not, in fact, be firm. In the first place, whatever the contemplation, the actual Underwriting Agreements are signed just moments before the syndicate is ready to offer the stock by requesting that the SEC declare the registration statement effective. Months of work could have already occurred, a preliminary registration statement could have been filed and a final version all prepared, and the deal could fall apart without any obligation on the part of the underwriters. The principal problem in most deals is pricing, which, for securities other than publicly traded stocks, occurs at the last possible moment before signing, in order to avoid undue market risks. If the Representative and the company cannot agree on price, there simply is no deal. In transactions involving stock for which there is already a public market, the pricing is done after the signing, but the Purchase Agreement is worded so that if there is no consensus as to price, there will be no closing. Furthermore, the Purchase Agreement contains a number of conditions to the underwriters' obligations. If the conditions are not satisfied, the underwriters can refuse to go through with the closing of the transaction.

A "best efforts" underwriting, is based on the underwriters doing their best to sell the issue, but having no obligation to purchase the unsold shares from the issuer; in essence, there is an agency relationship. Obviously, a firm-commitment underwriting is much more desirable to a company than a best-efforts undertaking because of the relative certainty that the securities will, in fact, be sold. Some best-efforts deals set a minimum level of sales which must be achieved before the distribution can go forward—for example, that 75% of the shares in the offering must be subject to purchase commitments before any stock will be sold.

Among the most important provisions of the Purchase Agreement are the following:

Representations and warranties   The company delivers the standard representations to the underwriters that it is duly incorporated, is in good standing, and has the power to conduct its business. It also represents that the stock being sold conforms with the description in the prospectus and will be duly authorized, validly issued, fully paid, and nonassessable. If there are any stockholders selling, they represent that they are giving good and marketable title, clear of encumbrances, to the purchasers of the shares being sold. In addition, the company represents that the registration statement is up to date, is correct, and has no material omissions.

Purchase commitment   The underwriters agree to purchase a specified number of shares from the company if the deal is a firm-commitment underwriting. Common stock which is thinly traded or is being initially offered to the public, debt securities, and preferred stock are usually priced the afternoon before the execution of the Purchase Agreement, and the actual purchase price is, therefore, reflected in the Purchase Agreement under those circumstances. However, if the company is already public and its stock is widely trading in the public market, the price will usually be determined in accordance with a formula, such as not less than $1 below the market price at the time the price determination is made. If formula pricing is used, the actual pricing is usually done at the close of trading on the day the Purchase Agreement is signed and the registration statement becomes effective. Therefore, only the formula, not the actual purchase price, is reflected in the Purchase Agreement in formula deals. At the time the issue is priced, each of the parties signs a pricing agreement stating the terms, including a determination of the underwriters' spread. However, if the parties cannot agree, the pricing cannot take place any later than a stated cut-off date.

To get a feeling for the structure of underwriter compensation by issuers, an examination of the actual spreads on issues in 1976, as compiled by *Institutional Investor* magazine, is illuminating. For initial public offerings of common stock, the spreads generally ranged from 6 to 8.5%. In sharp contrast, for established companies selling common stock, compensation was generally from 3.3 to 4.5%, illustrating the premium small companies must pay for raising capital, even when obtainable. On negotiated debt, the spreads were generally around 0.875% for an AAA company, although the spreads on some competitively bid debt offerings were somewhat lower. Of course, the size of the issue is fundamental in analyzing the impact of the spread, but because the spread is so relatively high in common stock offerings, these offerings can be quite lucrative. For example, a Texaco offering for $300 million of debt, with a spread of 0.875%, brought the underwriters $2.6 million, and Entenmann's Bakery going public, with an offering totaling $21.6 million and a spread of 6.2%, yielded $1.3 million for the underwriters.

Responsibility in the event of defaults Generally, there is a provision stipulating that if any underwriter defaults in its obligations to purchase its share of the issue, the other underwriters will increase their respective commitments to cover the default up to a stated percentage of their original obligation—for example, 10%. This provision fixes the maximum liability of individual underwriters in the event the syndicate "breaks" and there are defaults in purchase commitments. Sometimes, especially with issues of companies first going public, there is also the provision that in the event the full share of the defaulting underwriters is not picked up by the other underwriters, the company and the Representative have a stated time period—for example, 24 hours—in which to make new arrangements. If after that period, the complete share of the defaulting underwriters has not been picked up, the nondefaulting underwriters can get out of their puchase commitment without any liability under this type of provision.

Arrangements for the delivery of the stock The Purchase Agreement states the time of the closing on the deal and the manner of the delivery of the stock. Prior to the closing, the underwriters provide the names in which the shares shall be registered, and the company, in turn, agrees to have the shares available for inspection before the closing. At the closing, the shares being sold are exchanged for a check from the underwriters. The closing is usually scheduled 7 to 10 days after the execution of the Purchase Agreement and the effectiveness of the registration statement. If an offering contains a large number of shares being sold by stockholders, the closing may well be in Jersey City, New Jersey, across the river from Manhattan, rather than, as is customary, in New York City, in order to avoid the New York stock transfer tax.

Covenants   The company agrees that it will provide to the underwriters copies of all documents relating to the issue, will amend the registration statement if required, and will show any proposed amendments to the Representative before they are filed. Because Section 11(a) of the 1933 Act relieves an underwriter of any liability if an earnings report, which need not be audited, is issued by the company for a twelve-month period following the effective date of the final registration statement, there is a provision requiring such a statement by a specified time, usually about 15 months after the date of the agreement.

Another important provision in the Purchase Agreement relates to the expenses for the deal. Generally, the issuer is responsible for the printing expenses relating to the registration statement and the stock certificates and all fees and expenses, including counsel fees, relating to qualifying the issue under state blue-sky laws. Underwriters' counsel fees in connection with the preparation of the registration statement and the Underwriting Agreements and the costs of printing the Underwriting Agreements are generally not reimbursed by the issuer in offerings for larger companies. These expenses are paid for out of the underwriters' spread. If the company is first going public, however, the underwriters are in a better bargaining position and often do ask for both their attorney fees and printing costs to be paid by the company.

Indemnification   Under the indemnification provisions of the Purchase Agreement, the company agrees to hold the underwriters harmless from any liability relating to the offering, except for information provided by the underwriters for which they indemnify the company. In negotiating an indemnification provision, two issues are crucial: who will control the defense, and, if an indemnified party seeks to assert an independent position, who will pay for the legal expenses.

The mechanics of the indemnification provisions usually provide for the indemnifying party to control the defense. However, if any of the defenses of the two parties differ, the indemnified party is generally able to select, and have the indemnifying party pay the reasonable fees of, its attorney. If the offering is being made on behalf of stockholders, usually an insurance policy for liability is taken out rather than having indemnification provisions.

A number of cases have hinted strongly that indemnification provisions may be void as against public policy, the logic being that the federal securities acts would not have much effect if underwriters could remove themselves from any liability through indemnification provisions. For this reason, law firms will usually not give a flat opinion that Purchase Agreements are enforceable in accordance with their terms. Nevertheless, companies do seem to honor their indemnification commitments if they have the financial capability. As a practical matter, a company disavowing an indemnification clause would have a most difficult time locating an underwriter for future issues. The risks, however, are that eventually a litigious stockholder may be able to convince a court that a company should not be indemnifying the underwriter, whatever the desires of the company management, or that, in the event of insolvency, a bankruptcy court may refuse to recognize an indemnification claimant as a *bona fide* general creditor.

Conditions Other than the pricing terms, perhaps the key provisions in the Purchase Agreement are the conditions for closing. The two most important conditions are usually the "cold comfort letter" and the opinions of counsel.

The cold comfort letter has been a subject of intense debate between the legal and accounting professions for a number of years. Lawyers traditionally have wanted the accountants to do an exhaustive analysis of the prospectus and give an unequivocal opinion that it is accurate and complete, while the accountants have desired to say little, if anything, for fear of liability.

Usually, the accountants now state that they have reviewed the registration statement and found the audited financials to conform with the accounting requirements under the 1933 Act. In addition, specific information in the registration statement is described, and the accountants state that they have compared it with the records of the corporation and found them in agreement.

The comfort letter also states that "nothing has come to the attention" of the accountants which would cause them to believe that (1) any unaudited figures in the prospectus are incorrect or misleading or (2) there has been any change in the capitalization of the company, any decrease in its assets since the date of the balance sheet in the prospectus, or any decrease in net sales or income compared to the same period in the prior year except as contemplated by the prospectus. Obviously, the burden of diligence on an accountant in stating these no-knowledge conclusions is considerably less than a full-fledged audit where there is an active duty to investigate, but, nevertheless, the auditors cannot bury their heads in the sand.

In the event that there has been any such change, whether or not material, the condition is not fulfilled. However, the Representative is authorized by the underwriters to determine that the change was not material and waive the condition. If the change is material, all the members of the syndicate are entitled to withdraw from the offering.

This cold comfort letter is generally delivered both before the registration statement goes effective and on the date of the closing, when it is updated. The comfort is "cold" because the accountants do not state that the information in the prospectus is correct, merely that nothing has come to their attention indicating that it is wrong. A cold comfort letter's wording is always the subject of intense negotiation, even though the American Institute of Certified Public Accountants has issued guidelines on what accountants should and should not agree to say. Both the scope of the review and which specific facts in the prospectus will be compared by the accountants to corporate records are debated. Therefore, it is helpful to get a draft of the comfort letter as soon as possible.

The opinion of company's counsel is also often the subject of negotiation. Generally, an opinion is expressed about the due incorporation and good standing of the corporation and the due authorization and valid issuance of the stock. The counsel usually states that it has no reason to believe that the registration statement misstates a material fact or omits to state one and that the description of the capitalization of the company and the attorney's opinion in the registration statement are accurate. In addition, the opinion states that no governmental consents are required; the Purchase Agreement has been duly executed, authorized, and delivered by the company; the issuance of the stock does not conflict with any of the company's obligations; and, sometimes, that no contracts which should have been described have not been.

In the course of negotiating the opinion, the company's counsel will always try to limit the scope of their investigation and the breadth of their opinion. Instead of "there are no misstatements," the lawyers will try to get a "to the best of our knowledge" qualifier or even an accountant's "nothing has come to our attention which would indicate" type of clause.

Two questions always seem to come up: Should the opinion be only on the company or the company and all or some of its subsidiaries, and who should be giving the opinion, inside or outside counsel? If a company has significant activities in subsidiaries, it is important that they be covered. On the other hand, it would generate large amounts of paper work for outside counsel to become familiar with the workings of all the subsidiaries. Although underwriters generally prefer to get as much of the opinion as possible from outside counsel on the theory that they will be less intimidated by company management, a compromise is usually reached: The inside lawyer gives the opinion about due organization and valid issuance of the stock, but the outside lawyer gives the opinion relating to compliance with the securities law.

In addition to the standard conditions, some Purchase Agreements contain "outs" for the underwriters for conditions beyond the company's control, such as natural calamities, revolutions, bond moratoriums, trading suspensions on stock exchanges, and political developments with substantial adverse financial consequences. Perhaps the most common provision is the "market out" clause, which essentially provides that the underwriters may, at their option, be released from their purchase commitment if there are material adverse developments affecting the securities markets generally. Some of the larger investment banking houses have deliberately adopted a policy of not including "outs" other than the standard conditions in the Purchase Agreement. To them, the firmness of their commitment is a source of pride and prestige.

THE REGISTRATION STATEMENT

The SEC prescribes forms for companies registering securities. These forms are, in effect, general instruction sheets and are not blanks to be filled in by the registrant. Among the most common are Forms S-1, for companies registering for the first time and young or small companies; S-2, for companies in the developmental stage, which have no subsidiaries and have no substantial revenues or income; S-7, for mature firms; S-8, for employee stock plans; S-14, for exchange offers; and S-16, for secondary sales by major stockholders of mature companies. In addition, if an offering is for debt securities, the indenture must comply with the requirements of the Trust Indenture Act of 1939, and a Form T-1 must be filed to establish the eligibility of the trustee of the issue under the 1939 Act.

A registration statement contains two parts: Part 1 is the prospectus, the document a market purchaser receives from the broker, which contains a description of the company. Part 2 contains an itemization of expenses, lists of exhibits, and related matters which are ordinarily not given out to the public but are available for inspection at the offices of the SEC along with the exhibits filed. Each of the SEC's forms differs as to content, in both Part 1 and Part 2.

Form S-1 is used for all securities for which no other form is authorized. In effect, this means that it is used by companies first registering securities (other than certain firms in the development stage using Form S-2) and those not yet eligible for Form S-7. The theory of Form S-1 is that it has to be comprehensive because little public information is readily available about the concern, especially about a company registering securities for the first time. Although the pertinent form itself specifies the information to be provided, the SEC has also periodically issued releases which together constitute the SEC Guides for Preparation and Filing of Registration Statements, which should be carefully examined when writing a prospectus. The focus in this discussion will be on Form S-1, which, as indicated, is the most detailed form.

Recently, the SEC and its advisory committee on disclosure policy have focused on the interrelationship between the periodic reports required by public companies under the 1934 Act and the registration of securities under the 1933 Act. As a result, it is anticipated that eligibility for abbreviated prospectuses will be expanded and will become increasingly common. For example, Form S-7 is now available, assuming certain other requirements are met, to companies which had net income of $250,000 for 3 of the past 4 years, including the most recent year, in contrast to the previous requirement of net income of $500,000 for each of the prior 5 years. To indicate the contrast with other forms, an S-7 does not require all the information contained in a Form S-1 regarding the background and compensation of management or a detailed list of physical facilities on the assumption that any pertinent information has already been filed in a proxy statement, a 10-K, or a previous S-1. In addition, the required business description in an S-7 is much simpler and more general. Interestingly, however, some issuers eligible for an S-7 use the S-1 format, and many companies who do utilize the S-7 format include the detailed S-1 type of business description. The rationale for including the detail is based on its marketing appeal and on the desire to have detailed self-contained disclosure rather than requiring the investor to flip to the 10-K.

The SEC has also announced that it is exploring the possibility that Form S-16 (which is used in certain secondary offerings and is even more abbreviated than a Form S-7) be available in limited situations for primary distributions of securities of mature companies. In a Form S-16 registration statement, heavy reliance is placed on incorporating by reference the 1934 Act filings of the company whose securities are being sold, thereby making possible reduction of the bulk of the registration statement.

Among the items listed by the Form S-1 or required by the Guides are the following, which are described in narrative form without a specific answer-and-response breakdown:

The Prospectus

Immediately following the cover page, the Guides now require a short summary of the prospectus. Although not required for forms other than S-1, many S-7's also contain summaries. If the company is a speculative venture, the key risk factors must be highlighted.

Item 1: distribution spread A table on the cover page of the prospectus indicates the price per unit of the security being sold, the underwriting discounts and commissions, and the net proceeds to the registrant. The

Guides also require an explanation of the basis of price determination if a venture's stock has been sold to promoters and investors at a substantially lower cost. Gross expenses to the company from the offering are usually revealed in a footnote, but this figure is an understatement, since executive time is not counted as an expense.

Item 2: plan of distribution   The underwriters' names and the amounts they are purchasing are specified, as well as whether the deal is a best-efforts or firm-commitment underwriting. If there is a material relationship with the registering company—for example, if a partner in an underwriting firm is a director of the company—the information is disclosed.

Item 3: use of proceeds   The principal purposes for which the proceeds from the offering will be used are set forth. The SEC has devised a pie-chart format, which it encourages companies to use, showing graphically the percentage of the offering going into, for example, expenses, building and plant, a new research program, and repaying a loan. Often, this is quite a difficult section to draft because a firm's purposes may be contingent or tentative. Company executives like an answer such as, "The proceeds will be used for general corporate purposes," but this is not good enough and will draw an SEC staff comment.

Item 4: securities sales other than for cash   This item is inapplicable to the usual sale of stock for cash to the public. However, if, for example, there is an exchange offer or if assets are being acquired for stock in a nonprivate placement transaction, the terms are described.

Item 5: capital structure   The capital structure of the company is set forth in tabular form.

Item 6: summary of earnings   A 5-year summary, if the company has been in existence that long, of earnings in a comparative columnar form is required. Following the summary, unaudited "stub" earnings figures will be included, indicating results for the latest available period. If common stock is being registered, per-share earnings and dividends over this period must also be indicated. If debt or preferred stock is being registered, the annual interest or dividend requirement is stated. In addition, the SEC Guides now require that a discussion of the major events resulting in income changes over these years follow the 5-year income statement. This management discussion of income is a vital part of the prospectus because it is one of the few places where the numbers are analyzed. The Guides require that discussion of a change take place if an item increased or decreased by more than 10% over the prior period or if the change equaled in amount more than 2% of average income in the past 3 profitable years. Beyond any quantitative test, any material change in product mix or advertising, research, amortization, or investment policy must be reflected. Company management often likes to lift very vague descriptions from annual reports to fulfill these requirements, but they are generally not sufficient. Much prodding and rewriting must often be done to this section for it to meet the Guidelines standards and fulfill the underwriters' need for a document with no material omissions.

Item 7: organization   The year and the state of incorporation is indicated.

Item 8: parents of registrant   If the registering company is controlled by another corporation, the percentage owned and the name of the controlling concern is given.

Item 9: description of business   This item is the heart of the prospectus. Among the aspects of the business which are expected to be included are a general description of the company's activities and its record over the past 5 years including the following specifics:

1. An analysis of competitive conditions in the industry and the relative position of the company. Usually, the response to this is a brief statement that conditions are highly competitive. For a small company trying to capitalize on its proprietary position in new technology, however, the answer is generally more detailed.

2. If a material part of the business is dependent on a few customers, their names are stated and the nature of their relationship to the company discussed.

3. The principal products, markets, and methods of distribution of the company.

4. An analysis of the backlog of the company, including its dollar amount for the current and the past year and the amount not expected to be filled in the current year. For construction companies, for example, this disclosure is very important but must be handled with great care. Stating the raw backlog figures without explanatory detail regarding the basis of the computation may well constitute a material omission. For example, some key contracts may have cancellation clauses or, indeed, it may be industry practice to include projects in backlog without firm contracts being in hand. Or the backlog figures may mix apples and oranges: contracts whose dollar amounts are based on net revenues to the company and contracts whose dollar amounts include the gross amount which flows through a general contractor, very little of which ends up in the company's coffers.

5. The sources and availability of raw materials essential to the business. Before the shortages of the 1970s, responses to this question were quite brief. Then with the oil boycott and other raw material shortages, the disclosures became quite lengthy and complex. After all, a plastics

company which can't operate because of a petrochemical shortage and a nitrous fertilizer plant without natural gas are in trouble, and the public should know about the potential risk before it invests.

6. The importance to the business and the duration of patents, licenses, and franchises.

7. A description of research activities, including the dollar amount, the number of people involved and paid, and a description of new products.

8. The number of persons employed by the company.

9. The extent to which business is seasonal.

10. The impact, if any, of environmental protection laws. For many companies this is insignificant, but for others, especially manufacturing companies, it can be quite important.

11. For the last 5 years, the percentage of sales and income accounted for by each product line and class of product accounting for more than 10% (or 15% for a company with less than $50 million in sales) of income before taxes or sales.

12. If overseas sales are material, the nature of the business, its profitability, and the related risks should be described. Increasingly, in a multinational age, this disclosure area is becoming important. The revelations about corporate bribery in recent years have increased the need for attention to an adequate description of overseas operations.

13. If a company is registering its securities for the first time and has not received revenues from operations for 3 years, it also describes its plan of operation for the near future and its anticipated cash flow requirements.

14. Other material developments must be described. Whether or not a particular aspect of the business is picked up by the form, if the facts are material, they should be set forth.

Item 10: description of property The location and character of principal plants, mines, and other important physical properties are listed.

Item 11: organization within 5 years If a company has been formed within the last five years, a description of the relationship of the company with its promoters, including any payments made by the company to them, is required.

Item 12: legal proceedings Nonroutine litigation is described, including any in which 10% of the current assets of the company are at stake, the adverse party is an officer, director, or controlling person, or which are material environmental or civil rights suits by the government.

Items 13, 14, and 15: securities being registered The terms of the securities being registered are set forth. If the security is debt with many covenants or a complicated preferred, this description can run for several pages.

Item 16: directors and executive officers   A number of details are given about all directors and key executives. The names, any family relationship with any other insiders, the business experience for the past 5 years, criminal convictions or bankruptcy filings for the past 10 years, for each director or executive officer are listed.

Item 17: remuneration of directors and officers   For each director, each of the three highest paid executives (if their direct pay exceeds $40,000 each), and all directors and officers of the company as a group, the aggregate direct remuneration is stated, including bonus payments, retirement benefits, and other benefits other than insurance. The disclosure of this information and the item regarding security-holdings are certainly the disclosures that most irk entrepreneurs going public; through them, the world knows how much you make, and, if your wealth is basically tied up in the company, can compute your maximum net worth. Public scrutiny is at first hard to adjust to, but disclosure does not always stop titans of industry from occasionally making egregious overpayments to themselves.

Item 18: options to purchase securities   All the company's outstanding options are described, and, if the market value for any individual director or executive officer is above $10,000, the holdings and market value of options held by each such person is listed.

Item 19: principal holders of securities   For each person who owns of record or is known to own beneficially more than 5% of any class of securities and for officers and directors of the company as a group, the amount owned and the percentage of the class owned is indicated.

Item 20: interest of management and others in certain transactions   For any director, officer, or major stockholder of the company, the material interest (over $30,000) in any material transaction during the last 3 years or any proposed transaction is stated, unless the interest arises solely from ownership of less than 10% of another company's stock, the transaction is in the ordinary course of business, and the deal amounts to less than 10% of purchases or sales of the company registering its securities. The responses to this item contain highly interesting information when a public company is part of a web of interrelated firms controlled by key officers or directors of the public company.

Item 21: financial statements   The financial statements required in a prospectus are specified in the applicable form and must conform with SEC regulation S-X. Among other statements required is a balance sheet which need not be audited, dated within 90 days of the registration statement. However, the balance sheet may be within 6 months of the registration statement if the company has $5 million in assets, is not in default as to its debt, and files informational reports under the 1934 Act. If that recent balance sheet is not audited, an audited balance sheet dated within a year of the unaudited one must be included in the prospectus.

In addition, audited consolidated income statements and statements of sources and applications of funds for the previous 3 years of operations must be provided. A bevy of supporting schedules and unconsolidated statements must also be submitted, and the SEC requires updating of the prospectus if more recent results are released or the old statements became stale. These requirements call for considerable thought in advance of going public because a private company with unaudited financials may well find itself unable to meet the SEC's standards.

Information Not Required in a Prospectus

Part II answers are included in the registration statement, but not in the prospectus. Most of the time the answers are not interesting to the public, but they are publicly available. Sometimes, however, they can yield valuable tidbits, such as breakdown of expenses in a deal or a list of contracts filed as exhibits, some of which may be of interest to a competitor or a professional analyst.

Item 22: marketing arrangements   Any plans to stabilize the issue or to limit sales of similar securities, are disclosed.

Item 23: other expenses   A reasonably itemized list of expenses is provided, including applicable taxes, printing costs, and legal fees. It should be pointed out that the legal fees in this itemization represent only the legal fees to the company from its outside counsel and those legal expenses (usually for blue-sky surveys) it must pay under the Underwriting Agreements.

Item 24: relationship with registrant   If any expert has a relationship with the company, it is explained. In fact, the relationship is usually set forth in the prospectus itself.

Item 25: sales to special parties   If securities have been sold within the last six months at a different price, the facts are disclosed.

Item 26: recent sales of unregistered securities   Details are given of all private placements of securities within the past three years.

Item 27: subsidiaries   A list and the details regarding subsidiaries of the company are given.

Item 28: government concessions   The effect of government franchises or concessions must be described. Again, this information is usually given in the prospectus, anyway.

Item 29: indemnification   Indemnification provisions for officers and directors must be indicated.

Item 30: treatment of proceeds   Any unusual accounting treatment being given to the proceeds must be disclosed.

Item 31: index   All financial statements and exhibits being filed as part of the registration statement must be listed.

The registration statement must be signed by the company, its principal executive officer, its principal financial officer, its principal accounting officer, and by at least the majority of its board of directors. Included in each registration statement is the undertaking by the company that it will comply with the reporting requirements under the 1934 Act.

In addition to financials, extensive exhibits are required in connection with the filing of an S-1: copies of a corporation's charter and bylaws; all underwriting contracts; specimens of the securities; any debt instrument for more than 5% of the total assets of the company; if debt securities are being issued, the indenture and a cross-reference sheet between the provisions of the indenture and the Trust Indenture Act; all option plans, pension plans, and management bonus plans; voting trust agreements; an opinion of counsel regarding the transaction and material foreign patents—all must be provided. Copies of every material contract not made in the ordinary course of business must also be filed. In addition, any material contract made in the ordinary course of business, which is referred to in the prospectus, is a key component of the business, involves 15% or more of the company's assets, is a lease for significant property, or to which insiders are a party, must be submitted. Furthermore, any agreements where the amount of the contract or its importance to the business of the company are of a nature of which investors reasonably should be informed must also be filed.

These exhibits not only make a large pile of paper but also are quite sensitive, particularly the contracts. Other parties to the agreements may be reluctant to have their dealings subjected to public disclosure, and, understandably, competitors often find the details fascinating reading. There is a procedure under which details of contracts can be kept off the public record, but the SEC staff is quite conservative in providing this treatment, especially in light of the broad disclosure provisions of the Freedom of Information Act.

EXPENSES

Ongoing expenses relating to being a public company have already been discussed, but the mere process of becoming a public company by filing a registration statement is an expensive proposition. There are bills from printers, accountants, and lawyers and there is the drain on management time and energy, in addition to the underwriter's spread. By looking at the registration statements filed by similar companies, especially the Part 2 responses, a company can make a rough estimate of these expenses, although, certain items are not highlighted because they are contained within the underwriter's spread.

For example, printing expenses can be a shocker. Printing bills of $50,000 for even a relatively small offering are not uncommon. In addition to the printing of the registration statement and related documents, the certificates for the securities must also be printed, often by a different firm. A company learns by sad experience to deal with its printers in gingerly fashion. First, typing rather than printing early versions of the prospectus is a significant money saver. Since these drafts will be substantially revised, there is little point in incurring the large additional costs of printing at a premature stage. Second, use overtime most sparingly. It is extremely expensive.

However, using a printer inexperienced in financial documents may be a blueprint for disaster. All lawyers can tell horror stories of printers who stapled the cover of a registration statement to another company's prospectus or put the preliminary cover on the final prospectus. Having a good printer decreases the risk of something going wrong, but by no means eliminates it. Almost unseemly care and caution are dictated by sad experience: No one is pleased with 10,000 misprinted prospectuses.

Filing fees are another expense area. The SEC itself charges a filing fee of one-fiftieth of one percent of the maximum offering price of securities. So, for example, on the sale of $10 million of debentures, the SEC fee is $2,000. There are also NASD fees of $100 plus one one-hundredth of one percent of the maximum offering price, subject to a maximum of $5,100.

On offerings by smaller companies and secondary sales by insiders, underwriters often demand indemnity insurance. Premiums can be quite expensive, ranging up to 1% of the issue and, indeed, may be quite difficult to obtain.

Legal expenses can be considerable. Outside counsel may charge from $20,000 to $80,000, depending on the complexity of the deal and the amount of work done. Curiously, the legal bills may be less for a larger company; many tasks, such as corporate cleanup and exercise of due diligence, do not have to cover as extensive an area or time period, since much of the work has been done in connection with previous offerings. The bills for the underwriters' counsel are usually, but not always, paid out of the underwriters' spread.

Aside from their spread, the underwriters sometimes ask for reimbursement of all of their costs and almost always get the costs of their blue-sky work, including qualification fees and legal analysis, repaid. In addition, underwriters, especially in smaller companies, sometimes seek first refusal rights on future offerings or options to purchase "cheap" stock.

Finally, another major expense item is accounting expenses. If a company has never had auditors preparing SEC-type schedules, it may be surprised to find that the fees can easily run above $40,000. All in all, when a typical 6% underwriters' spread is added to these expenses, going public can easily be a million-dollar proposition, or more, for a company selling as little as $15 million in stock.

Timetable for
a Public Offering

To get a better feel for the registration process, it is useful to go through the steps which take place in a public offering. To show the interrelationship between the 1933 Act registration statement and the continuing reporting obligations under the 1934 Act, the following representative timetable is for a common stock offering in 1978 by a company which already has registered its securities and is listed on the New York Stock Exchange. It is assumed that the company is thinking of closing in the spring and that meanwhile it is making its customary filings with the SEC. Because of the intricacy of the procedures and the fact that all this information has not been gathered by the SEC in one place, references to some of the pertinent rules and releases of the SEC under the 1933 Act have been made for future convenience.

BY JANUARY 1: The broad strategy of the offering is planned by the company with the assistance of the investment bankers. Hurdles to a successful offering, such as, for example, the uncertain status of an important acquisition, are analyzed and plans are made for coping with the problems. If debt is being offered, a company which feels it deserves a better rating than it currently has may present its case to Standard & Poor's and Moody's, the leading rating agencies.

BY JANUARY 23: The board of directors of the company holds its quarterly dividend meeting. Upon advice of its investment bankers, the board decides to split the common stock two for one and increases the dividend. The increase in the dividend signals that the board believes the company is growing stronger. If the increase is merely a public relations gimmick, it may backfire in the long term. Usually this sort of increase is of value only when earnings seem to be steadily rising. It then indicates a constant payout-ratio policy with increases in dividends in dollar terms as earnings grow. A stock split by itself is, in theory, meaningless. However, investment bankers seem to believe that, as a practical matter, certain price ranges are more attractive to the market, particularly to odd-lot (less than 100 shares) buyers.

BY FEBRUARY 17: The company's counsel delivers (with all attachments, exhibits, and annexes) to the underwriters' counsel the basic due-diligence material, including copies of (1) all SEC filings made by the company or filings pertaining to the company made by others (of which the company has copies) since January 1, 1973, including proxy statements, Forms 10-K, 10-Q, 8-K, any registration statements or amendments, and the 13D, Form 3, and Form 4 filings of security holders of the company; (2) any registration statement, as amended, on Forms S-1 or S-7 since January 1, 1968; (3) all other communications to stockholders by the company or any subsidiary acquired by the company since January 1, 1973, including annual reports and quarterly reports since January 1, 1973; (4) certified charters, bylaws, and minutes of the board of directors of the company, each of its subsidiaries, and all committees thereof, including the executive committee, the policy committee, the audit committee, the finance committee, and the compensation committee, if any, since January 1, 1973; (5) all major contracts, leases, debt instruments, and acquisition agreements since January 1, 1973, credit or financing agreements, and guarantees or other agreements; (6) all descriptive booklets or brochures about the activities of the company, news releases about major events, and copies of articles about the company; (7) all annual letters to the management or to the audit committee from auditors of the company or any of its subsidiaries since January 1, 1973; and (8) such other documents as the underwriters or their counsel may reasonably request.

The listing of all these documents is an attempt to define the scope of a reasonable investigation for due-diligence purposes. Collecting the documents by themselves, of course, is not enough. Something must be done with them by someone. But precisely what is often elusive. Obviously this is an enormous stack of papers, especially if the company is in a field where there are large numbers of contracts—for example, the construction or the leasing business. The first problem is to try to make a rough cut as to what are major documents. One way to do this is to set a dollar amount and a term cutoff for the contracts, so that all documents involving payments of more than $1 million or with a term exceeding 3 years are examined. The larger the company, the greater the amount a contract has to involve to be material.

In scanning the documents, a great deal of time can be spent digesting the irrelevant. When analyzing contracts for the purposes of a registration statement, the focus should be on potential liability and ways for the other party to back out of the deal. For example, a registration statement which indicates that a construction company has a substantial backlog is inaccurate if it does not reflect which contracts may be easily canceled. Similarly, if there may be substantial liability when a job does not meet some contractually stipulated performance standard, disclosure is necessary.

BY FEBRUARY 23: The 10-K financial statements prepared by the auditors and a draft of the 10-K and proxy statement text are sent to the underwriters and their counsel by the company. These materials give a view of recent developments, and in the event that any of the material contradicts the approach anticipated in the registration statement, the problems are discussed before any definitive material is filed.

BY FEBRUARY 24: The company pays its dividend.

MARCH 1:
1. A draft of the annual report to shareholders is given to the underwriters and their counsel.
2. The auditors deliver full S-X financials to the company. As previously noted, these S-X financials, which are the forms used for registration statements, include detailed schedules required by the SEC in addition to standard balance sheets and income statements.

FEBRUARY 17–MARCH 10: Representatives of and counsel for the company and the underwriters and representatives of the auditors discuss the approach being taken in the draft registration statement and any issues raised by the due-diligence materials, the 1977 financial figures and the text of the draft proxy statement, the 10-K, and the annual report to shareholders, and they inspect certain of the company's facilities and projects. Usually the inspection is conducted by the underwriters themselves rather than their counsel. This is a "kick the tires" theory of due diligence. Whether a whirlwind tour of a chemical company's five plants in four states in one day makes any practical sense is another question.

FEBRUARY 27: The preliminary proxy statement is filed with the SEC.

BY MARCH 3:
1. The company's counsel delivers a draft of the registration statement (with complete S-X financials) to the underwriters, their counsel, and the auditors.

2. The underwriters' counsel delivers proofs of the underwriting documents to the company, its counsel, and the auditors.
3. The underwriters' counsel commences a blue-sky survey to examine the legality of selling the issue in various jurisdictions.
4. The company's Form 10-K is prepared for filing.

MARCH 5–14: Representatives of and counsel for the company and the underwriters and representatives of the auditors meet to discuss the drafts of the registration statement and the Underwriting Agreements (including the provisions relating to the cold comfort letters) and to ask the officers of the company any questions they may have. The writing and rewriting of a prospectus are the heart of the public offering process. If a company has previously registered securities, the natural starting place is the previous prospectus and other SEC filings, such as the 10-K. Aside from the ease of marking up something which already exists, the SEC staff has a tendency in analyzing prospectuses to ask why any part of the previous registration statement has been omitted, perhaps because it is the easiest comment to make. Then, recent prospectuses by similar companies are scanned for ideas.

As in any other industry, there are fashions in the writing of registration statements. Partly, the patterns reflect the underwriters' changing notions of market appeal. For example, one year the underwriters may decide that a detailed discussion of foreign operations will be appealing or that a thorough analysis of a bank's exposure on bad loans will be helpful because things are not quite as bad as analysts suspect. The next year, all prospectuses may have full-color photos of factories and products. Styles also reflect, however, the actual comments of the SEC or companies' perception of what they will be. For example, in the plastics industry, a paragraph about the shortage of petrochemical raw materials was a "must" during the oil crisis.

Any competent company counsel tries to do a thorough job on the first draft of the prospectus which is circulated to the underwriters. Usually, it is the culmination of three or four previous drafts which have been commented upon by company officials. Nevertheless, especially for a company which does not register securities frequently, the document is often completely rewritten by the time the meetings with the underwriters are completed.

As the underwriters go through the prospectus and review their counsel's notes on the due-diligence investigation, they ask questions of the company officials, and the answers are often reflected as riders to the prospectus. Of course, this questioning can be quite pro forma, but underwriters generally try to ask at least some tough questions, if only for the record. In the last few years, for example, pointed inquiries regarding bribery have been quite prevalent.

Deciding who is to ask the questions can be difficult. Dealing with lower-level personnel or even company counsel is not sufficient. Even if these persons wish to be cooperative, they often do not have a firsthand knowledge of the facts. Furthermore, they are only acting as relay posts, repeating, in turn, the same questions themselves. Because of their relative lack of leverage within the organization, it is extremely doubtful that they can probe these issues as forcefully or as effectively as the underwriters directly. Indeed, senior management often has a built-in tendency to skim material presented to them by their lower-level staff. Often the drafts of the prospectus sent to management are virtually ignored until the underwriters focus their attention on the subject.

MARCH 15: Representatives of and counsel for the company and the underwriters approve the forms of the registration statement and the Underwriting Agreements to be submitted to the board of directors of the company.

MARCH 16:

1. The board of directors of the company meets to (a) approve the general terms of offering (except final terms as to price, underwriters' discounts, commissions, etc.); (b) appoint a committee to determine and approve final terms of the offering, approve the registration statement and any required amendments to it, and approve and authorize execution of the Purchase Agreement; (c) approve the present form of registration statement and authorize the execution and filing of the registration statement and any required amendments; (d) authorize certain individuals to sign the registration statement and amendments; (e) extend the authority of the transfer agent and registrar to cover the shares to be offered; (f) authorize the application for listing on the New York Stock Exchange of the shares to be offered; (g) authorize compliance with blue-sky laws, as required, and adopt resolutions required by blue-sky authorities; (h) appoint an agent for service of process; (i) authorize officers to take all further necessary action in connection with the offering; and (j) obtain signatures of officers and directors of the company to a power of attorney authorizing certain persons to sign the registration statement and any amendments to it on their behalf.

2. The company distributes the most recent draft of the registration statement to officers for comments on its accuracy as revised.

BY MARCH 20: The preliminary registration statement and the Underwriting Agreements are printed in form for filing with the SEC.

1. The company and the directors (or attorneys-in-fact) sign the registration statement.

2. The auditors execute consent and report regarding the company's financial statements contained in the prospectus.

3. All available necessary exhibits are prepared.

Printing all the documents required is a major part of any registration effort. Selection of a printer who does not staple the cover page to another company's registration statement is imperative. But even with a good printer, it is important in these transactions that a prudent sense of paranoia is developed because Murphy's law (whatever can go wrong will go wrong) is definitely applicable. Registration statements with missing pages, misplaced lines of type, blurry pages, and typographical errors are, unfortunately, quite common and highly embarrassing.

BY MARCH 21:

1. The company's counsel files the preliminary registration statement package with the SEC. There is usually a "packaging party" at which each side gets the opportunity to check the material going to the SEC. A messenger goes to Washington to the SEC and then goes on to file the documents at the NASD office. As soon as the messenger indicates that the package has been filed, the documents are printed for distribution to the prospective underwriters. Before this point, no offerings of the securities can be made without violating Section 5 of the 1933 Act. Once the preliminary package is filed, the "red herring" preliminary prospectuses, with their legend in red ink stating that they cannot be used for sales, can be distributed to the public. The preliminary prospectuses, of course, do not contain any pricing terms. No actual sales can be made until the registration statement is amended to reflect the SEC comments and the pricing terms and becomes effective. During this "waiting period," the company should avoid initiating publicity other than customary announcements.

The SEC has exacting specifications as to the contents of the registration package, set forth in Regulation C under the 1933 Act. Specifically included in the package, pursuant to Rules 402(a)(1), 402(a)(2) and 402(b) of Regulation C, are three copies of the registration statement with all exhibits, one of which must be manually signed and the other two signed or conformed, ten additional conformed copies, and ten extra copies of the Underwriting Agreements. Also included are a Rule 404(c) cross-reference sheet, which compares items required in the pertinent form to the location of the responses in the prospectus, and a certified check for the SEC's filing fee. A cover letter sets forth responses to appropriate items of two important SEC releases, Releases No. 4936 and No. 5231, which specify items that should be discussed in this cover letter. Among the items included in the cover letter are

(a) a cross-reference sheet to items in the Guides; (b) a discussion of any particular disclosure or accounting problems; (c) an indication of the desired timetable so that the SEC knows when its comments are required; (d) a statement regarding eligibility for Form S-7, if used; (e) a representation regarding review of Release 4936; (f) a reference to any previous registration statement which was the basis of the current filing; (g) a representation regarding the filing of all 1934 Act reports; (h) a response to Item 10 of Form S-7, if appropriate, which explains the omission of certain financial statements; (i) responses, if appropriate, to Release No. 5170 regarding environmental or civil rights litigation which has not been disclosed in the prospectus because it is not material and (j) a copy of a letter sent to the SEC's Office of Public Information pursuant to Rule 458. This letter summarizes the offering in a one- or two-sentence description, which is reproduced in the SEC's weekly news digest.

2. The Representative files appropriate documents, including the company's certified check in payment of the fee, with the National Association of Securities Dealers.

3. The underwriters' counsel delivers the preliminary blue-sky memo to the Representative and commences steps for qualification in the states designated by the Representative.

MARCH 22:

1. The Representative sends invitations to prospective underwriters to join the syndicate, enclosing (1) the registration statement, (2) the preliminary prospectus, (3) a questionnaire regarding the underwriters' activities in the issuer's stock, (4) a power of attorney, if required, for the execution of the Underwriting Agreements, and (5) the preliminary blue-sky memo.

2. The auditors distribute a revised draft of the cold comfort letters.

3. The counsel for the company distributes a draft of its opinion letter.

4. The counsel for the company distributes questionnaires, prepared by the underwriters' counsel, among the officers, directors, and principal stockholders of the company, concerning their background.

5. The company's counsel distributes a draft of a supplemental listing application for common stock to be filed with the New York Stock Exchange. If a company already has listed securities, it must file a supplemental application. Usually there is a discussion with representatives of the Department of Stock List as to whether there will be any difficulties in listing.

BY MARCH 24:

1. The company's counsel submits the supplemental listing application for common stock to the New York Stock Exchange.

2. The final proxy statement is filed with SEC and mailed to share-holders along with the annual report.

MARCH 27: The NASD indicates its approval of this transaction.

MARCH 30–APRIL 7: Informational meetings are held in various cities to discuss the company and the offering, including a Due Diligence Meeting on April 7. The Due Diligence Meeting, as distinct from a general informational meeting, is a vestigial curiosity. The assumption is that underwriters can show their due diligence defense by attending a meeting at which a company representative, usually the chief executive officer, makes some general statements about the company which are reflected already in the prospectus. The personnel attending are often at the lowest level in their hierarchies, and a penetrating question is seldom asked by the underwriters. Indeed, they usually ask only two or three questions. Informational meetings, including the Due Diligence Meeting, are, however, useful for marketing purposes, especially for a company which may not be familiar to security analysts and institutional investors in a particular region, and these individuals often ask the better questions. In fact, the underwriters rely on the Representative to perform their duties of due diligence.

BY MARCH 31:
1. The underwriters return their questionnaires.
2. The company receives questionnaires from its officers, directors, and principal stockholders; one set is forwarded to the counsel for the underwriters.

APRIL 7–12:
1. The SEC's comments are received orally, followed by a letter of comments on April 9. Usually, arrangements are made in advance with the SEC staff as to the mechanics of transmitting comments.

   The SEC uses four different types of review procedures in analyzing registration statements submitted to it, depending on which procedure it feels is appropriate under the circumstances. If the preliminary filing is obviously in terrible condition, the issuer is notified that review is deferred and no further staff time will be allocated to that registration statement. The second type of procedure is called cursory review. No written or oral comments are given by the SEC under cursory review. The theory is that after perusing the registration statement the staff feels its efforts could best be allocated elsewhere in reducing the backlog of pending registration statements. The third type of procedure, summary review, is similar in concept to cursory review in the sense that the SEC staff's analysis is limited. However, unlike cursory review, summary review includes some comments. The most complete accounting and legal analysis of a registration statement is called customary review. If this procedure is used, the SEC's comments may well be quite extensive. Even under summary review, the SEC's points can run for a couple of pages.

The contents of an SEC comment letter can range from insightful remarks about accounting treatment to more or less meaningless nitpicking. Certainly, these comments should be thoughtfully considered, but if they seem inappropriate, it is always possible to discuss the matter further. Blind deference to the SEC is not necessary; the staff can and does make mistakes, but it is always willing to listen to a responsible point of view and is quite reasonable in considering its positions.

2. Changes in the registration statement are agreed upon with the SEC staff, and the timing for effectiveness is cleared. Now the company is prepared to file an amendment to the original registration statement to make it effective. If the transaction is other than a formula-price deal, the filing will be known as the price amendment because the terms of the offer will be specified. Unless the preliminary filing has already been amended to get clearance of new wording from the SEC, the price amendment will be labeled Amendment No. 1.

3. Two business days before the proposed effectiveness date unless a later filing is allowed by the SEC, the company's counsel files requests for acceleration of the effectiveness of the registration statement, as amended, by the company and underwriters (pursuant to Rule 461). Without acceleration, the amendment would be stale by the time it became effective; without acceleration, a registration statement does not become effective until 20 days after the filing of a price amendment, obviously an unacceptable situation. A letter from the Representative stating, in effect, that the preliminary prospectuses had been widely distributed (pursuant to Rule 460 and Item 19 of Release 4936) is also submitted. The wide distribution of preliminary prospectuses is a condition to the SEC allowing a registration statement to become effective. If a preliminary prospectus is materially amended, a recirculation of an amended prospectus, an expensive proposition, may be required by the SEC or considered advisable by the attorneys involved. In addition, letters from the Representative, the company, and the auditors acknowledging that they realized the registration statement had been subject only to cursory or summary review, if received (pursuant to Release 5231), are also required.

4. Diligence material is updated.

5. A committee of the company's board of directors approves the terms of Amendment No. 1 and the Underwriting Agreements

and authorizes execution of the Purchase Agreement and takes other necessary action. If the issue is for debt or the company does not have either debt or a strong public market, the price terms are set the day before the issue becomes effective. For most common stock issuances of larger, publicly traded companies, a formula price rather than a set price is used. The formula essentially states that the price will be no higher than the market price at the time the price determination is made. Therefore, although Amendment No. 1 is the basis for effectiveness (assuming no previous wording change amendments), its pricing terms will reflect only the existence of the formula. The actual pricing for a formula deal usually takes place on the afternoon of the day the issue becomes effective, after the close of the market.

APRIL 13: This is the day the registration statement becomes effective— the most important and hectic time in the public-offering process.

1. The auditors deliver their first "comfort" letter.
2. 8:30 A.M.: The underwriters sign the Agreement Among Underwriters. In large deals, swarms of underwriters gather in the elegant offices of the Representative to sign the Agreement Among.
3. 9:30 A.M.: The company and the Representative sign the Purchase Agreement. Since the prospectus in its final form lists the underwriters, both the Agreement Among and the Purchase Agreement must be executed before the registration statement is filed. A messenger is usually waiting in Washington at the SEC's offices ready to file, and calls periodically to find out whether all the documents have been signed.
4. 9:30 A.M.: Upon the signing of the Underwriting Agreement, the counsel for the company, by a transmittal letter which conforms with Release 5231, files Amendment No. 1 with the SEC (three copies, one of which must be manually signed and the other two of which, signed or conformed; eight additional conformed copies of which five are "red-lined" for changes; three sets of additional exhibits, including the consent and opinion of the company counsel; and ten copies of the Underwriting Agreements, pursuant to Rules 402, 471, and 472), together with, among other items, a response to each staff comment, a marked copy of the SEC letter of comments (if any), and a statement as to the status of the NASD review of the underwriting arrangements. Copies of the letters and of Amendment No. 1 go to the chief of the SEC branch examining the registration statement.
5. 10:00 A.M.: The registration statement is declared effective by the SEC. The company notifies the Representative of the effectiveness,

confirming its notice in writing pursuant to the Purchase Agreement by a copy of the effectiveness order. If the deal is not based on a formula price, the press releases, telegrams, and notifications (which will be described as happening at the end of the day of effectiveness in a formula transaction) occur immediately after effectiveness, and the order can be given to print the final prospectus.

6. 4:30 P.M.: If a formula price is used, a committee of the company's board of directors approves the terms of the price agreement in accordance with the formula, and the company and the Representative execute it.

7. 4:30 P.M.: The Representative sends telegrams to Selected Dealers; the underwriters are notified as to terms and allotments; and a press release as to the pricing is issued.

8. 5:00 P.M.: The definitive prospectus with the final pricing terms is printed for general distribution.

9. The underwriters' counsel completes the blue-sky qualifications and delivers the supplemental blue-sky memo to the Representative.

APRIL 14:

1. The company's counsel files ten copies of the final prospectus with the SEC pursuant to Rule 424(b) and sends a copy to the New York and Chicago offices of the SEC. In a formula deal, this 424(b) prospectus will be different from the prospectus contained in Amendment No. 1 because the actual price terms will be specified.

2. The underwriters publish the tombstone ad for the deal.

3. The Representative notifies the underwriters and the company of the date of delivery of the common stock and designates a place for inspection of the certificates.

4. Copies of the final prospectus, Amendment No. 1, and the supplemental blue-sky memo are distributed to the underwriters.

APRIL 19: The New York Stock Exchange approves the supplemental listing of the common stock being sold, subject to official notice of issuance.

APRIL 20: The counsel for the company and the underwriters and their counsel hold a preliminary closing.

APRIL 21: The closing takes place, including delivery of the stock certificates, the updated comfort letter, and the various legal opinions.

APRIL 24: The company's annual meeting is held.

POSTCLOSING ACTIONS:

1. The company's counsel prepares and distributes a bound history of the offering.
2. Within 15 days of the closing, the company files a Form 8-K with the SEC and sends a copy of the form to the Representative.
3. The company sends copies to the Representative of all reports and financial statements furnished by the company to the SEC or to holders of any class of the company's securities.
4. Pursuant to the Purchase Agreement, the company makes available to its security holders, as early as practicable, in accordance with Section 11(a) of the 1933 Act, financial statements concerning a period of at least 12 months beginning after the effective date of the registration statement.

An Overview
of the Securities Laws

Having examined how the securities laws in fact function, one should step back and ponder whether it all makes much sense. Recent developments and new academic theories have raised fundamental questions about the federal disclosure system which will affect the shape of future innovations in this field. It would be nice to say that there are easy answers to the myriad problems in the securities regulation field, but, unfortunately, they don't exist. What can be done, however, as a first step is to sharpen the focus on objectives and sketch possible alternative approaches and their drawbacks.

THE DISCLOSURE APPROACH

The basic issue is whether the assumption of the 1933 Act is sound: that disclosure is an effective remedy to the ills affecting the securities markets. As William Douglas pointed out, all the disclosure in the world is completely useless if no one reads it. The vision of a public eagerly digesting and capable of absorbing every footnote in a prospectus is simply not realistic.

Furthermore, the federal securities laws were passed as reactions to the 1929 crash; yet they certainly have not prevented dramatic gyrations in the 1970s. They do regulate manipulative devices and compel disclosure of historic facts, but the goal of stability in the financial markets has not been achieved. In theory, a system with full information should not result in prices which behave like a yo-yo. However, this behavior may not so much demonstrate that the system is bad as show the great uncertainty and imperfectibility of financial and economic predictions.

One alternative to a disclosure system is no securities regulation mechanisms at all. There are academics who argue that there is no evidence that disclosure has had any economic impact and who maintain that the private market mechanisms would be as effective in dispersing information. This analysis, however, is too glib because it ignores the fact that the very existence of a healthy market is partly a function of the confidence investors have in the SEC-created regulatory environment. Furthermore, disclosures going beyond SEC requirements are premised on the existence of the SEC standards.

The polar possibility is the imposition of a system which requires all offerings to be fair as determined by the bureaucracy. Aside from being burdensome, this technique does not solve the problem of wide fluctuations in prices after the initial offering of the securities. Besides, such an approach has an inbred bias against speculative companies, and although some of those firms never make an economic contribution to our society, some may be the future IBM's.

As unsatisfactory as it may be, a disclosure system may be the best available alternative. This conclusion, however, does not negate the possibility that some aspects of the alternatives models are useful. For example, rules restricting the selling of speculative securities to unsuitable investors can be strengthened, and a greater effort can be made to deregulate controls which seem to have little purpose.

THE OBJECTIVES OF DISCLOSURE

Even assuming that a disclosure system is maintained, questions still remain as to what is disclosed to whom and when. In thinking about the problem, it is necessary to focus on the objectives of disclosure. Three objectives seem of particular importance:

1. The protection of the unwary public from fraud and from unknowingly entering into risky ventures. As was stated by the House Committee considering the 1933 Act, "The purpose of these sections is to secure to potential buyers the means of understanding the intricacies of the transaction into which they are invited."*

---

*House of Representatives Report No. 85, 73d Congress, 1st Session, p. 3 (1933).

2. Treating the small investor equitably as compared to insiders and institutions.

3. The promotion of a more nearly perfect market by the dispersal of information obtained from the company through full and fair disclosure. As the report of the House Committee on the 1934 Act stated, "[T]he hiding and secreting of important information obstructs the operations of the markets as indices of real value. There can not be honest markets without honest publicity."* Unfortunately, however, the SEC's emphasis has been limited to the wide dispersal of information a company generates and the prevention of insider tips. Until recently, a fundamental reexamination of the type of information disclosed was lacking.

Today, objectives of protective and equitable treatment dominate the need for better information, but the system is not static. The need for reform has been recognized by, among other groups, the SEC's Advisory Committee on Corporate Disclosure in its 1977 findings, and change is inevitable.

THE DISCLOSURE AUDIENCE

One of the curiosities of the present disclosure system is that it requires a myriad of detailed historical information for the use of a hypothetical average investor. The technical dexterity required to comprehend the material would be beyond the background of this mythical investor, anyway. On the other hand, the detail does not cover the type of data of most value to a professional or institutional investor—projections, future plans, and current worth.

Today, the stock market is, in fact, dominated by institutional purchasers such as mutual and pension funds, not individuals. At the end of 1976, major institutions held 40% of the total of $933 billion in stock outstanding. In addition, the individuals who do invest often rely on stock analysts for information, not SEC filings. The question, then, is what to do about a disclosure system oriented to the protection of relatively unsophisticated individuals which inundates them with complex material.

One approach is to make mandatory the provision of simpler documents which summarize the data and highlight key risks to the general public and offer detailed disclosures upon request. The theory behind this bifurcated approach is that much information is trickled down from specialists such as stock analysts to the general public. The SEC has been contemplating moving toward this method as regards complicated merger-offering documents. On the other hand, it has moved away from it as regards annual financial reports. The annual reports to stockholders

*House of Representatives Report No. 1383, 73d Congress, 2d Session, p. 2 (1934).

used to be quite simple, as contrasted to the 10-K's, which were really designed for analysts and professional investors. Now, many of the important details from the 10-K are contained in the annual report.

The fundamental problem with the bifurcated approach is that as a practical matter, it does not treat the sophisticated small investor equitably as compared to institutional investors. The cost of duplicating materials from SEC files and time delays in obtaining supplementary data are an unfair burden. If the bifurcated approach is to be viable, mechanisms have to be devised to put the sophisticated small investor in the same position as institutional representatives.

THE CONTENTS OF DISCLOSURE

The question of whom the disclosures are for is inextricably intertwined with the nature of the information. The other objective of the disclosure system—the spread of useful information to investors generally—is not satisfied by the type of data traditionally contained in a prospectus.

At the heart of any disclosure document are the financial statements. Historically, there have been two fundamental problems with the data contained in SEC filings. First, the data have been based on historical costs and performance rather than on current market values and future projections. Second, the permissible treatment of comparable information varies widely, with the SEC essentially having delegated the regulation of accounting principles to the accounting profession.

Historic versus current values   Since the 1967 Wheat Report, the SEC has recognized that it has a significant challenge in modernizing its approach. Perhaps the most significant step to date was the adoption in March 1976 of an amendment to Regulation S-X, the SEC accounting standards, which requires large companies to disclose information about the impact of changing costs on their business. Specifically, all companies with inventories and gross plant aggregating more than $100 million (if those assets represent 10% or more of total assets) must disclose the current cost of replacing inventories and productive capacity and the amount of cost of sales and depreciation computed on the basis of replacement costs. These disclosures may be made either in a footnote or in a separate section of the financial statements.

The SEC itself noted when releasing the amendment, "[D]ata, based on current replacement costs, may represent the first step toward a revised system of accounting based on current values." The business community initially reacted quite negatively to the rule, pointing out the extra auditing costs and the difficulties in using replacement cost as the basis for any meaningful analysis. Whatever the failings of the concept, it is a first, important step toward revising financial reporting.

Accounting standards In its release adopting the replacement cost amendment, the SEC indicated that it was relying on the accounting profession itself to initiate changes in accounting standards to more adequately reflect current values. This historic reliance on the accounting profession to regulate itself has become increasingly controversial. For example, the Senate Government Operations Subcommittee on Reports, Accounting, and Management issued a report in January of 1977 which lambasted the SEC and the accounting profession. Senator Lee Metcalf, the chairman of the subcommittee, made the following points summarizing the report:

> Corporations presently have substantial discretion in choosing among alternative accounting standards to report similar business transactions. As a result, the amounts of earnings or losses reported to the public can vary drastically depending on which accounting alternatives are chosen. . . . In particular, I am disturbed by two . . . findings. The first is the extraordinary manner in which the SEC has insisted upon delegating its public authority and responsibilities on accounting matters to private groups with obvious self-interests in the resolutions of such matters. The second is the alarming lack of independence and lack of dedication to public protection shown by the large accounting firms.*

Of course, the Metcalf report was quite controversial, and it may well assume a perfectibility of accounting policy which can not exist. Indeed, when the government has attempted to impose its own standards, as it has in the railroad industry, the result in terms of clarity and economic sense has been far worse than the result of generally accepted accounting principles as adopted by the accounting profession.

The Financial Accounting Standards Board (FASB) is now the policy-making body for accounting principles. It has been the target of attacks not only from critics who claim it has done too little but also from those who allege it has done too much and has been too responsive to SEC pressure. Indeed, it has been argued by defenders of the present system that even a zealous SEC can be more effective by preserving the FASB than by taking over itself the burden of promulgating accounting standards: "In areas where the SEC's chief accountant feels the need for action . . . he can move like a guerrilla fighter. Where the Board has been slow he can . . . step in, fire his guns, and then retire."†

In addition to pressuring the FASB, the SEC issues accounting releases in areas where it feels action is required, such as the disclosure of

---

*Letter to Sen. Abraham Ribicoff, quoted in Bureau of National Affairs, *Securities Regulation Reporter,* Jan. 19, 1977, p. H-1.

†Thackray, "Are the Days of the FASB Numbered?" *Institutional Investor,* October 1976, p. 66, at p. 156.

replacement costs. In another example, the SEC issued in September 1975 Accounting Series Release No. 177, which provides that when a business enterprise changes an accounting principle or practice previously followed, the next quarterly report must contain a letter from the firm's accountants indicating whether or not the change is an alternative which is preferable under the circumstances.

The accounting profession protested because under generally accepted accounting principles there is often more than one "acceptable" alternative treatment. Arthur Andersen & Co., in fact, filed a suit to attempt to block enforcement of the Release. Obviously, the fundamental underlying issue is the general flexibility of accounting standards. Whatever the merits of the conflicting claims, the flexibility of accounting standards and the relationship of the SEC to the accountants will continue to be a source of controversy for years to come.

Projections, plans, and other analytical data   Perhaps, historically, the most serious flaw in SEC reports (after the lack of financial statements reflecting current value) has been the absence of projections, plans, and the analytical data of most value to analysts. By contrast, a standard private-placement memorandum is replete with this sort of information. The fear has been that the general public would be unable to appropriately discount this information. In 1975, the SEC did propose stringent rules for companies wishing to make projections, essentially stating that any forecasts given to analysts should be disclosed to the public and were subject to the 1933 Act and the 1934 Act liability. The proposal lapsed because it was felt by executives that it would have the impact of discouraging all disclosure.

In 1977, the SEC's Advisory Committee on Disclosure recommended that the SEC should formally encourage projections of management. Specifically, a "safe harbor" rule was suggested which would protect management from liability for projections unless the claimant could show they were not made in good faith and were not accompanied by suitable cautionary language.

Similarly, in my opinion, statements as to future plans and dividend and financing policies should also be included in SEC filings. However, there should also be a continuing record of how past predictions compared to actual results. Additionally, technical data of use to analysts and sophisticated investors should be included in disclosure documents. For example, critics have pointed out that a stock's volatility as compared to the market (its Beta coefficient) could be described, or perhaps, more simply, a graph comparing the stock's performance to some suitable market index could be included. Of course, it will take some time for these changes to be fully implemented, but clearly the nature of disclosure is changing.

THE TIMING OF DISCLOSURE

A number of critics over the years have pointed out that requiring spasmodic revelations in a 1933 Act registration statement makes less sense than a system of continuous disclosures integrating the reporting requirements under the 1933 and the 1934 Acts. The SEC has begun gradually to adopt this tactic for larger companies by making available shorter 1933 Act registration forms for firms which have been making regular 1934 Act filings.

A humorous article by Lee Seidler and Jeremy Wiesen points out that there are drawbacks to this approach: "All companies subject to such requirements should hire a person with a Ph.D. in Instant Ethics and Situational Morality who makes hourly judgments on the materiality of corporate developments."* There are, however, more serious risks. Generally, the 1934 Act filings are not drafted with the same care and investigation as 1933 Act disclosures, if for no other reason, because the underwriters and their counsel are involved. Although continuous disclosure is the wave of the future, a periodic, in-depth corporate review of the type required by 1933 Act statements retains merit.

The concept of integrating more closely the 1933 and 1934 Acts may also one day be reflected in statutory changes. The American Law Institute over a number of years has been preparing a new Federal Securities Code under the direction of Harvard Law Professor Louis Loss. The Code's central concept is to regulate through one comprehensive statute the entire securities field. Although the impact of the proposed Code may one day be tremendous, it is currently still in the discussion stage, with drafts circulating for comments. Given the recent changes in the securities regulation field, however, it is clear that major innovations can, and must, be made before the adoption of the Code.

---

*Seidler and Wiesen, "The SEC's Fight Against Unemployment," *Harvard Business Review,* January-February 1976, p. 122, at p. 124.

Mergers, Acquisitions, and Tender Offers

These things are rather bloody, you know.

—THOMAS MELLON EVANS, a veteran of corporate takeovers,
  discussing tender offers with a rival bidder,
  Forbes (Feb. 1, 1976)

FOURTEEN

Mergers and Acquisitions

The urge to merge has been a fact of American economic history since the coming of the industrial revolution. Over the years, the rationale, style, and intensity of successive merger waves have varied, but the fundamental instinct to grow by acquisition remains. In the early 1970s with the market decline, the most recent merger boom tapered off from its frenzied pace of the 1960s. The halcyon days of the 1960s may not return in the near future because many of the assumptions upon which that merger movement was predicated have changed; yet in 1977 there was a boom in cash tender offers based on new factors such as excess corporate cash balances. History teaches that periodic surges of mergers will continue to be the pattern of the future.

THE MERGER MOVEMENT

There have been three major merger movements in American history, each terminated by a stock market collapse. The first merger wave occurred around the turn of the century, ending with the panic of 1907. Most of the mergers were horizontal in the basic industries such as steel, tobacco, chemicals, and canning. The second merger movement was touched off by the boom of the 1920s and ended with the great crash of 1929. Again, most of the mergers were horizontal. The merger wave of the 1960s was, however, different in nature. Most of the mergers were, in fact, not between competitors but involved companies in unrelated industries. By the end of 1968, the height of the merger movement, the 200 largest industrial corporations controlled more than 60% of the total assets held by all manufacturing firms—a share equal to that held by the 1000 largest firms in 1941.

THE MOTIVATIONS FOR MERGER

The advantages of acquisitions and mergers are quite complex and are often distorted by the proponents or opponents of the movement. Critics of the merger movement, such as Ralph Nader, allege that there are serious public policy disadvantages to further concentration. If competition is eliminated, these critics claim that consumer prices will rise, reflecting an oligopolistic price pattern (although even this conclusion is hotly debated in the academic journals). Furthermore, these critics feel that 200 firms should not control such a large proportion of the American economy. On the other hand, the critics maintain that the asserted advantages of mergers are either nonexistent, are available through less restrictive alternatives, or are results of imperfections in the economic system which create distortions in the structure of industrial organizations. For these reasons, critics like Nader urge a more vigorous antitrust policy. Other commentators, like John Kenneth Galbraith, point out that historically antitrust has been largely ineffective, particularly in restructuring existing oligopolies, and recommend tighter government regulation as a more effective control mechanism.

Whatever the merits of mergers from the public policy perspective, there are tangible advantages from an executive's point of view.

Manufacturing Efficiency

The classic statement of the "bigness is better" assumption was made by Joseph Schumpeter: "[T]he large scale establishment or unit of control must be accepted as a necessary evil inseparable from . . . economic progress. What we have got to accept is that it has become the most powerful engine of that progress."* Studies have been made by economists, most notably Harvard's Joe Bain, which indicate that the typical industry can consist of many firms, even when each firm has attained minimum efficient scale. These findings challenge the Schumpeterian assumptions about efficiency.

On the other hand, there have been recent technical breakthroughs, such as the application of linear programming, which are increasingly useful in managing the allocation of resources as the units involved become larger. Otherwise, there might be suboptimization. In addition,

*J. Schumpeter, *Capitalism, Socialism and Democracy*, 3d ed., Harper & Row, New York, 1950, p. 106.

technology changes so rapidly that past assumptions as to the nature of the product being produced become rapidly outmoded. For example, the resources required to build a supertanker are quite different from those needed to build the old-style oil barge. Furthermore, markets are now worldwide and may require larger firms. Yet many consultants today urge that large firms use profit centers because if management units are too large, there may be administrative inefficiency.

In any event, the predominant mergers of the 1960s were conglomerate rather than horizontal. Obviously, few manufacturing gains could be expected from merging firms in unrelated industries. All of which leads to the murky conclusion that sometimes manufacturing efficiency is a factor in mergers, but less often than one might suspect.

Other Efficiencies

Manufacturing efficiencies are only one aspect of a modern enterprise, and it ignores commercial realities to judge mergers simply on that basis. Financing, management, research, and marketing are all vital to success.

Finance   The financial area is one where obvious efficiencies of size exist, despite the protestations of economists that they in theory should not. In the 1970s small and medium-size firms had incredible problems trying to raise capital. The first problem is the expense. The prime rate is the rate banks charge their most credit-worthy customers. Even with a healthy balance sheet, a smaller company presents more of a risk to a bank than a larger, more diversified firm. For example, its product may face competition, or its management may become ill. Naturally then, the banks charge a premium over the prime rate to these smaller firms.

Money is not only expensive; during crises, it may be unavailable. In times of really tight money, lenders will take care of the needs of larger firms first. The public market, which was accessible to small companies in the early sixties, periodically dries up, as it did in the early 1970s. Indeed, the cyclical lack of money for financing results in a larger firm having more "staying power" in the face of adversity than a smaller concern. Unfortunately, even a well-managed small firm may find itself insolvent in a cash crunch.

The theoretical argument can be made that institutional investors should be able to get the diversification benefits of investing in larger firms by buying securities of many different smaller firms, and, therefore, money should not be so scarce. Maybe so, but the world does not seem to work that way. One reason is that institutions are inclined to purchase securities in large blocks, and in smaller firms this investment could be illiquid. A purchase or sale of such substantial holdings by itself would affect the market valuation. Recently, even venture capitalists have been reluctant to commit money to the smallest firms because the ability to get money out is most unclear. When the public market is dead, the only way for a small firm owned by a group of investors to provide for the necessary events of life—death, divorce, living expenses—is either going public or selling out to another corporation.

This raises another financial benefit of mergers which, though indirect, is quite important. The availability of the merger route as a means to realize on an investment is an important motivation in starting and putting capital into a small business in the first place. If it were over-restricted, there might well be a disincentive for future venture capital transactions.

Management   Another possible area of efficiency is that of management. A small firm may not be able to afford in-house expertise in, for example, law, finance, or computer techniques. In addition, a large firm just by the sheer number of managers has more depth and is less dependent on a few key individuals. A death, a retirement, or a job switch generally affects a large concern less than a small one. Furthermore, the salary of the chief executive officer in a small firm could only be, for example, $75,000, although, at least on a part-time basis, what was really required was the expertise of higher-priced talent. The theory then goes that each unit of a diversified enterprise can draw as necessary on a central management pool.

There is some degree of validity to this approach. Modern techniques of business management can be acquired by looking at the methodology of sister companies, and insights can be gathered from headquarters. Of course, there is also always the possibility that the company being acquired is being mismanaged and that, with the help of skilled personnel, it can be turned around. There are, however, countervailing arguments. Some companies are not subject to the standardization of the large conglomer-ate and need the creative flair and enterprise of an entrepreneur to prosper.

A related argument is that the threat of a possible takeover bid may discipline incumbent management into performing better. With stock-holders often quite powerless, the possibility of a tender offer may be one of the few means available of encouraging a more productive record.

Diversification   If a conglomerate does have able management, an added advantage is that the structure can result in an efficient allocation of capital despite differing conditions and a reduced vulnerability to the whims of circumstance. For example, if one operation is seasonal, it can be offset by another with a different timing pattern to its cash flows. Simi-larly, the timing of cash cycles on investments and products can be kept in better balance, and priorities can be shifted between varying industries. For example, compare a company which is both a retail chain and a steel manufacturer to two separate concerns in these industries. The independent steel company and the retail chain must each devote its financial and managerial capacities to the one industry. On the other hand, the conglomerate can reallocate capital as the situation demands. Of course, this assumes a management capable of running entirely different businesses at once, a rare quality.

A variant on this diversification theme is the financially strong company in a low-growth industry seeking a higher return on new investments by entering new fields. In theory, again, this diversification can be done at the investment level by stockholders, but that is not realistic. First, much financing is made possible by retained earnings. Second, the firm able to get financing does not necessarily have the most economically worthwhile projects. Third, this diversification by acquisition has been encouraged by relatively high cash holdings of large companies and the higher cost of internal expansion versus purchase of a going concern.

Marketing With national media such as television and mass circulation magazines, a company promoting its overall image can spread the costs over more products to the degree it is larger. Even on specific product advertising, firms get volume discounts. Indeed, unless billings are high, it's very hard to get a quality advertising agency to work on an account. Recently, there has been a trend toward more spot advertising and toward regional editions of national periodicals, but there remain advantages from mergers. Certainly twenty mattress companies across the country joining together in one marketing program are getting better marketing buys than one strong regional firm.

Perhaps more important than costs is the concept of market presence. The public is aware of the identity of the larger concerns, and it is hard for a small firm to establish a reputation.

Purchasing Even though the actual plant may be no more efficient, a large firm is more likely to get volume discounts for its production needs. For example, Sears has more clout in negotiating with manufacturers than the corner appliance store, even though the local firm may be otherwise as efficient.

Research Large firms may have more money to spend on such luxuries as research labs, which sometimes achieve technical innovations with commercial potential. However, economists have studied the impact of size on research and innovation and have found that larger firms do not have a disproportionate role in major inventions. Indeed, the leading study by Jewkes, Sawyers, and Stillerman found that, if anything, the contribution of larger firms was relatively minor. Therefore, this purported advantage is a relatively weak argument.

Bargain hunting Some acquirers may simply see a good deal as motivation enough for a merger. Either the market for the target's stock may be depressed or the bidder may feel that it can get better performance from the assets.

Earnings and Other Advantages

Regardless of public policy implications or real or imagined efficiencies, there are many other motivations to merge. Among the least high-minded is the understandable desire of executives to preside over a larger entity. Aside from the increase in power and prestige, it may result in increased salary and benefits to the managers.

Of course, if a corporation acquires a firm with good potential at a bargain price, the acquirer makes a good move for itself, regardless of public policy implications. The analysis of what is a bargain and what is good earnings potential is, however, much more complex than it initially appears to be.

In the 1960s, for example, it was quite common for an apparent high-growth conglomerate to acquire firms which were selling at a lower price-earnings multiple for stock at a slight premium. If the market did not alter its perception of the multiple for the conglomerate, the result was both instant growth and a boost in stock market price.

As an example, take a diversified growth firm selling at twenty times earnings. If it were to acquire a firm equal in earnings which was selling in the market at eight times earnings, it might have to pay a premium, perhaps ten times earnings. Earnings would have mathematically doubled for the firm as a whole, assuming that no write-down of the purchase price is required by accounting principles under the particular circumstances. But the total number of shares outstanding would not have doubled because of the difference in price-earnings ratios. Thus, for example, if the acquiring firm had 1 million shares outstanding, it would only have to issue an additional half a million shares to make the deal. As a result, the earnings per share would dramatically rise because of the acquisition: an increase of 33%, as the following table illustrates.

GROWTH IN EPS BY ACQUISITION

	Acquirer	Target	Merged Firms
P/E	20	8–10	20
Earnings	$1 million	$1 million	$2 million
Shares outstanding	1 million	1 million	1.5 million
EPS	$1	$1	$1.33
Market valuation per share	$20	$10	$26.67

This effect could become even more pronounced if securities other than common stock were offered. For example, companies such as LTV specialized in devising hybrid securities to be issued in connection with mergers. If debt or preferred stock were issued the earnings per share would nearly double, although, of course, an allocation has to be made for debt servicing or payment of preferred dividends.

In addition, stodgy, old-line companies often are replete with opportunities for discovering buried earnings. For example, depreciation or capitalization policies might be very conservative and can be altered to produce more beneficial results. A revaluation of optional accounting policies might yield some lucrative nuggets in addition to the possibility that some assets may be understated.

Although it is difficult to fathom, a company can maintain big growth in the short run by acquiring low-growth firms. As the table indicates, mere acquisition can bring favorable earnings-per-share growth results, even though the separate firms may not, in fact, have been growing. As a result, the acquiring firm at first impression seems even more worthy of a high multiple which allows it to make future acquisitions to perpetuate its growth record.

In the business schools in the 1960s, there was much talk of "synergy"— two units together would make a whole somehow greater than the separate parts. To some degree this sort of analysis obscured a shell game that the financial world would sooner or later discover.

In the first place, in order to work the game had to go on in perpetuity. But as the expression goes, nothing is forever. When the long string of earnings increases was broken, the price earnings multiples declined. Acquisitions became difficult and expensive, and the mass of all the so-called Chinese paper, the hybrid securities issued to target company stockholders, began to impose a heavy burden.

Second, a key presupposition was that the stock market would treat the growth in EPS from acquisitions as being the same as if it were from internal growth. If a company merited a high P/E because of internal growth, the acquisition of more slowly growing companies would only dilute its momentum. Gradually, the P/E's of the conglomerates began to shift downward.

Third, the use of the leverage of hybrid securities became less efficacious. Again, analysts began pinpointing the effect undue leverage was having on earnings and began discounting the results. Meanwhile, the government began to limit the tax deductibility interest on certain debentures issued in merger transactions, and, as will be discussed, accounting authorities began to reform the treatment of acquisitions to more realistically reflect costs.

Fourth, in the mad rush to make deals, some were necessarily rotten.

Companies began to sag under the weight of high interest costs and low internal growth from ill-thought-out acquisitions.

In the end, the merger game worked for some companies and was a disaster for others. LTV suffered, but Gulf & Western survived and began to thrive. So far, in the 1970s, corporate acquisition policy seems more thoughtful than in the go-go years of the 1960s, with many companies trying to tailor a coherent diversification strategy. The point, however, is not that mergers are good or bad; rather, a sophisticated sensitivity to the complex factors involved is required, as well as a sense of modesty. After all, many companies on acquisition sprees have bought some real dogs.

ANTITRUST CONSIDERATIONS

Antitrust analysis is a key element in a merger strategy. Many a wheeler-dealer has been vanquished on this battlefield through lack of anticipation of the nature of the risks. On the other hand, some executives overcompensate for the risks and out of intellectual intimidation don't enter into deals they should have entered: They simply do not understand the antitrust process.

The Antitrust Risk

The classic antitrust snafu story is the saga of Jimmy Ling. In the go-go years of the sixties, Mr. Ling managed to create the conglomerate of conglomerates in LTV: meat-packing, sports equipment, and aerospace technology were all under the same corporate umbrella. To build this empire, Ling had embarked on a seemingly endless string of acquisitions, issuing increasingly creative mutations of hybrid securities to selling stockholders. Then, Ling met his match in the Justice Department.

Reacting in part to the howls of the other large steel manufacturers, the Justice Department challenged the LTV takeover of Jones & Laughlin, a large but sluggish steel company. Pending determination of the suit, LTV was not allowed to exercise control over J&L, tying up vast amounts of cash in J&L stock without offsetting cash flow from dividends. The LTV house of cards then began to topple. Cash to pay interest on LTV's pyramid of securities became scarce; everything was tied up in J&L. Finally, a negotiated settlement was reached with the Justice Department. LTV agreed to spin off some other subsidiaries but keep J&L. It was, however, too late; the time delay brought about the eventual downfall of Ling.

Therefore, in analyzing the antitrust aspects of mergers, it is imperative to have a good grasp on the nature of the principal risks. These key risk elements may be summarized as follows.

Disclosure In late 1976, Congress passed the Hart-Scott-Rodino Antitrust Improvements Act. Under the provisions of the Improvements Act and the regulations promulgated to implement it, firms involved in substantial acquisitions must file notification forms with both the Federal Trade Commission and the Antitrust Division of the Justice Department. Specifically, acquisitions by firms with net sales or total assets of at least $100 million of the voting stock or assets of companies with net sales or total assets of at least $10 million are covered by the Act, if at least 15% or $15 million or more of the stock or assets of the acquired firm is being sought. Joint ventures are regarded as acquired companies under these regulations. Therefore, a commitment by a large firm to invest $10 million or more within a year in a joint venture is subject to the requirements of the Act.

After notification of an intended transaction, the parties are subject to a waiting period of 30 days (15 days for cash tender offers) before the deal can be consummated. Both companies involved in the deal must file notification forms. In the case of a tender offer, the target company must file a notification form within 15 days of the acquirer's notice (or within 10 days in the case of a cash tender offer). Among the information contained in the notification form are a description of the transaction, all background studies relating to it, detailed product-line breakdowns, a listing of competitors, and an analysis of sales patterns.

During the waiting period, the government may ask for additional material and, based on it, may request a 20-day extension (or 10 days for cash tender offers) of the waiting period from a federal district court. In the event the government reacts adversely to the information it receives, the Act sets up a procedure for facilitating the immediate hearing of a preliminary injunction motion.

An alternative to the procedure under the Improvements Act is for the parties to a deal to seek formal clearance from the governmental authorities. In the past, many firms, especially sellers, have been reluctant to do this because it focuses the attention of the regulators on the transaction and puts governmental officials in a delicate position because by granting a clearance they seem to be endorsing the transaction. Understandably, however, buyers who are risk adverse often prefer seeking a clearance. Otherwise, they bear the risk that one day after the deal is consummated, the acquisition will be challenged.

Through either the notification program or clearance requests, a great deal of information is submitted to the government. Furthermore, the enforcers often follow up with more questions. Even to a public American company, detailed inquiries about market shares and profit margins by products are discomforting. To private companies or to most foreign concerns, the possibility of material disclosures can be a deal breaker. If a suit is actually commenced, the barrage of inquiries and subpoenas seems limitless, both in number and scope. Even if you may not be frightened by the disclosure problem, the other side to the deal may well be.

Expense   An antitrust proceeding can be incredibly expensive, basically because it consumes so much time. Of course, if the transaction or the challenge to it is terminated at the preliminary injunction stage, the costs, though high, are not stunning because the time involved is limited. Many disputes are not, however, resolved at this level. For example, the FTC or Justice Department is perfectly free to challenge a merger after the notification period has run and the deal has been consummated. If fully litigated, a government merger suit can take 8 to 10 years to be finally resolved. Expense, however, cannot be thought of merely in terms of legal bills. The drain on management time and energy can dwarf those fees. In addition, if a private suit is brought, there is also the possibility of having to pay treble damages.

Lost flexibility   As the LTV situation illustrates, antitrust litigation may result in the loss of corporate flexibility while the suit continues. Even assuming the lack of injunctions, it is difficult for a firm to do the most elementary planning when its asset structure is seriously in doubt. Furthermore, investors and creditors will naturally reflect the ambiguity of the situation in their decisions.

Although the risks are substantial, they can be exaggerated. First, even if sued, a company may well settle the case without a significant divestiture, or it may win in court. Even if an acquisition is lost after a suit, much of the economic benefit of a good investment will have accrued, and, probably, a sizable profit can be made on resale. Second, not that many suits are actually brought. So a theoretical antitrust problem may not be realistically, a litigation risk. A client should therefore press his or her attorney to give not only the abstract legalisms of the situation but also a judgment of the practicalities. Then an executive can make an informed decision whether the possible rewards are worth the risks.

Administration of the Antitrust Laws

The merger laws are administered by two branches of the government: the Antitrust Division of the Justice Department and the Bureau of Competition of the Federal Trade Commission. This bifurcated authority on its face makes no sense, although a host of legal articles solemnly argue that nothing could be more appropriate than some competition in enforcement of antitrust laws. A more sophisticated defense advanced by supporters of antitrust enforcement is that the two existing bodies have more political clout separately than when combined. Reformers have periodically pointed out the inanity of it all—split resources, duplication, lack of coordination, etc.—with no impact, so schizophrenic government policy in this field will probably remain institutionalized.

Certainly, the Federal Trade Commission is the more colorful of the two branches. The FTC was established in 1914 as an independent regulatory agency to combat the abuses of businesses. Over the years, it has varied from being a vigorous and imaginative enforcement agency to, more often, a phlegmatic repository for political cronies. Every few years, another reform group springs up to salvage the FTC, but the impact of the reports of these groups has historically been fleeting. Recently, however, the FTC has been in an upswing.

As an administrative agency, the FTC brings complaints which have first been recommended by the staff and approved by the Commission. Each complaint is heard by one of the FTC's hearings examiners, and the Commission as a whole then votes whether to accept or reject the hearing examiner's findings. The decision of the Commission can then be appealed in the federal circuit courts. In theory, by having hearing examiners and Commissioners who specialize in the trade regulation field, the FTC should be able to make more sophisticated and better decisions than the courts.

Among the problems in implementing this theory is the fact that many of the Commissioners and hearing examiners have not been of the highest caliber. In addition, as a system, there is the inherent difficulty of Commissioners who decide, on the basis of staff recommendations, whether or not to bring complaints and then later judge the ultimate merits of those actions. Indeed, much of the significant byplay at the FTC occurs at the complaint issuance and settlement level. In antitrust, the art of negotiation is every bit as important as prowess in the courtroom.

The Antitrust Division, by way of contrast, brings its proceedings through the federal court system. Since the days of the Roosevelt administration, when Thurman Arnold reinvigorated the division (after the Supreme Court indicated that the President's alternative program of economic regulation, the price-fixing codes of the National Recovery Act, were unconstitutional), the Antitrust Division has generally had the better reputation of the two enforcement branches.

The Substantive Law

Most nonlawyers find it very disconcerting when they discover that law is not a certainty. Antitrust is probably one of the most uncertain areas of the law, and, therefore, one of the most frustrating to corporate executives. In the merger field, there are few bright-line rules, only guidelines from precedents.

There are three basic forms of mergers: horizontal (between competitors), vertical (between customers and suppliers), and conglomerate (between firms in unrelated industries). The law is most developed in the horizontal area and most uncertain as applied to conglomerates.

Section 7 of the Clayton Act is the principal statute governing mergers. As amended by the Celler-Kefauver Act of 1950, it provides that "no corporation . . . shall acquire, directly or indirectly, the whole or any part of the stock . . . [or] the whole or any part of the assets of another corporation . . . where in any line of commerce in any section of the country the effect of such acquisition may be substantially to lessen competition, or to tend to create a monopoly." Before the 1950 amendment, only stock acquisitions were covered, and it was unclear whether the statute applied to mergers other than horizontal acquisitions.

In examining any merger, a universal factor is the determination of the relevant market, as determined geographically and by product. To date, the Supreme Court has generally gone along with the narrow market definitions sought by the Justice Department and the FTC. The problem of market definition will be discussed in more detail in the description of horizontal merger policy, but is applicable to horizontal and vertical deals as well.

Horizontal mergers   In the horizontal-merger field, the history of court decisions is one of a movement toward a tough quantitative test of illegality without consideration of offsetting redeeming factors. The first major case decided by the Supreme Court under the amended Section 7, *Brown Shoe,* involved the merger of the Brown and Kinney shoe chains. Although the Court in its 1962 decision considered many factors, there was a primary emphasis on market share in the analysis of the impact of the merger at the horizontal level among competing retail branches. Significantly, the Court seemed to indicate that even a 5% level of market control after a merger could, under certain circumstances, be regarded as anticompetitive.

In its 1963 decision in *Philadelphia Bank,* the Supreme Court went a step beyond *Brown Shoe* and articulated a presumption that high market shares resulting from a merger will reduce competition. The Court held that such an increase in concentration will be enjoined in the absence of evidence clearly showing the merger was not likely to have anticompetitive effects. To appreciate the breakthrough of *Brown* and *Philadelphia Bank,* it must be understood that many academics and corporate lawyers urged the courts to adopt a "rule of reason" in the merger field. Rather than any bright-line rules, an analysis which considered and balanced all pertinent factors was advocated. The Court rejected this argument in *Philadelphia Bank* on the theory that permitting too broad an economic investigation would defeat the congressional intent of limiting the increase in concentration.

The cases since *Philadelphia Bank* became increasingly specific about what would be considered unacceptable concentration levels. In the 1964 *Alcoa-Rome* decision, the Court firmly established the principle hinted at in *Philadelphia Bank:* that in a concentrated industry even slight increases in concentration may be considered illegal. Thus, Alcoa's acquisition of Rome was deemed in violation of Section 7, even though it added only 1.3% to Alcoa's approximately 28% control of the national aluminum conductor market. A later appeals court case, *Stanley Works,* established the converse proposition: a firm with 1% market share could not acquire the leading firm with 24% of the market.

In *Von's Grocery,* the Supreme Court in 1966 expanded the *Philadelphia Bank* quantitative standard to firms with relatively small market shares if the industry was exhibiting a trend toward concentration. Noting that the number of single-store groceries was declining in the Los Angeles area, the Court held that a merger resulting in a firm with a total of 7.5% of the Los Angeles market was illegal.

In the last days of the Johnson administration, Guidelines were issued as to which mergers were likely to be challenged by the Justice Department. Although they are not definitive, the Guidelines are useful to give a rough feel of the antitrust problems involved in a merger. The Guidelines indicate that the Justice Department will challenge mergers between firms accounting for the following percentages of the relevant market:

When the four largest firms have more than 75% of a market:

Market Share of Acquiring Firm	Market Share of Acquired Firm
4%	4% or more
10%	2% or more
15% or more	1%

When the four largest firms have less than 75% of a market:

Market Share of Acquiring Firm	Market Share of Acquired Firm
5%	5% or more
10%	4% or more
15%	3% or more
20%	2% or more
25% or more	1% or more

However, the Guidelines indicate that other factors are also taken into account in determining whether to prosecute a case. For example, the Guidelines state that a stricter test will be applied in industries with a trend toward concentration. Such a trend is considered to be taking place if the share of any subgroup of the eight largest firms in an industry has increased by approximately 7% or more within the 5 to 10 years prior to the merger. The Justice Department indicates in the Guidelines that it will challenge any acquisition by any firm in such a subgrouping if its own market share exceeds 2%. In addition, the Department will ordinarily attack the acquisition of a particularly innovative or disruptive competitor by a larger firm, according to the Guidelines.

As discussed, the product and geographic market definitions may be critical in the determination of the legality of a merger. Starting with *Brown Shoe*, the Supreme Court indicated that in defining submarkets it would consider as important factors industry or public recognition of a submarket as an independent economic entity and the product's characteristics such as uses, required production facilities, customers, and sensitivity to price changes in competing products. Thus, the Court in *Brown Shoe* held that there were separate submarkets in men's, women's, and children's shoes; in *Alcoa-Rome,* aluminum and copper cable were treated distinctly; and in *Clorox,* household liquid bleach was deemed to be a product with no close substitutes.

Some federal lower courts have in the past extended the Court's narrow interpretations of markets even further: For example, florist aluminum foil has been recognized as distinct from other lines of aluminum foil, and paper-insulated power cable has been deemed different from other cables. Recently, however, some courts have examined more seriously assertions of cross elasticity—that the supply, demand, and pricing of one product, such as oil supplied to utilities, is necessarily related to the marketing of another product, such as coal.

In geographical markets, *Brown Shoe* again established the basic concept that the commercial realities of where competition takes place is the governing factor. In *Brown,* the Court indicated that every city with a population of 10,000 might be considered a geographical market. Subsequent decisions have split as to whether a particular small town fit the "section of the country" standard in Section 7, but the general principle remains true that geographical markets may be determined on quite a localized level.

In recent years, there has been a reluctance to extend the progeny of *Philadelphia Bank.* For example, in the *General Dynamics* case, the Supreme Court approved the merger of two coal companies, finding a cross elasticity with other forms of energy, and in *Marine Bancorporation* it held that an acquisition by a large banking organization in Washington state of another bank within the state had not increased concentration within any applicable market. This broadening of the definition of product and the application of less strict market definitions may change the legal status of some horizontal mergers. However, despite some loosening of standards, horizontal mergers are still judged by tough criteria.

Vertical mergers   In the vertical-merger field, the courts have relied heavily on the precedents established under Section 3 of the Clayton Act, which deals with exclusive distribution contracts. The basic concern of the courts in vertical mergers is that an acquisition by a supplier of an outlet for its products will foreclose the supplier's competitors from a segment of the market.

Over the years, the line of cases on vertical transactions has evolved multiple criteria rather than the quantitative test for horizontal mergers articulated by *Philadelphia Bank.* The *Brown Shoe* decision itself stated that the market foreclosed to competitors by a supplier acquiring a customer was a significant but not dispositive factor in evaluating the legality of a vertical merger. Trends, the actual economic effect on competitors, the barriers to new entries, all should be considered in vertical integration situations, according to the *Brown* Court.

The Guidelines indicate that the Justice Department will ordinarily challenge a merger between a supplying firm accounting for 10% or more of sales in its market and one or more purchasing firms accounting in total for more than 6% of the total purchases in the market unless there are no significant barriers to entry into the market such as capital or technological requirements.

However, the cases indicate that the courts may enforce a stricter standard depending on the facts of the situation. For example, in the 1966 *Standard Oil (Potash)* case, an oil company's acquisition of a potash producer was held to be illegal, even though only 1% of the potash market was foreclosed. The court felt that despite the small market percentage involved, the effect, based on the facts of a concentrated market and the high likelihood of Standard Oil entering into the industry on its own, would be anticompetitive.

Conglomerate mergers   The most vexing area of merger law concerns conglomerate deals. Piercing through the rhetoric of the cases, one key area of concern is simply the overall tendency toward economic concentration. Unfortunately for the sake of clarity, neither the statutes nor the cases explicitly cope with this problem; there is no clear legal basis for a position that bigness or overall concentration is per se bad. Therefore, the Justice Department and the FTC have induced the courts to declare transactions void for reasons which are really tangential to the basic thrust of the pure conglomerate problem, the concern about overall concentration levels. Instead, the courts attempt to focus on the product or market-extension or preferred-access aspects of the cases. Former Assistant Attorney General for Antitrust Richard W. McLaren attempted to raise some of these issues, but his major cases, as will be discussed, were settled before any clear precedents could be set. The overall concentration issue is one whose time will come, but at this point, both proponents and opponents seem to prefer skirting the issue in litigation, if not in congressional hearings. In Congress itself, a series of bills has been introduced to break up the leading companies in heavily concentrated industries, sure to foment controversy for years to come.

Perhaps the leading case in the conglomerate field is the Supreme Court's 1967 *Clorox* decision. Clorox had some 48% of the national sales market for liquid bleach and was acquired by the nation's largest advertiser, Procter & Gamble. The Court found that Clorox had largely achieved its dominant position through advertising, since, in fact, liquid bleaches were chemically identical. Holding that the acquisition was illegal, the Court reasoned it was more likely that potential new entrants to the market would be dissuaded from entering the bleach business and smaller competitors would fear to compete if Procter & Gamble kept Clorox than if Clorox, remained independent. Furthermore, Procter & Gamble was regarded as the most likely potential entrant into the market, and the Court felt that this loss of potential competition exacerbated the entrenchment of Clorox's position. Procter & Gamble was therefore ordered to divest Clorox.

Similarly, in other cases, courts have stopped giant diversified firms acquiring industry leaders in concentrated markets where the conglomerates are considered potential competitors. In the *S.O.S.* case, a federal appeals court in 1967 held that the acquisition of S.O.S. by General Foods would raise entry barriers in the concentrated steel wool market and decrease competition. More recently, in *Kennecott Copper,* courts have stressed the importance of potential competition, holding that potential entrants have a procompetitive effect on the market even though it is unlikely they would enter the industry under current conditions.

Another factor examined in conglomerate cases is reciprocity, a seller's using its own buying power as a lever to induce purchasers to buy the seller's products in preference to those of its competitors. In the 1965 *Consolidated Foods* decision, the Supreme Court held that the acquisition by Consolidated, a wholesale and retail food marketer, of Gentry, a garlic and onion powder supplier, was illegal. The Court reasoned that buyers of garlic and onion in the food-processing business would favor Gentry in order to spur their sales to Consolidated, reinforcing Gentry's leading role in the market. However, the Court was careful to point out that the possibility of reciprocity by itself is not sufficient to make a merger illegal; in addition to the opportunity for reciprocity, there must be a factual finding that it is likely (given past practices and industry patterns) and that in the particular market setting, the result of the reciprocity is likely substantially to lessen competition.

The Guidelines for conglomerate mergers also focus on potential entrants and reciprocity. Because of the novelty of other aspects of conglomerate mergers, the Guidelines themselves admit that further specificity was impossible. For example, the Guidelines indicate that a merger between a likely entrant and any of the following firms will be challenged:

- any firm with 25% or more of the market
- one of the two largest firms in the market (where the two largest firms share 50% or more of the market)
- one of the four largest firms in a market, if the target has at least a 10% market share (where the eight largest firms have 75% or more of the market)
- one of the eight largest firms in which the share of these firms is at least 75% of the market, if the target doesn't have an insubstantial market share and is rapidly growing and there are no more than one or two likely entrants

As to reciprocity, the Guidelines indicate that a merger will be attacked where 15% or more of the purchases in a market in which one party to a merger sells is accounted for by firms which, in turn, make substantial sales in markets in which the other merging firm is a leading buyer.

A series of suits brought by the government in the late 1960s and early 1970s against ITT and other conglomerates indicate the rather confused current status of conglomerate merger law. None of these cases reached the Supreme Court, as they were all settled by consent decrees after the lower court decisions. In the ITT cases, ITT agreed to spin off Hajoca Corp., the Fire Protection Division of Grinnell, Canteen Corporation, and either Hartford Fire Insurance Company or three other acquisitions, ITT Levitt & Sons, Hamilton Life Insurance Co. and ITT Avis (which were the spin-offs chosen by ITT) as part of consent decrees entered into with the government after all the lower court decisions went against the Justice Department. There was some wording in the opinions limiting the scope of some of the doctrines being expanded by the Antitrust Division. In *Grinnell,* the court indicated that there must be showing that Grinnell was the dominant competitor in any market; in *Canteen,* the court stated in the *dicta,* side comments to its opinion, that even if an opportunity for reciprocity existed, a probability of its occurrence must be indicated. As a result of the settlements rather than an appeal of these fundamental issues to the Supreme Court, conglomerate mergers are still an unresolved area of law.

Common issues   In any merger suit, two issues repeatedly come up in the minds of executives as questions to their lawyers. First is the question of postacquisition evidence. Unfair as it may seem, courts have had a tendency to use it against a defendant, but rarely in its favor.

The second issue, is the impact of the economic results on antitrust. Although the Guidelines clearly state that the economics of a transaction will not ordinarily be considered in evaluating a merger, there is one exception, the failing-company doctrine. If a target company is clearly failing with no reasonable prospect of remaining viable and no offer of acquisition has come from a noncompetitor, the Department may not decide to challenge a deal it might otherwise attack.

Special Situations

Joint ventures Since the 1964 Supreme Court decision in *Penn-Olin,* joint ventures between two or more corporations are essentially treated as though the firms involved had merged that aspect of their businesses. Indeed, the notification requirements under the 1976 Improvements Act treat a joint venture exactly like a merger. Often the ancillary documents to the joint venture, such as technical licenses and marketing agreements, cause greater antitrust difficulties than the basic joint venture agreement itself and must be carefully drafted.

Banks and bank holding companies Banks present a special and complicated situation under the antitrust laws. Unlike other regulated industries such as common carriers, which are exempt from Section 7 because of the jurisdiction of the special government agencies which supervise their activities, banks and their parent holding companies are subject to both Section 7 and regulatory agency oversight. In reaction to the *Philadelphia Bank* decision, Congress passed the Bank Merger Act of 1966 which, aside from legalizing past bank mergers, mandated that any merger the Attorney General did not challenge within 30 days of its approval by the pertinent regulatory agency could not be challenged under Section 7. In addition, the 1966 Act also stated that anticompetitive effects could be outweighed by a finding of meeting the "convenience and needs" of the community to be served. However, this defense is not applicable to the acquisition by banks of nonbanking businesses under the Bank Merger Act and the Bank Holding Company Act.

Private Suits

Under Section 16 of the Clayton Act, private parties are entitled to sue under Section 7 and recover treble damages. Recently, private claims have become popular in defense of tender offers. However, competitors, as well as target companies, have standing to sue. Over the next few years, there is little doubt that private merger damage suits will become increasingly prevalent. Thus, the government is not the only party to fear regarding antitrust matters. Competitors and target companies in hostile tender-offer situations may raise antitrust issues.

The liabilities of a private defendant are not, however, unlimited. For example, Purex Corporation sued Proctor & Gamble claiming damages as a result of the acquisition by P&G of Clorox, which had been held illegal by the Supreme Court. However, a court in 1976 held that, in fact, any damages were not discernible and refused to award Purex any money.

Similarly, the Supreme Court in *Brunswick v. Pueblo Bowl-O-Mat* held in 1977 that for a private party to recover damages in a Section 7 suit, it must show actual injury to itself—not merely a violation of Section 7. Thus, competitors of bowling alleys acquired by Brunswick were held by the Court not to be entitled to treble damages, even if the acquisitions were illegal under Section 7 unless actual, rather than possible, injury to competition could be demonstrated.

FIFTEEN

Tax, Corporate Law, and Accounting Considerations

Added to the complexities of whether a merger or acquisition is fundamentally sound and not in violation of the antitrust laws are the tax, corporate law, and accounting wrinkles in the transaction. These factors can have a substantial economic effect and often are the decisive elements in considering a deal.

Assuming that all or nearly all the voting securities or assets of a target company are being acquired, there are five basic forms of structuring transactions:

1. A statutory merger
2. The purchase of stock of the target in exchange for voting stock of the acquiring firm
3. The purchase of the assets of the target in exchange for voting stock of the acquiring firm
4. The purchase of the assets of the target for cash or nonvoting securities
5. The purchase of the stock of the target for cash or nonvoting securities

Each of these forms has distinctive benefits and disadvantages stemming from the intertwining factors of antitrust, tax, and securities law and accounting principles. The corporate law and tax impact of each of these procedures will be discussed in turn, and then accounting aspects will be highlighted.

TAX AND CORPORATE LAW FACTORS

The first three transactions described—mergers, the stock for stock, and the voting stock for assets exchanges—are tax-free reorganizations under the Internal Revenue Code. In order to qualify for this tax-free treatment, the transactions must be carefully conducted and must have an independent business purpose other than being tax free. Under the Code, the sellers will have no recognizable tax gain or loss, and the acquiring corporation will use the old tax basis of the target company in the acquired property. In the 1960s, tax-free transactions were assumed to be preferred. After all, if a stock had run up in price, one might want to hold on to the new security and not pay taxes on the sale of the old stock. This was especially true of securities held by persons thinking of their heirs, because before the Tax Reform Act of 1976, property passing at death had a tax basis for the heirs equal to fair market value. Only an estate tax was payable on that value; no one paid a capital gains tax on the appreciation in value.

In the 1970s two difficulties were perceived with this preference for tax-free transactions. First, there often was a loss rather than a gain on the security; therefore, stockholders often wanted a recognizable event so that the tax loss could be used to shelter other income on their tax returns. Second, even with a tax burden, cash was often regarded more highly than a security which may or may not have been worth its estimated value. Today, tax-free transactions are an alternative, but not necessarily the right solution.

A Statutory Merger

The first common form of tax-free reorganization is a statutory merger or consolidation, known in legal slang as an "A" reorganization for Section 368(a)(1)(A) of the Internal Revenue Code which describes it. The Code states that if there is either a merger (one firm merging into another firm) or a consolidation (two firms jointly merging into a newly created third firm) which complies with the requirements of the applicable state statutes, the result will be a tax-free transaction. For the purposes of this discussion, consolidations will not be treated separately unless they have distinct features from mergers. Although the Code provisions are relatively simple, in tax law simplicity seems to be a metaphysical impossibility. The courts interpreting these provisions and the Internal Revenue Service have naturally added some gloss of their own.

The continuity of interest and other tests   In theory, the parties to a merger may receive consideration in cash, stock, debt, or any other form of payment. This flexibility in terms is one key advantage of an A reorganization and is in sharp contrast to the other tax free vehicles. The IRS, however, has limited the scope of freedom as to the means of payment by requiring that there must be a "continuity of interest" by stockholders of the merged corporation. As a rough rule of thumb, the "continuity" test is satisfied if the former stockholders of the acquired company get stock in the surviving entity equal in value to 50% or more of the value of the stock which was surrendered. The rest of the consideration may be cash, debt, or other forms of payment.

This continuity test was originally based on the judicial view that the reorganization provisions of the Code did not contemplate tax-free treatment to a transaction which was in substance a sale rather than a reorganization. Thus, deals in which parties received cash and notes in exchange for their stock were treated by the courts as being taxable. Perplexingly, the definition of what comprises a continuing interest includes any form of stock—including nonvoting preferred. Long-term debt, however, is not considered to contribute to continuity even though the interests of a long-term debt holder are very similar to those of a holder of nonvoting preferred stock.

In addition to there being a continuity of interest test, courts also tend to integrate a series of transactions and consider them as one deal. This step-transaction doctrine lets courts often pierce the veil of the form of a transaction and examine its substance. For example, in an A reorganization, if stockholders receive cash to redeem their stock immediately before or after a merger, a court may deem the payment to be part of the merger terms and count the redemption against the stockholder in applying the continuity-of-interests tests. All of which is very sensible except that the Guidelines as to when a court will use this doctrine are most unclear. The step-transaction concept is even more important as applied to the other forms of tax-free reorganizations because of their more rigid standards as to the form of payment involved.

Corporate requirements In terms of corporate requirements, a merger agreement under Delaware law, for example, must generally first be approved by a vote of a majority of the directors and then be submitted to the stockholders for approval of each involved company. However, under Delaware law, no approval by the stockholders of the acquiring firm is required if the stock had already been authorized and less than 20% of the outstanding stock of the acquirer will be issued. In any event, the New York and American Stock Exchanges both require a vote by the stockholders of the acquiring company if the value of the stock and cash being given in connection with an acquisition equals about 20% or more of the acquirer's outstanding voting stock, and in addition the listing agreement may require a vote if an officer, a director or a major shareholder of the acquiring company has an interest in the acquired firm. Of course, varying state laws have procedures which must be complied with, and all this gets rather complicated when the corporations involved are incorporated in different jurisdictions. In addition, the acquired company's bylaws or certificate often requires a high quorum for merger approvals and must be carefully checked.

The merger or consolidation agreement specifies the terms of the deal and the conditions for the transaction becoming effective. Upon effectiveness, the surviving corporation (in the case of a merger) or the new company (in a consolidation) issues securities in the appropriate ratios to the former security holders of the merged firm or the consolidating companies. The assets and contract rights (unless otherwise specified in those documents) as well as all the liabilities, direct or contingent, disclosed or not, of the merged concern, pass automatically by operation of law to its successor, the surviving company. Although this succession avoids the need for complicated assignment documents, it also poses the danger that the acquirer will be subject to the undisclosed liabilities of the target. Furthermore, some contracts specifically provide that they do not pass to a successor, and this provision can raise serious obstacles to the merger.

Once a merger has been approved by the required number of shareholders, there is a cram-down effect. Even those stockholders who voted against the merger own only securities in the merged or consolidated enterprise or seek their remedy through appraisal rights, discussed below. The old corporate entity no longer exists. Thus a key advantage of the statutory merger is that no minority stockholders remain; they have been forced out.

The disadvantage of this merger procedure, however, is the formalities involved. As discussed, the directors of both companies must approve the deal. The target's directors may well be recalcitrant. Therefore, in contested situations, the statutory merger route often doesn't work. In addition, at least the target's stockholders are entitled to vote on the merger question at meetings. If it isn't time for the annual meeting, the expenses of calling a special meeting for a public company are high. The public stockholders must be provided with a proxy statement describing the transaction and a prospectus outlining the terms of the securities which they are going to receive, unless they qualify for private placement treatment. Form S-14 is an abbreviated registration form adopted by the SEC which, in essence, wraps around the required proxy statement which is then also used as a prospectus. The S-14 joint proxy statement-prospectus approach satisfies the requirements for a registration of the offering company's securities.

Inevitably, an A reorganization involves a substantial waiting time between the conception of a deal and its implementation, especially if publicly held companies are involved. Aside from giving stockholders adequate notice (usually about 30 days in advance), both the proxy statement and the S-14 must be cleared through the SEC before the holders can even be sent the pertinent documents. Mechanically, the proxy statement is sometimes filed with the SEC first for review because it is generally given confidential treatment in preliminary form, assuming that the filer is not otherwise compelled to issue a press release. However, recent cases under the Freedom of Information Act indicate that under exceptional circumstances the public may gain access to these filings. After the SEC has given its comments on the proxy statement under this procedure, the S-14 is filed and, like all other registration statements, is available for inspection and is announced in the SEC's news digest. Of course, if secrecy is no problem, as is usually the case, both filings are made at the same time.

Usually, the opinion of an investment banker as to the fairness of the transaction is included in the proxy. This opinion is designed to insulate directors from any charges they did not fully protect their shareholders in a deal. It is in the best interests of the directors to hire a firm with a record of taking vigorous, independent positions in such situations, because its views will be more persuasive to a court.

If a stockholder of either company involved in a merger should oppose it and is not satisfied with the securities being received, most state statutes provide the remedy of appraisal rights under specified circumstances. Under the Delaware statute, for example, unless the certificate of incorporation otherwise provides, there are several broad exceptions to the general right of appraisal. Specifically, there are no appraisal rights as a result of a merger (other than a short-form merger, as will be discussed) for a stockholder of a company listed on a national securities exchange or whose stock was held of record by not less than 2000 shareholders if the stockholder received in return stock in the surviving company or shares in a listed firm or one with 2000 shareholders. If there are appraisal rights, the proxy rules require that they be described in the proxy delivered to the voting shareholders.

Appraisal procedures must be handled quite gingerly. First, the methods of evaluation used by courts can often differ considerably from market value. For example, in Delaware, market value, book or liquidation value, and dividend yield are all weighted. In many states, the appraisal procedures often tend to be quite archaic, based on traditional precedents that may be inapplicable to today's economy. Second, the statutory requirements for eligibility are quite intricate and can be easily muffed. Some statutes, for example, require that a shareholder desiring appraisal rights must vote against the merger and file a request complying with technical statutory standards for requesting an appraisal within a specified time frame.

Triangular mergers   A twist on the familiar form of an A reorganization is the "triangular" A, which, in essence, permits the acquiring company to set up a wholly owned subsidiary into which the acquired firm is merged. Shareholders of the acquired company receive stock of the parent company of the acquiring subsidiary. The key advantages of the triangular A are that no vote of the stockholders of the parent corporation is required, and only the subsidiary, not the parent, is exposed to the liabilities of the target company. In order to be eligible for a triangular A, which is authorized under Section 368(a)(2)(D) of the Code, a transaction must meet all the criteria for an A reorganization. In addition the subsidiary must acquire "substantially all" of the assets of the acquired company.

Section 368(a)(2)(E) allows a very useful variation of the triangular A, the reverse triangular A. In essence, the subsidiary of the acquirer is merged into the acquired company, which continues to exist as a subsidiary of the purchaser. The key attraction of the reverse triangular A is that assets such as contracts and franchises which may be restricted as to their transferability remain with the acquired company.

Stock for Stock Exchanges

The second tax-free form of reorganization, commonly known as a B reorganization after Section 368(a)(1)(B), involves the acquisition by one firm of a controlling stock interest in another company in exchange solely for its own or its parent's voting stock. Consideration other than voting stock such as cash or debt securities, which is called "boot," is absolutely forbidden. In contrast to an A reorganization, the continuity of interest in a B transaction is 100% because all of the consideration is voting stock. When control is acquired, the target concern becomes a subsidiary of the acquiring company. For the purposes of a B reorganization, control is defined by Section 368(c) as the acquisition of at least 80% of the voting stock and 80% of the shares of all the other classes of stock of the acquired concern. The tax basis to the shareholder of the target for the shares received is the same as their basis in the shares exchanged.

Generally, B reorganizations are approved by stockholder and director votes of the target company. With this approval, the transfer of control as required by the Code is assured and a cram-down effect is created. Sometimes, an exchange offer without the approval of the target company is used because of hostile target company management. However, without the 80% control, the tax-free nature of the transaction will be jeopardized. Therefore, a condition is sometimes put into the offer stipulating that it will not be consummated unless the requisite 80% control is attained.

A key advantage of a B reorganization is that it allows the acquirer to maintain the corporate existence of the target, thereby retaining in the acquired company any valuable contract rights or franchises which cannot be assigned. On the other hand, unless there is a stockholder vote, this preservation of the corporate shell does not result in the squeezing out of minority shareholders, unlike a merger or a B reorganization with a vote.

One method of eliminating minority shareholders is to have a merger following sometime after the B reorganization. Often such a merger will utilize a "short form" procedure which does not require a stockholder vote. For example, in Delaware if the parent company owns 90% of the outstanding shares of each class of stock, the board of directors of the parent may approve a short-form merger of the subsidiary into the parent without any vote on the part of the minority holders of the acquired concern's stock. The minority stockholders may be, however, entitled to appraisal rights. Other states have differing requirements, and, of course, certificates and bylaws may have specific provisions on the subject. However, as will be discussed, a merger for the sole purpose of eliminating minority holders may well prove troublesome in litigation.

The stock of the acquiring corporation in a B reorganization must be registered in order for it to be offered to the target's shareholders, if it is a public company. Often the acquirer qualifies for the simplified S-7 form or the transaction is voted upon by the shareholders making it eligible for S-14 treatment. Otherwise, a full-blown S-1 registration statement must be utilized, which is much more detailed than the S-14 wraparound type of statement used in connection with mergers.

Corporations which frequently are involved in acquisitions use a technique called "shelf registration," which limits the scope of the problem of filing of a new registration statement with every merger or acquisition. Generally, securities can be registered only if it is contemplated that they will be offered in the proximate future. However, the SEC Guides permit a company engaged in a continuing program of acquisitions to register a reasonable number of securities for future offerings and put those registered but unissued securities "on the shelf," with the registration statement being periodically amended after its filing to keep it current. Thus, if at a later period an acquisition opportunity arises, the already registered securities from the shelf are used without the delays of first commencing the registration process at that time. Of course, if a stockholder vote is required, a proxy statement is still necessary.

From the tax point of view, a B is the least flexible and most fragile form of reorganization. For example, the "solely for voting stock" requirement of a B reorganization is strictly applied, even to incidental costs in a transaction. The acquiring company has been allowed by the IRS to assume expenses directly related to the reorganization, such as printing and legal fees. However, costs not directly incurred in connection with the deal (such as general corporate financial advice) or by the target company (such as legal services for large shareholders) cannot be absorbed by the acquirer. If they are, the transaction will lose its tax-free status. Similarly, employment contracts which arguably provide cash payments for the stock of officers of the target company can also jeopardize B status. Without extreme care, disasters are quite possible in the tax field. Not surprisingly, in large transactions, requests for rulings from the IRS as to the treatment of proposed deals are quite common.

Stock for Assets

Under a C reorganization, named after Code Section 368(a)(1)(C), the exchange of voting stock of a company or voting stock of its parent for substantially all the assets of a target company will be a tax-free transaction.

Mechanically, the board of directors and the stockholders must approve the transaction. Under Delaware law, for example, a majority vote is required for the sale of all or substantially all the assets of the company. Unlike a merger, stockholders objecting to the asset transfer generally have no appraisal rights. If the stock for the acquisition has already been authorized, no approval is required from the stockholders of the acquiring corporation unless the 20% rule of the national exchanges is applicable, as has been previously discussed. After the transfer of assets takes place, the shell of the target company is generally liquidated, and the stock of the acquiring corporation, which has been registered on a Form S-14, is distributed to the stockholders of the target company in exchange for their stock.

In issuing rulings regarding C reorganizations, the IRS applies a quantitative test to determine whether substantially all a target company's assets have been transferred. According to the IRS, substantially all the assets of the target company in this context means 90% of the net assets at their fair market value and 70% of the gross assets at fair market value.

In addition to this quantitative test, the IRS has also been quite zealous in attempting to apply the step transaction test to C reorganizations. For example, if assets had been disposed of by the target company shortly before the asset acquisition, the two transactions may well be regarded as one integrated plan by the IRS. If too high a percentage of the assets were sold before the reorganization, the deal might not meet the C "substantially all" standard.

In theory, a C reorganization is not entirely limited to the acquiring corporation offering voting stock; up to 20% of the value of the assets may be accounted for by boot—payment other than stock, such as cash or debt securities. However, if any "real" boot such as cash passes, all assumed liabilities (including, for example, long-term debt) are treated as boot.

Therefore, the amount of "real" boot which can be transferred is, as a practical matter, very limited. Thus, a C reorganization is more flexible than a B reorganization as to boot, where none is permitted. However, it is considerably more restrictive than an A reorganization. When boot is received in any reorganization, that part of the transaction is taxable.

One key advantage to the acquisition of assets, as opposed to that of the stock of the target company, is that the liabilities being assumed can be carefully selected. For example, if the target company previously sold defective products or broke its contracts with impunity, the acquiring company has the option of not assuming the contingent liabilities. In contrast, when stock is purchased, the acquiring company owns the target with both its assets and its liabilities. But in that situation, the liabilities are insulated within the acquired subsidiary. If a merger takes place, however, the assets and liabilities are merged into the acquiring company. So an assets-for-stock deal has much to recommend it if there is concern about the assumption of liabilities. A note of caution is, however, appropriate. A recent case has suggested that a purchaser of assets continuing the business will be liable for suits regarding products manufactured by the seller of the assets. Although this is not the majority view, the risk should be recognized.

Not assuming the old corporate shell is also a weakness in the acquisition of assets. Every asset has to be specifically assigned, including every contract. Many contracts have clauses which state that they may not be assigned without the consent of the other party. So an assets deal can create enormous burdens, and quite often these problems are not merely administrative. For example, a key supplier with a no-assignment clause may well see the assets deal as a perfect opportunity to renegotiate the contract. To avoid this sort of problem, assignment clauses which state that the contract may be assigned to a successor to all or substantially all the company's (or division's) business are quite useful.

The Purchase of the Assets for Cash or Nonvoting Securities

The purchase of assets for cash or for nonvoting securities will both be taxable transactions. Both require the assent of management and stockholders if the assets involved are all or substantially all the assets of a corporation. In addition, the complexities of any asset transfer must be handled, including the chore of getting consents to contract assignments. On the other hand, however, unwanted liabilities can be excluded. Of course, if the deal is for securities, a registration statement is necessary.

Taxable transactions As noted, however, there are situations when a taxable event is preferable to a tax-free reorganization, for example, when most stockholders have losses. But there are other situations when the criteria of a C or other reorganization simply cannot be met. If a corporation is selling off a particular division (which is not itself set up as a subsidiary corporation) to a purchaser, the test of all or substantially all of the assets being sold may not be satisfied. Or a corporation may prefer to issue all nonvoting securities because of the dilution in earnings per share that issuing voting equity might cause. In either event, a taxable acquisition can have distinct advantages.

The legal documents Since the documents related to an assets acquisition are among the most complicated legal instruments, it is useful to briefly highlight some of their most important features. Other acquisition documents are similar but have unique attributes. For example, if stock is being offered to the owners of a privately held company, the stock may be unregistered, and the contract may contain registration provisions similar to those used in venture-capital deals. Of course, deals for the target's stock do not have detailed transfer provisions, but the representations regarding its financial conditions are similar.

After the business parties have achieved a general understanding a nonbinding letter of intent is often signed. Although generally quite vague, it is useful in the letter to highlight the key terms of the deal—it saves days of arguing when the actual contract is being negotiated.

The negotiation of the purchase contract itself can be a long and arduous process. This brief discussion will focus on the unique attributes of purchase contracts. The prior discussion of venture-capital investment contracts discusses legal agreements in a broader context.

In the negotiation of a purchase contract, the fundamental questions are what exactly is the buyer purchasing and in what condition is it purported to be in. In the simplest case, a buyer is purchasing a distinct division "as is" with no representation as to condition and with related liabilities which are clearly discernible. Often, however, the buyer wants representations as to the quality of the assets. Furthermore, it is often very difficult to determine exactly what assets and liabilities belong to this "business." In addition, there is the need for a myriad of consents to assignments of anything from bank loans and sales office leases to union contracts. The result is a situation which is often complex and entangled.

The contracts themselves may start with recitals which state the background of the contract and the assumptions of the parties entering into it. Although these passages are not operative by themselves, they do add a gloss to the contract which may assist a court in interpreting its provisions.

Generally, the representation section follows. A key issue is whether the representations survive the closing. Otherwise, the accuracy of the representations is merely a condition to closing the deal. If it is later discovered that they were inaccurate, the buyer's recourse is limited except, possibly, for a fraud claim. The rationale for nonsurvival is strongest when the buyer has an adequate opportunity to inspect the assets before the closing.

If, as usual, the representations survive the closing, they have two functions. First, they flush out the pertinent facts about the acquisition. If there are material errors or omissions, the buyer can refuse to close. Second, after the acquisition, there is the possibility of a monetary adjustment if the representations are not true. Naturally, the buyer tries to make the representations as extensive as possible, while the seller attempts to limit them. In addition to financial statements, the seller represents as to the existence and status of various types of assets from real estate to sales contracts to patent rights. Details about category of assets are usually attached as exhibits to the purchase contract. Although some commentators have suggested that much of the detail in purchase contracts is extraneous, it does focus the attention of both parties on the assets to be transferred and the problems relating to them. For example, a listing of all material contracts and leases should be prepared and the documents should be read by the buyer, to know about their assignability, financial terms, and any unwanted liabilities related to those instruments such as liquidated damages clauses. Indeed, often the hardest negotiations in asset deals come only after the backup documents have been thoroughly digested.

After the section on representations, the conditions to closing are stated. Aside from the standard legal opinions and certificates, there may also be outs for suits brought or threatened and challenging the deal, representations which were not accurate and complete in all material respects, and the inability to obtain specified consents to the transfer of certain vital contracts.

In negotiating the purchase contract, there are several recurrent difficulties. One problem is having a mechanism available for adjustments in the price, for unforeseen events which occur after the closing, and for inaccurate representations. Sometimes, part of the purchase price is reserved for later payment. When a selling corporation has assets other than those being sold, there is recourse against it for any misrepresentation. However, if the selling corporation's only assets are being sold, and it is going to be liquidated soon after the closing, a potential action against it may be meaningless. Sometimes, therefore, the major shareholders of the selling company will themselves agree to be liable in the event any representations are untrue, although they should certainly attempt to place limits on the scope of their potential exposure. Another technique is to place a portion of the cash price in escrow. Adjustments can be made to this amount against receivables which prove to be noncollectible, inventories which are obsolete, erroneous representations, and undisclosed liabilities. Alternatively, some method of evaluating all these uncertain elements has to be calculated in advance and may well involve a painstaking inventory and receivables analysis. In addition, a pension specialist should examine the potential liabilities relating to employee retirement plans and the actuarial assumptions relating to their funding.

Another difficulty is the contracts, leases, and loan agreements which require consents. Usually, the consents are routinely given, but even if the buyer assuming the agreement is as responsible as the seller, there are sometimes holdouts.

Sometimes if a contract is unfavorable, the holdouts will demand that the agreement cease or that prices be negotiated. Similarly, labor contracts must be carefully examined to make sure that new negotiations are not triggered. Of course, in any regard, great efforts should be made to contact union representatives to assure a smooth transition.

Defining exactly what business is being purchased is another fundamental problem. Buyers may not wish to assume unprofitable operations, leases on inefficient sales offices, and money-losing contracts, but, of course, sellers do not want to continue to absorb the costs. So, compromises or price adjustments must be made.

The Purchase of Stock for Cash or Nonvoting Securities

The prime advantage of a purchase of stock for cash over other taxable-acquisition transactions is the lack of cumbersome corporate and transfer procedures. No authorizations are required from anyone. As will be discussed, any pertinent tender-offer statutes must be complied with, but there are no stockholder meetings and proxy statements. In addition, no assignments of contracts and transfer of property are needed, since the corporate shell is being acquired. However, liabilities are being assumed that may be unwanted, and there is always the problem of dealing with minority stockholders who did not sell pursuant to the offer.

Other Tax Factors

In addition to a discussion of the varying forms of reorganizations, there are other critical tax factors in making policy decisions regarding mergers.

The installment purchase Assuming a taxable transaction, the timing of the seller's tax liability can be quite important. At the taxpayer's option, sale proceeds can be reported on an installment-sales basis if certain criteria are met. Essentially, this enables a taxpayer to defer payment to the government of the taxes on the profit. Internal Revenue Code Section 453 provides that profit from a sale may be reported on the installment basis if the payments during the year of the sale do not exceed 30% of the selling price. Payments during the year of sale are defined to include cash and readily marketable debt. The taxable income in each year is the proportion the installment payment received in that year bears to the total profit.

Aside from being able to earn interest on the money which eventually has to be paid in taxes, a deferral may result in some of the profit being taxed in a lower bracket than it would if all of it was bunched in one year, assuming a taxpayer was not always in the 70% bracket. Even for the 70% taxpayer, the deferral has advantages. For example, the rate of tax on capital gains is normally one-half a taxpayer's marginal rate, so it could range up to 35%. However, the capital gains rate is subject to a limit of 25% on the first $50,000 of gains in a tax year. Therefore, by spreading a gain, it may be possible to have more of the gain fall within the $50,000 limitation. Furthermore, spreading the profit over a number of years may limit the amount due under the minimum tax on tax-preference items. For this purpose, 50% of capital gains are tax-preference items, in any one year. Essentially, the chance of exceeding the $10,000 (or one-half the year's tax liability, if greater) annual exemption from this minimum tax is increased.

In structuring an installment sale, a stumbling block is the interest component. Unless a minimum interest rate (at least 6%) is stated, the IRS, pursuant to Section 483 of the Code, will impute interest at a greater rate (7%).

Liquidation upon sale of assets   After a corporation has sold its assets, the proceeds are usually distributed to the shareholders in the form of a liquidation of the corporation. Obviously, it is imperative in such a trans-action to avoid double taxation, a taxable gain at both the corporate and individual levels. Section 337 of the Code provides that there will be no recognition of loss or gain by a corporation if the sale of the assets occurs after adoption of a plan of complete liquidation and, if within 12 months after the adoption, all the assets, except those retained to meet outstanding claims, are in fact distributed. Section 341 of the Code, however, states that the general nontaxability will not apply to such transactions if a "collapsible corporation" is involved. Essentially, a collapsible corporation is an entity designed to distribute to its stockholders at capital gains rates property whose sale by the corporation would have been taxable as ordinary income.

In negotiating a transaction, one factor to be taken into account in fixing a price is determining who will bear the burden of paying the recapture on investment tax credits. The recapture arises because assets are being sold before their life as computed for investment tax credit purposes has expired. If the purchaser were to buy the stock of the target and then liquidate it, the purchaser would pay the recapture. If on the other hand, the assets are sold, the selling company is responsible for the recapture.

Earn-outs   In haggling over price in an acquisition, one useful device is an earn-out. The setting is familiar: The entrepreneurs state that their little company has a spectacular future, and the sky is the limit on their price demands. The acquiring company is skeptical. A reasonable compromise is to make the final price a function of future earnings. Of course, there are a number of difficulties in structuring this sort of transaction. The seller is worried that the buyer can manipulate the books to show earnings are low or that the buyer may direct the company's best personnel or most innovative product ideas to some other division. Even if the seller retains an employment contract, there are still the difficult problems of intercompany pricing and allocation of central overhead. Sometimes sales are used as a measure, but again there are difficulties. Margins may change on sales, product lines can be transferred, and, from the buyer's perspective, if the sellers retain employment agreements, they can hype sales without commensurate profits.

As a result, it is quite usual to incorporate page after page of technical descriptions of accounting methods and the basis for intercorporate charges in earn-out agreements. These provisions seem to always require a great deal of negotiation, but in the end, if there is bad blood, lots of legalese is not going to solve many problems. Perhaps an arbitration clause and some language that profits and sales will be determined for the purposes of compensation on a basis substantially consistent with prior accounting practices is the best that can be done. But a wise seller and a prudent buyer will insist on a floor and a ceiling, respectively, on what the price paid will be.

In structuring an earn-out, there are important tax considerations. The installment method is frequently used in earn-outs. Care must be taken that a set maximum price is stated; otherwise, the IRS will regard the installment requirements as not having been met because it is unclear whether 30% of the final purchase price has been paid in the first year. The IRS has recently attempted to limit the use of the installment method in earn-outs, and the current situation should be checked with a tax expert before proceeding with such a transaction.

If tax-free treatment is desired, all the consideration must be paid within 5 years, and at least 50% of it must be paid in the initial distribution. A ceiling on the amount of total payment is a necessity; otherwise the 50% test cannot be satisfied. The use of certain escrow accounts may lower the amount which must be paid in the initial distribution, and a tax expert should be consulted as to the drafting of such a device.

Loss carry-overs   One of the vital considerations in structuring an acquisition is the preservation of the tax-loss carry-over, if it exists. Under the Code, a corporation can use its losses in the previous 7 years as a deduction against current profits, thus lowering taxes. To have a loss carry-over, a corporation need not have been unsuccessful. For example, a company with heavy start-up and development expenditures may well have a glowing future but have accumulated loss carry-overs. Or a corporation may have valuable assets, such as patents, which were not well exploited, and the company cumulated deficits. Of course, the firm could also basically be an economic failure.

In theory, each $1 of carry-over should have a net after-tax value of 48 cents, the amount of taxes saved by a corporation in the usual 48% bracket if the carry-over can be used. But the particular facts of a situation may make that carry-over worth anything from that 48 cents per dollar to nothing to an acquiring corporation.

Section 269 of the Code states that if the acquisition of a corporation or of control of a corporation is for the principal purpose of avoidance of federal income tax, the tax benefits which would otherwise accrue to the acquirer will be disallowed. This provision is the key stumbling block in many a deal-maker's vision of a cheap tax haven. Simply stated, a tax-loss carry-over may not be as usable at it seems.

Among the typical situations which are blocked by Section 269 are the following:

- the acquisition of a shell corporation with a loss with no going business and the use of its carry-forward to shelter the income of an unrelated business
- the acquisition of a loss corporation followed by the pumping of other businesses into the corporation in order to boost its profits so that its carry-over will be usable before it expires

How can the loss carry-over be preserved? Section 381 states the basic rule that upon certain liquidations of a subsidiary into a parent corporation or in an A (statutory merger) or a C (assets-for-stock) reorganization, the carry-over will be preserved. Of course, in a B reorganization (stock for stock), the carry-over is preserved because the original structure of the loss corporation still exists—all that has changed is the ownership. But although 381 states a basic rule, it is naturally riddled with exceptions and intricate requirements.

First, the 7-year applicability of carry-overs is not what it seems. The corporation's gross carry-overs should be broken down by the specific years when the carry-overs expire. Then one gets a rude surprise. The tax year for a corporation distributing its assets or transferring them in a reorganization ends when the transfer takes place (Section 381(b)(1)). As a result, there is usually a short additional "stub" year, which decreases by a year the longevity of the tax carry-forwards. For example, if a loss corporation is acquired in October, its tax year ends then. Assuming the calendar year is the normal tax year of the acquiring company, another tax year takes place from October through December 31, and a year of tax carry-over has been lost. Only if the reorganization takes place on December 31, is the stub year problem avoided for companies reporting on a calender-year basis.

Second, even though a corporation files a consolidated return for its subsidiaries, the loss carry-forward cannot be used against consolidated income. Treasury Regulation 1.1502-31 states that a loss sustained prior to a corporation's acquisition by the parent company can be carried over only as regards its own income and should not be used to reduce income of other corporations on the consolidated return.

Third, if there is an A (statutory merger) or C (stock for assets) reorganization, the carry-over will be preserved only if there is sufficient continuity of interest. For this purpose, Section 382(b) of the Code, as amended by the Tax Reform Act of 1976, states that a carry-over in either the acquiring or acquired corporation will be completely preserved only if the stockholders of the loss corporation receive 40% or more of the total fair market value of the outstanding stock of the acquiring corporation used in the deal. For every 1 percent less than the 40% which is received, the amount of available carry-over is reduced $3\frac{1}{2}\%$, but below the 20% level, the reduction is $1\frac{1}{2}\%$ for each percentage point decrease. Thus, if there is only a 15% continuity of interest, only 22.5% of the carry-over is available (100% minus [20% $\times$ $3\frac{1}{2}$ plus 5% $\times$ $1\frac{1}{2}$]). Before January 1, 1978 (the date these provisions of the 1976 Act took effect), the Code required a 5% reduction for each percent less than 20%; above 20%, the carry-over was completely preserved.

Triangular mergers were especially useful in loss carry-over situations before the Tax Reform Act of 1976. The Code had a provision which allowed large firms to make relatively small acquisitions by deeming the stock of the parent to be the stock of the acquiring subsidiary for the purposes of determining fair value. Thus, a subsidiary of ITT with stock worth $1 million could acquire a loss corporation and give its stockholders $200,000 in ITT stock and completely satisfy the continuity test. Indeed, ITT directly could never have satisfied the test itself under these circumstances, since it wouldn't be paying directly 20% of the value of its stock. Beginning in 1978, the effective date, triangular mergers will be judged as if the parent were the acquiring party.

Fourth, until July of 1978, if any one or more of the 10 largest stockholders of a loss corporation increase their ownership through purchases by 50 percentage points or more after the beginning of the tax year or after the beginning of the prior tax year, the loss carry-over will be disallowed if the company changes its business. The practical impact of this provision, Code Section 382(a), is to keep stockholders from purchasing control of a loss corporation and then changing its business.

Beginning in July of 1978, if any of the fifteen largest stockholders of a loss corporation increase their ownership through a purchase by more than 60 percentage points after the beginning of the tax year or after the beginning of each of the two previous tax years, the carry-over is reduced. For every percent of ownership in excess of 60%, the carry-over is decreased by $3\frac{1}{2}\%$, and above 80%, it is reduced $1\frac{1}{2}\%$ for every additional percent of ownership. These are complicated provisions whose impact is unclear. In carry-over situations, they would seem to encourage either a merger or a B reorganization because these transactions would not be considered "purchases." Alternatively, a company could acquire less than 60% control while the carry-over was being used and later increase its ownership after the 3-year test period was no longer applicable.

The standard manner of getting the benefit from a loss corporation if no other method is available is to eventually liquidate the subsidiary. Treasury Regulation 382(b)-1(a)(6), however, states that the IRS may view the entire transaction as one with the purpose of tax avoidance. For this reason, most businesses wait 3 years before they will liquidate a subsidiary with a loss carry-over. Indeed, under Code Section 334(b)(2) any transfer before 2 years have passed would clearly destroy the carry-over.

Related tax provisions   In addition to the A, B, and C forms of reorganization discussed, the Code in Section 368 also classifies additional transactions as tax-free reorganizations. A transfer by a corporation of all or a part of its assets to another company which is either owned by the transferring company or a shareholder is a tax-free "D" reorganization if it meets certain specified criteria. Among the transactions allowed by this provision are spin-offs and split-ups complying with the detailed provisions of Code Section 355. A recapitalization, an "E" reorganization, and a mere change in identity, form, or place of organization, an "F" reorganization, are also tax-free.

ACCOUNTING CONSIDERATIONS

Accounting for mergers and acquisitions has been an explosive issue for more than 20 years, especially in the areas of the amortization of goodwill and the concept of pooling.

Purchase Accounting

If a firm buys a piece of equipment for cash, the cost of the asset is reflected on the company's books at its purchase price. Similarly, when a company purchases another concern's stock for cash, the total price paid is reflected under the "purchase" method of accounting. However, often the price paid is above the book value of the target company's assets. The difference between the purchase price and the book value is considered "goodwill." In order to fully reflect the cost of the transaction, the buyer under the purchase method enters both the book value of the acquired firm and the related goodwill on its balance sheet. Thus, for example, if a company has a book value of $10, and it is purchased for $15, $5 would be goodwill. Goodwill is quite common in acquisitions because book values often do not reflect the current value of a concern; book value only purports to be an indication of historical costs. Furthermore, earning power may make a firm worth more than the value of its assets, even if the book value was an approximation of current asset values. All too often, however, book values do not even indicate the current value of the assets themselves.

The critical question then is how the frequently arising goodwill should be treated. If it has to be written off or amortized (tangibles such as plant and equipment are depreciated, intangibles such as patents and goodwill are amortized), there could well be an important effect on earnings. For example, if a firm were purchased with a book value of $40 million and a purchase price of $80 million and earnings of $16 million a year before taxes, the amortization of the $40 million in goodwill could well have a dramatic impact. If the $40 million in goodwill were amortized over, for example, 20 years, earnings before taxes would be lower by $2 million.

Naturally, executives actively involved in either selling or buying companies have historically opposed the amortization of goodwill. The theoretical basis for this position is that the goodwill lasts as long as the company. On the other hand, critics have pointed out that if the individual assets were purchased for cash, accounting conventions clearly require that the costs of the assets be depreciated over time. The retort to this argument is that goodwill is not being generated by the individual assets but rather by the business as an ongoing entity.

Pooling

Accountants have felt that the purchase method is not appropriate for all merger transactions, especially stock-for-stock transactions. Pooling is an alternative accounting concept under which the purchase of a company is essentially ignored for accounting purposes in certain limited circumstances; rather, the two independent concerns involved in a merger are treated as though they had always been together. The purchase price is not reflected because the assets of the companies are pooled. For example, if a company with assets of $30 million purchases a company with assets of $20 million for $30 million in voting stock, conventional "purchasing accounting" would state that goodwill of $10 million was present in a company with $60 million in assets. Under pooling, however, the goodwill would be ignored, and the total assets would be $50 million. If goodwill has to be amortized, pooling accounting—which avoids the creation of goodwill—can make an important difference in earnings results.

The original theoretical foundation for the pooling approach was that two companies of roughly comparable size involved in a stock-for-stock purchase should be treated as though they joined one another and were pooled rather than evaluated in the context of a purchase. Over the years, however, because of the favorable earnings impact, companies of grossly disproportionate size used the pooling method and the stock-for-stock standard was diluted. The American Institute of Certified Public Accountants came out with study after study over a period of 20 years which suggested criteria for limiting the use of pooling, including rough comparability of size among companies.

At the height of the 1960s merger wave, critics, including the Federal Trade Commission, argued that pooling increased the incentive to merge by jacking up earnings. The SEC finally brought pressure on the AICPA to reform. In a first draft opinion, the AICPA did, indeed, state a comparability-of-size test for pooling. The howl from the nation's leading companies and their accountants was, however, overwhelming. As a result, a rough compromise was fashioned in the final AICPA opinions, Accounting Principles Bulletins 16 and 17, now the governing rules in this area, are vital to any merger analysis.

Under the APB standards, if a merger is not eligible for pooling treatment, it must be treated as a purchase; if the purchase price is greater than the book value, goodwill will be created, and that goodwill must be amortized over a period not greater than 40 years.

In order not to be treated as a purchase and to be eligible for pooling treatment, a merger must meet, among others, the following criteria:

1. Each of the combining companies is independent and has not been a division or subsidiary of another company in the last 2 years.

2. The deal is completed within 1 year in one transaction.

3. The consideration involved is voting common stock for substantially all of the target company's voting stock.

4. No shares of its own stock are reacquired by the surviving company except for its stock option and compensation plans pursuant to a systematic pattern of reacquisitions established for 2 years.

5. No contingent payments are permissible; earn-outs are inconsistent with pooling treatment.

Therefore, in thinking about the economics of a transaction, it is important to take into account whether the structure of the deal will be eligible for pooling treatment. The earnings impact can be substantial.

SUMMARY

The following table briefly summarizes the key factors to be considered in evaluating the different forms or reorganizations:

	Advantages	Problems
1. (a) "A" (Statutory Merger):	1. Most flexible as to consideration 2. Tax free 3. Squeezes out minority stockholders	1. Continuity of interest test 2. Intricate corporate procedure 3. Need proxy statement 4. Parent may be assuming unwanted liabilities
(b) Triangular "A":	1. Simplifies corporate procedure for parent 2. Liabilities limited to subsidiary; parent protected	
(c) Reverse Triangular "A":	1. also allows target to pay boot such as legal fees	
2. "B" (Stock for Stock):	1. No corporate procedures absolutely necessary unless stock unauthorized, but must meet control test 2. Tax free	1. Need registration statement (and proxy if having vote) 2. No boot allowed 3. Only voting stock can be used 4. Retain unwanted liabilities 5. May have problems with minority holders unless have vote
3. "C" (Assets for Stock):	1. Liabilities don't have to be assumed 2. Limited boot O.K. 3. No problems with minority holders	1. Must acquire substantially all assets 2. Intricate corporate procedure 3. Need plan of liquidation and proxy statement 4. Transfer of assets and contracts complicated
4. Stock for Cash:	1. Fast	1. Taxable 2. Retain unwanted liabilities
5. Assets for Cash:	1. Liabilities don't have to be assumed 2. No problems with minority holders	1. Taxable 2. Intricate corporate procedure 3. Need plan of liquidation and proxy statement 4. Transfer of assets and contracts complicated

SIXTEEN

Tender and Exchange Offers

The mid-1970s were the years of the tender offer. With the slump in stock prices, American and foreign companies saw a unique opportunity to acquire firms with high potential in a bear market. Tender offers were quick and effective. Without warning, a chief executive could wake up in the morning and find a huge two-page ad in the paper announcing a surprise attack.

Things have changed since then. First, market conditions, of course, have varied over time. Second, management has become increasingly sophisticated in devising means to fend off tenders. Third, largely because of political pressure from incumbent management, most key states, including Delaware, have passed statutes which take much of the surprise element out of a tender offer, as does the Antitrust Improvements Act of 1976, which requires advance notification. But the bear market did leave a legacy of making a tender offer a respectable instrument of corporate policy. Leading investment bankers now anxiously compete for sizable fees, even though in the past it was somehow thought to be bad form to be involved in what are often mudslinging contests.

STRUCTURING THE OFFER

Tender offers, of course, can be friendly or contested. Indeed, a firm can tender for its own shares. Offers can be for cash or for another security, in which case they are commonly referred to as exchange offers. The common denominator is that cash tender offers and exchange offers are both made directly to all public security holders of a company. By contrast, a merger is, in effect, carried out between the corporations themselves.

What Is a Tender Offer?

When is a purchase a tender offer? This issue repeatedly arises, but there is no clear answer. Much, of course, depends on the facts. A doctrine known as the "creeping tender offer" integrates as part of the offer purchases made before the formal announcement. Once an offer is announced, as will be discussed, any side private purchases are illegal during the term of the offer and may invalidate the entire tender offer. The net effect of the creeping tender offer doctrine is to make the statute governing tender offers, the Williams Act, applicable to preannouncement purchases—thereby making many of these purchases illegal. Commentators have postulated that unless there is a period of, for example, 60 days separating these early purchases from the announcement of the offer, a creeping tender may well be deemed to have taken place. However, no court has yet taken this position and, as will be discussed, the actual practice in tender offers is quite different. Even if the purchases are themselves legal, there is still the issue of whether the buyer had an obligation to inform sellers as to the probability of a tender offer.

Although the creeping tender offer theory is interesting, the fact remains that the key to the success of many offers is the ability to scoop up the shares of key stockholders immediately before public solicitation commences. The defensibility of this tactic may well depend on the number of people involved. Once the number exceeds ten or fifteen, the offer comes dangerously close to being a creeping tender if a public offer soon follows. If no tender offer is contemplated in the near future, the numbers could rise to general private placements levels, say thirty-five offerees. Of course, all solicited persons must meet private placement eligibility standards.

These deals to acquire the shares of major stockholders raise a number of other problems. First, everyone involved has serious problems under the 1934 Act's Rule 10(b)-5, which makes it fraudulent not to disclose accurately material facts in connection with the purchase or sale of securities. The insiders selling have a duty to disclose their knowledge about the company, but, on the other hand, this disclosure may be deemed to be a breach of their fiduciary obligations to the company. Meanwhile, the purchaser, which, as discussed, may have a duty to disclose its intent to make a tender offer, must itself disclose in the subsequent tender offer any nonpublic information it previously received from the insider sellers.

Second, acquiring more than 10% of the shares in a private purchase may subject any shares subsequently bought in a tender offer to the short-term-profit squeeze-out provisions of Section 16(b) of the 1934 Act in the event such shares are sold within 6 months of the purchase. Thus, the flexibility of a defeated offeror is more limited, if pre-tender purchases have exceeded the 10% threshold.

Third, the relationship between the price paid the insiders and that offered to the public is quite sensitive. Although professors have railed against the concept for years, most modern cases have allowed large block holders and insiders to receive a "control premium." On the other hand, the issue is likely to be litigated, and inevitably the pure control premium issue becomes muddied with the related problem of a breach of fiduciary duty on the part of the insiders. Was the insider paid the premium for the block as such or for not fighting a deal which takes advantage of the public shareholder? As a result of the delicacy of this issue, many insider purchase agreements have a provision which stipulates that if a tender is made, it will be at the same price as that offered the insiders—or a higher price.

In short, what is and what is not a tender is a difficult and dangerous subject, with the law in the area in constant evolution and convolution. Unfortunately, practical judgments have to be made. The result is uncertainty and a field day for the lawyers.

Selecting a Target

In making a tender or direct exchange offer, it has necessarily been decided that the alternative of structuring a deal through the corporate target itself, such as a merger, assets acquisition, or consensual B reorganization, has critical failings. In some cases, the transaction is friendly, but a stock-for-stock transaction is preferred to a merger for tax or accounting reasons or a cash deal is insisted upon by some major stockholders of the target company. When the deal is unfriendly, however, a cash tender or an exchange offer are the only practical choices; the other forms of corporate acquisition in effect require the cooperation of incumbent management.

If an offer is likely to be hostile, the target company must be selected with extreme care. The following are among the key factors to be considered, assuming the basic financial judgments have been made:

Stock ownership A detailed analysis must be made of who owns the corporation's securities and what their feelings are likely to be about incumbent management. The first step is a determination of the ownership by management, officers, and employee benefit programs whose investment decisions are controlled by management. Related, but distinct, is the block owned by all other employees. Employees may or may not have strong feelings of loyalty to present management, but officers almost always will. Then a breakdown is needed of the types of other key holders: For example, what percentage are institutions versus individuals, what are their average holdings, and how long have they held the securities? The objective is to first determine the "float" in the market—the trading shares that will easily flow to the highest bidder and then those which can be acquired with a little work.

Some companies are simply very hard to crack: Management owns a high percentage of the stock, employees are loyal, stockholders have held the stock for years and have prospered, and the trading float is thin. Following financial reverses, however, stockholder loyalty often disappears. For this reason, tender offers are often made to companies which are underachieving; a disillusioned stockholder is usually willing to sell.

Corporate structure The corporate structure of a target firm can be a key factor in determining the success of an offer. A potential acquirer must study the provisions of the bylaws and charter of the target. Provisions for a staggered board, the inability to remove directors without cause, or high quorum requirements for approval of mergers could make life very difficult for the would-be acquirer, even if the offer itself is relatively successful. Provisions such as cumulative voting can be a double-edged sword. They make entry onto the board easier but make elimination of minority opposition on the board more difficult.

Analysis of possible defenses Possible defenses to a tender offer will be discussed in detail later, but obviously an acquirer should analyze the probability of likely strategies. For example, are the executives signed to long-term contracts, are there substantial authorized but unissued shares available for defensive mergers, will there be a competitive bid, etc.? Also, an acquirer must be aware of the weaknesses in its own position: Are there likely to be sensitive and blurry disclosure issues; is the antitrust situation clear; are there any other regulatory hurdles, such as required state or federal commission approvals; and can the record of the acquiring company's management be easily attacked?

Assembling a Team

A tender or exchange offer is a fast-paced, complex, highly charged, and extremely dangerous situation. The consequences of a mistake in judgment can be much greater than merely the failure of an offer; liability for damages and expenses in suits can be staggering. Not surprisingly, perhaps the most important step in preparing for an offer or defending against one is assembling a top-notch team.

The lawyers   The instinct of most companies is to save a little money and rely on their general counsel. Unless their attorneys are specialists in corporate finance, this may well be an expensive mistake. Unlike many other transactions, an offer is so briskly paced that there is not enough time to learn on the job. Another related problem is the depth of resources. In an offer, speed is critical. A small firm with other pressing commitments has very serious problems shifting its resources quickly. Indeed, even many large New York firms tell clients that although they will prepare the papers, another firm will have to conduct the litigation, if any is necessary, because of prior commitments.

As a result, a specialized breed of highly paid tender-offer litigators has developed. Their firms are geared to the sudden, in-depth challenge, and their prices are steep. Usually, they coordinate their efforts with those of the company counsel. As a defensive tactic, some major corporations have gone so far as to put one of the more notable of these firms on retainer, so at least it won't be leading the attack. In many offers, all these lawyers are unnecessary; the issues are resolved elsewhere than in a courtroom. However, the fact that one side knows that the other has able counsel on tap may influence the negotiations. Furthermore, as in any potential struggle, reserves are a good idea.

The dealer-manager   The dealer-manager is almost always an investment banker. Occasionally, especially in bids for their own stock, companies will not have any dealer-manager at all. Being a dealer-manager can be quite lucrative—flat fees can run in the hundreds of thousands of dollars, and that is only the beginning. Often, the dealer-manager gets an additional fee for all shares tendered and can also get an extra "soliciting" fee for all shares it collects itself. On a major transaction, total compensation of more than $1 million is not uncommon. Part of the explanation of the high fees is that dealer-managerships often represent payments for other services provided over the years. Another factor is that if the deal is unsuccessful, the payment to a dealer-manager is considerably less because there are no solicitation fees. In addition, the fee reflects the possibility of liability for the dealer-manager in the event of a litigated offer.

Companies tend to sign the dealer-manager agreement at the last minute before the offer is made; until that point, the dealer-manager is at risk for time and expenses. Cautious dealer-managers attempt to get a letter from their clients at an early date specifying at least the coverage of expenses if the dealer-manager agreement is never signed.

What do dealer-managers do for all this money? Sometimes a lot, sometimes not much. Of course, often the fee reflects compensation for proposing the transaction to the acquirer, a "finder's fee." However, if it performs its job well, a skilled dealer-manager can be crucial to the success of an offer, even if the client has already picked the target.

First, using its trading expertise, it can appraise who the stockholders are and tailor an offer to that constituency. Should there be a minimum acceptance figure, should cash or securities be offered, will the commitment to purchase be unconditional? All are difficult questions requiring a sophisticated expertise.

Second, the very name of a well-regarded investment banker may add credibility to an offer, especially if deals managed by it have been successful in the past. Indeed, the lack of impressive bankers may stiffen the resolve of the opposition.

Third, the contacts of the investment banker with the critical arbitrageurs, who will be discussed, and with the institutional holders are very important in soliciting acceptances. Again, effectiveness is partly credibility and experience.

Fourth, and perhaps most complicated, is the issue of pricing. Having set all the other terms, how much should be paid directly to the shareholders and how much to the soliciting brokers who get a fee for each share they surrender? In theory, the final offering price (there is the possibility of amending the price during the offer) should be the lowest possible which assures success. The issue then is how much of a premium over market price is needed to jar the shares loose and discourage competing bids. A dealer-manager's insights can be quite helpful in making this determination. The impact of acute judgments can be quite significant. For example, in an offer for 5 million shares, a lowering in pricing of 50 cents results in a $2.5 million savings.

Finally, the general experience of the dealer-manager can be quite helpful in organizing a team, developing a strategic approach preparing an offer, and even negotiating with the target's management. At some firms, the investment bankers working in the merger field are specialists with an invaluable knowledge of the technicalities and techniques in the field. In addition, often the counsel to the dealer-manager is much more experienced in the tender offer field than the company counsel and will take the leading role drafting the papers. These services can be of particular use to companies with little offering expertise of their own. Especially in the context of a complex, contested offer with rival bidders, a capable investment banker can be critical.

Pricing and term strategies will be discussed in more detail, but it should be pointed out that some dealer-managers occasionally may be overgenerous with their clients' money in recommending pricing terms in order to assure a successful transaction. This is partly a reflection of the compensation structure under which a dealer-manager loses a large portion of its fee in an unsuccessful offer and partly a result of the common perception among many dealer-managers that their clients are very averse to the risk of losing in a takeover bid, even if assuring a victory is costly. Of course, in an offering for a limited number of shares, if a flood of securities are tendered, a dealer-manager would be quite embarrassed, since it obviously recommended too high a figure. The point is that a company must retain an independent critical judgment, be able to clearly define and articulate its objectives to its investment bankers, and, of course, select bankers with a genuine interest in the long-term relationship with the company, rather than in the one quick deal.

Soliciting agent   There are only a handful of firms which specialize in the mass solicitation of security holders, the most prominent being Georgensen & Co. and D. F. King & Co. Working for a flat fee rarely exceeding $25,000, these firms utilize telephone banks and direct mailings to inform small stockholders about the tender terms. In addition, their regional offices serve as distribution points for documents and information regarding the offer.

Depositary   The depositary, usually a bank, is responsible for the mechanics of accumulating the tendered securities and the payment for them. From the offeror's perspective, it is extremely important that the depositary is up to date in its records because the determination of whether or not to extend an offer will depend on that data.

Forwarding agent   Usually, the forwarding agent is a bank in the New York area (often in New Jersey to avoid the arguably applicable New York Stock transfer tax) if the depositary is located elsewhere. The forwarding agent has a very limited function: to forward the securities submitted to it to the depositary, keeping track of the raw numbers. Sometimes, the depositary will use its New York City office as the forwarding agent.

Approaching the Target

The days of the blitzkrieg tender are numbered. With the Antitrust Improvements Act of 1976 and state notification statutes, the sudden tender offer completely unknown to management is becoming rare. Given this situation, it nearly always makes sense to have a conversation with the target's management before launching a hostile offer. If the friendly conversation carries the implied threat of a hostile offer, commentators have often referred to it as a "bear hug." The key to the bear hug is that it plays on a recalcitrant company's officers' and board's fiduciary responsibilities to the shareholders to seriously consider the offer. Of course, a serious bidder is in a much stronger position if it already has picked up a block of stock in a private purchase.

Once an offeror has decided to make the appropriate state filings, a press release announcing its intentions is appropriate. However, it may be advisable to issue press releases regarding meetings with the target's management as a strategic ploy. One variant on this technique is to inform the stock exchange of these meetings and have them press for a release from the target. The hope is that the publicity will produce higher trading in the stock placing more shares in the hands of the arbitrageurs. Of course, the risk is that rival bidders will become interested.

The Terms of the Offer

Cash versus securities With the assistance of the dealer-manager, the offeror must necessarily begin the structuring of the offer with an analysis of its own requirements. First, it must decide whether to use an exchange offer with securities or a cash tender offer. Historically, cash offers have been much more sudden and a more effective surprise attack because there was no built-in delay period before the offer could be made; in contrast, securities have to be registered with the SEC. Not only is there delay in getting the SEC to declare the registration effective, but the preparation of the registration statement itself is quite time-consuming. This difference in time factor, although still present, has decreased because of the passage of state tender offer laws and the Antitrust Improvements Act of 1976, both of which may require a notification period before an offer is made.

Of course, there are other fundamental differences between a cash and a securities deal. Some exchange offers, stock for stock, may be tax-free "B" reorganizations if the requisite control is obtained. Cash must be raised; securities merely authorized and issued. By accepting securities, the target company's security holders are necessarily subjecting them-selves to the risks of the acquirer's business.

Obviously, the choice of which securities to issue in an exchange offer is critical and depends on the needs of the acquirer and the target's stock-holders. In the merger boom of the 1960s, it was highly popular to issue convertible subordinated debt on the theory that the additional leverage would increase earnings while not unduly restricting debt capacity. How-ever, in 1969, Section 279 of the Internal Revenue Code was passed. It limits the deductibility of convertible subordinated debt issued in connection with acquisitions for highly levered companies.

If a company's securities are less than blue chip, an exchange offer introduces an additional element of uncertainty into a deal: valuation. Owners of the target's securities may be willing to sell, but not for what they regard as "Chinese paper." Cash results in a simpler deliberative process: Is the price right?

The role of soliciting dealers and arbitrageurs In structuring the offer, the role played by two key groups, the arbitrageurs and the soliciting dealers, must be considered. All brokers who are members of the National Association of Security Dealers (NASD) and certain foreign brokers who have agreed to abide by NASD rules are usually eligible to be soliciting dealers. The function of a soliciting dealer is simple: to try to get as many acceptances of the offer as possible. For every security that a soliciting dealer tenders, a fee is paid, which can range from 0.3 to 2% of the tender price, but averages about 0.8% (25 cents a share on a $30 stock). So when a broker calls up clients telling them to hurry and tender their stock, they should be a little skeptical. The broker is hardly disinterested, but is, rather, a paid agent of the offeror.

Occasionally, offers will attempt to clamp down on soliciting fees. Sometimes there are limits on the payment of fees to soliciting dealers for large blocks. As a practical matter, this often does not work because it is only with the greatest effort that stocks can be traced back to their original beneficial owners. In some cases, companies have totally eliminated the solicitation fee, especially in friendly deals.

Arbitrageurs are middlemen who take positions in a stock being tendered for in the hope that ultimately they can tender it for a handsome profit. These profits are based on two components: (1) the difference between the market price and the tender price and (2) the solicitation fee paid all soliciting dealers. The spread which usually exists between the market price and the tender price, even after the tender has been announced, reflects the risk that not all shares tendered will be accepted. First, there is always the risk of government suit or defensive action by the target company. Second, the terms of the offer may themselves create the risk of nonacceptance by, for example, stating that if a stated minimum number of shares are not tendered, the deal is off or by setting a maximum as to the number of shares which there is a firm commitment to purchase with the possibility of rejection or pro rata purchases above that number.

Arbitrageurs used to hedge against the risk of proration by the practice of short tendering. Essentially, the arbitrageur would tender a greater number of shares than owned by guaranteeing delivery at a future date. Of course, the arbitrageur by short tendering had an increased probability of successfully selling securities in the event of proration; on the other hand, the investing public's chances proportionately decreased. Rule 10b-4 under the 1934 Act, however, now prohibits this practice.

The assumption of arbitrage is that the estimates of the arbitrageurs as to the success of an offer will be better than the general market's evaluation of the risks. In fact, there is some basis for this assumption, for arbitrage is a dangerous but extremely lucrative business. The advantages the arbitrageurs have over the general public are their experience in past, similar situations and the fact that they have a finger on the pulse of market reaction. For example, the arbitrage department of a brokerage house knows how its customers, at least, are reacting to an offer.

Even if there is no gap between the market and the offer price, an arbitrageur can still make money as a soliciting dealer. Although once considered possibly illegal under the federal securities laws, arbitrageurs are now clearly permitted to receive soliciting dealer fees on shares which they purchase according to 1934 Act Release No. 9395, which was issued in 1971. Recently, however, some state authorities have raised questions about the legality of such payments under their tender statutes. Toward the end of tender offers, it is not uncommon to see the market price at a slight premium above the offer. Assuming no reflection of the possibility of a competing bid, this represents the fact that until the market price equals the offer price plus the solicitation fee, the arbitrageurs can earn a profit.

By the end of a successful offer, a large portion of the trading float is in the hands of the arbitrageurs. Thus any offer must be structured to contemplate their needs. In addition, if a competing bid is made, the arbitrageurs often play a decisive role in determining its success.

Minimum requirements and maximum obligations   Given these key actors in tender offers, there are two basic structuring questions: Should there be a minimum requirement below which the offeror is not obligated to buy securities, and should there be a maximum obligation beyond which there is no firm commitment to purchase?

The chief danger of a high minimum is that it may prevent arbitrage. If the market price moves up above its preoffer level, an arbitrageur takes a substantial risk: If the offer fails because the minimum number of shares were not tendered, the price will decline back to its old level. Therefore, arbitrageurs lack an incentive to pick up the float.

On the other hand, there may be advantages to a conditional offer. For example, the market price near the end of a firm commitment offer with no sizable obstacles in sight tends to go above the offer price because of the solicitation fees. This premium market price, it has been argued, may actually discourage the general public from tendering out of anticipation of a potentially higher bid and the thought that the securities can always be sold in the market. With a conditional offer and a market price below the tender price, the public may have more incentive to tender.

Second, there is the risk that without a minimum, the acquirer will become an inadvertent investment company. Under the Investment Company Act of 1940, one definition of an investment company is one which owns investment securities exceeding 40% of its assets; however, securities issued by majority-owned subsidiaries which are not themselves investment companies will not be regarded as investment securities.

If a company is deemed to be an investment company under the Investment Company Act, it must register with the SEC; an unregistered investment company may not legally conduct any business. Thus, there is a serious risk that in certain situations involving a major acquisition, the Investment Company Act will be violated unless there is certainty that the target company will be majority owned. In such situations, a 50% minimum standard is sometimes used in the offer.

Of course, this problem will be inapplicable unless the target is large in comparison to the assets of the offeror. However, it should be noted that often a firm has investment securities other than those of the target company which would be used against it for the 40% test.

A more general problem is simply being stuck with the securities of a company in which the offeror has less than majority control. For example, a hostile offeror with 15% of a target company is in a no man's land. There is no control; indeed, a rival bidder or insider may have a larger block. Yet, the market for resale of such a large block may be illiquid and registration may be required of the securities involved—all in all, not an enviable position. Similarly, a minimum control level may be desired for tax reasons to qualify as a B reorganization or to allow a consolidated return, for accounting purposes or to satisfy loan convenants.

A maximum obligation provision has applicability to an offeror who wants to purchase all the shares of the target for cash. Some firms, however, which ultimately desire full ownership do not wish to pay cash for that total position. Rather, they seek a strong initial position, perhaps majority control, and contemplate the future possibility of, for example, a merger. Also, as discussed under the 1976 Tax Reform Act, a shift in ownership above 60% can reduce the usability of tax-loss carry-overs. When companies tender for their own shares, maximums are almost always stated; unless completely becoming a private company, a firm usually does not want to unduly tighten the public market. It must, however, be remembered that even with a maximum limit on the firm obligation to purchase, the offer usually retains the right, at its·option, to purchase additional securities tendered on a pro rata basis.

Pricing Pricing, whether in terms of cash or the value of the securities being exchanged, is perhaps the most difficult aspect of structuring the deal, and the skills of a sophisticated investment banker are invaluable. Premiums over the market price in tender offers vary from hardly anything to more than 100%. A study by Prof. Fred Ebeid indicates that the median premium for noncontested offers examined was 10.5% and for resisted bids 19.7% in the mid-1970s. Since then, however, the premiums have been rising dramatically. For example, recently, premiums in the vicinity of 90% have been quite common. The most common figures in contested offers have recently been in the neighborhood of 80%. Pricing strategy depends on the facts. Of course, the relationship between the price and the solicitation fee must be carefully examined, as will be discussed. A contested offer with potential rival bidders is likely to result in a higher premium than an uncontested deal. Pricing, then, is meant not only to placate the tendering stockholder but also to preempt a rival from entering into a bidding contest.

Professor Ebeid found that there was no correlation between the level of the premium and whether or not contested offers were successful. This analysis, however, is somewhat misleading because it does not eliminate the possibility that any given offer might have had a different result at varying premium levels.

Pricing strategy is complicated by the possibility of amending an offer. On the face of it, one can test a low bid and always raise it. There are a number of problems with this approach, however. First, there is the possibility an unsuccessful low bid will attract a competing bidder. Related to this problem is the confusion in market perception: It is very difficult to determine, especially in an exchange offer, whether the offer was unsuccessful due to the level of consideration or because of the offeror. Second, the offer may ultimately be more expensive than a well-priced initial offering because of an additional premium which will have to be paid above the initial price, and that higher price under the federal securities laws would have to be paid to all tendering shareholders, even if they tendered under the initial offer.

One common difficulty is the prospect of a tender creating an artificially high price in a thinly traded stock. Despite all precautions, it is not uncommon, especially in friendly tenders, to have the market anticipate a tender. This may not reflect any conspiracy so much as a widely spread analysis that a company is a likely tender target or common knowledge that the target has had many visitors from other companies lately. One tactic in this sort of situation is to let the speculation die down by delaying the offer. Another is to offer at a low premium on the theory that the securities are readily available at that level because the assumed premium is already reflected in the price. One word of warning: If wholesale leaks and tips are obvious, seriously consider holding up the deal and consulting your lawyer. Insider games will only result in much aggravation, bring in the SEC in full force, and may ultimately threaten the success of the offer.

Solicitation fee There is a trade-off between the premium level and the amount of the solicitation fee. If the premium above market is high and the prospects for a successful offer are good, presumably solicitation should be easier, and a relatively lower solicitation fee is warranted. In a few deals, the solicitation fee is even eliminated. Cynics, however, will argue that a cushy solicitation fee is the key to success. Brokers can be quite persuasive when their own money is at stake.

LEGAL LIMITATIONS

Federal Securities Regulation

In reaction to the rising tide of take-overs in the 1960s, Congress adopted the Williams Act in 1968 (named after Senator Harrison Williams) and later amended it to expand its coverage. Today, Sections 13 and 14 under the 1934 Act and the related regulations form an intricate web of restrictions on offers which are an integral factor in structuring a deal.

Section 13(d) is the basic protection against a creeping tender. Within 10 days of acquiring indirect or direct beneficial ownership (the right to determine how securities will be voted) of 5% or more of any class of equity securities, the purchaser must file with the SEC, with the pertinent stock exchange (if the stock is listed), and with the company—a Schedule 13D. This Schedule discloses the manner in which the securities were acquired, the purchaser's future plans regarding the target and the purchaser's background. The statute is broadly worded and interpreted so that the holdings of a group of related purchasers will be aggregated. If there are increases above 2% by a party filing a 13D or material changes in the information disclosed, an amendment is required. The essential point is that initial purchases, even assuming they are not integrated into the tender, have to be less than 5% or within the 10-day lapse period, to avoid full public disclosure of intent before a tender offer is formally announced.

Section 14(d) covers a direct cash tender. When the Williams Act was passed, it was felt that the public needed the same sort of protection on cash offers as was provided in exchange offers through the registration process. Any person making a tender offer which will result in the offeror owning more than 5% of any class of equity security must file a Schedule 14D-1 including all solicitation material with the SEC. If a position of over 5% has been accumulated in the last ten days and a tender offer is being announced, a combined Schedule 13D and 14D-1 is usually filed.

Having required these disclosures, the law attempts to assure their accuracy. Section 14(e) is an antifraud provision which specifically provides that the disclosures required under 14(d) may not contain an untrue statement of a material fact or omit to state a material fact. In addition, Rule 10b-5, the general antifraud provision, is also applicable.

A series of statutory sections and regulations limit the actions of the offeror during the tender. Among the most important of these provisions are the following.

Directors If a majority of the directors of the target company are to be elected or designated other than at a meeting of security holders pursuant to any arrangement or understanding, Rule 14(f)-1 requires a full-fledged proxy statement be transmitted at least 10 days before such persons can take office. The objective is to provide to the public full disclosure about such back-door arrangements.

Other purchases Once an offer is announced, a purchaser may not buy any security subject to the offer except pursuant to its terms. Rule 10b-13 is intended to prevent preferential deals once the tender is underway. Thus, if there is a desire to pick up large private blocks separate from the offer, this must be done before or after the tender, but not during it.

Terms of offers Section 14d contains a number of technical provisions to protect the public as regards the fairness of the terms of the offer. Under Section 14d(5), a person accepting a tender offer may withdraw that acceptance until the expiration of 7 days from the time final copies of the offer are sent to security holders and at any time after 60 days from the date of the original offer. Offers are often kept open longer than 7 days because of state law requirements, or stock exchange rules (the New York Stock Exchange requires 10 days, the American 14). Section 14d(6) provides that if too many securities are tendered for a limited offer, the cutbacks will be pro rata for shares tendered during the first 10 days, and Section 14d(7) stipulates that any increase in the price during a tender shall inure also to the benefit of those who have already tendered. In structuring an offer, care must also be given to the short-term trading-squeeze-out provisions of Section 16(b) of the 1934 Act which have been discussed. Particularly troublesome are extensions after a 10% position has already been acquired and, as discussed, a scoop-up of privately held shares before the tender offer resulting in an over-10% stake.

The SEC has proposed a series of amendments to its rules regarding tender offers. Perhaps, most important is a proposed provision which would make the furnishing of a recent stockholder's list mandatory. In addition, the SEC has proposed a longer withdrawal period, more detailed information from incumbent management defending an offer, and clarification on the point that a short-form ad may be published as to the offer which would inform stockholders where they can get the offering documents.

Margin Rules

The limitations on the financing of securities purchases embodied in the Federal Reserve Board's margin rules are applicable to tender offers. Regulation U restricts the ability of banks to lend money for the purpose of purchasing margin securities which will serve directly or indirectly as the collateral for the loan. For example, a negative pledge, a promise not to make certain uses of the margin securities, sometimes inadvertently constitutes a Regulation U violation. In addition, under Regulation T, brokers may neither lend themselves any money on nonmargin securities or arrange loans on any securities which they cannot lend on. In contested offers, it is especially important that all the nuances of the margin rules be carefully examined because violations are frequently alleged.

Antitrust Notification

As has been discussed, the Antitrust Improvements Act of 1976 requires prenotification to the FTC and the Justice Department under certain circumstances of proposed tender offers for at least 15% or $15 million of the stock of the target firm. The minimum 15-day waiting period imposed by the Act, coupled with the often longer waiting periods under state statutes, has all but eliminated the surprise, short offer for major firms. Of course, many firms are not subject to the provisions of the Act. For example, a concern with $90 million in sales and $50 million in assets bidding for another firm with $50 million in sales and $25 million in assets would not be required to file a notification statement. One of the firms involved must have sales or assets of $100 million or more and the other must have sales or assets of $10 million or more.

State Regulation

An increasingly important role is currently being played by state legislation in the tender offer field. Under pressure from local businesses, state officials reacted to the large number of tenders by passing laws which, in effect, have a delaying impact on hostile tenders. Most of these state statutes are, however, by their terms inapplicable to offers recommended by the target's management.

There are two basic models for these statutes, which have been adopted by over half the states: a pure notification statute such as Delaware's and a registration and hearing procedure law such as Ohio's, Indiana's, and New York's. Under the Delaware procedure, 20 days before the offer commences, the target management must be notified of the intent to make the offer. As a result, sudden surprise attacks against Delaware corporations are a thing of the past. In addition, the Delaware law makes certain disclosure requirements, most of which are satisfied by compliance with federal law. However, Delaware also requires a copy of an offeror's financial statements for the past year to be delivered to the target's management in the event a tender is for less than all the outstanding shares. Since such financials are often not available for two months after the end of a fiscal year, the net effect is to ban limited tenders during that period.

The registration-type statutes are more complicated. If an offer is not recommended by incumbent management, a detailed registration statement must be submitted to the state authorities, and hearings may be held regarding the offer. In some states, such as New York, the pertinent state official decides whether or not to hold the hearings. In others, such as Idaho, a hearing must be held if demanded by the target's board of directors. Delaware claims jurisdiction only over companies incorporated under its laws; Ohio is far bolder, asserting jurisdiction over companies which have "substantial assets" within the state if they also have a "principal place of business" within the state. Ohio has interpreted these phrases rather broadly so that any firm having material contacts with that state may well be deemed to be covered by that statute. Indiana asserts jurisdiction if a corporation is either organized in the state or has its principal place of business or a substantial portion of its total assets there. Some states also assert jurisdiction if a certain number of stockholders of the target reside there. For example, Arkansas claims jurisdiction over all offers to companies with more than thirty-five Arkansas residents as shareholders.

There are many common problems as to these state filings. First, inconsistent as it may seem, states may assert that a corporation has more than one "principal place of business." Therefore, a company with executive offices in New York, may still be deemed to have its "principal place of business" in Ohio. Second, the meaning of substantial assets is also most unclear. Third, the relevance of the state of incorporation of subsidiaries is an issue which is just beginning to emerge. Fourth, if there is a hearing, the determination of "fairness" is most elusive. Fifth, once caught in the web of the state registration and hearing process, it may take months to emerge. Every time a material amendment is made in reaction to comments, the time periods usually begin to run again. In addition, the comments of the various states may well be inconsistent.

Often, these statutes do not seem to be applicable, but the situation is gray. The nonfiler then takes the risk that in a contested offer, the target company will raise the filing issue as a defense, which will result, anyway, in a time delay.

Serious questions have been raised as to whether these state statutes are preempted by federal securities laws and whether the states' attempt to stretch their jurisdiction is unconstitutional. The SEC and at least one court have taken this position. For now, however, a state-by-state analysis (based on the descriptions in the target's 10-K) of whether the local statutes are applicable and what their requirements are is imperative for any successful offer.

Mechanically, if a state statute is applicable, an announcement is usually made of the intention to make an offer, subject to compliance with the applicable state requirements. A Schedule 14D-1 is filed with the proposed form of offer, which is amended and updated before the actual offer is made. No solicitations of tenders may take place during this period.

The Chris Craft Litigation

The 1977 Supreme Court decision in *Piper v. Chris Craft* illustrates the pitfalls of a contested offer and the changing status of the law in the field. In 1968, Chris Craft began making purchases of Piper Aircraft stock and made friendly overtures to Piper management. The Piper family, however, opposed the Chris Craft offer and exchanged their 31% stock interest in Piper Aircraft for stock of Bangor Punta Corporation, a rival bidder. As part of that deal, Bangor Punta agreed to make an exchange offer to gain control of Piper. In addition to the Piper family block, Bangor Punta also made three block purchases of about 7% of the Piper stock from institutional investors. In the end, Bangor Punta emerged with 50% of the Piper stock and Chris Craft 42%.

The contested offer brought about a host of litigation. After a series of reversals, a circuit appeals court held that Bangor Punta and its investment banker were liable for over $36 million in damages to Chris Craft. The award was granted on the basis of alleged market manipulation in purchasing the institutional blocks of stock and the making of a misleading statement as to the value of a railroad subsidiary of Bangor.

This dramatic award of the circuit court was, however, reversed by the Supreme Court. After an extensive review of the Williams Act, the court held that a rival bidder does not have standing to sue for a damages recovery under the fraud provision of the Williams Act, Section 14(e). The Court held that the purpose of the Williams Act was to protect investors confronted with a tender offer—not competing bidders. As a result of the *Chris Craft* case, civil liabilities due to rivals in a tender battle is not any longer an effective deterrent to the making of offers. One by-product of this situation is that the SEC may intervene more actively in offers in the future to fill the policing vacuum created by the Chris Craft holding.

KEY DOCUMENTS

State Filings

If a state law such as Delaware's requires notification to incumbent management, a very brief letter will suffice, attached to which can be the draft of the terms of the offer. In other states such as New York and Ohio, a registration statement on file with the state authorities is required although cross-references can be made to the 14D-1. In either event, the offeror can file simultaneously a Schedule 14D-1 announcing a present intent to make an offer at a stated price at a specified future date. When the actual offer is made after the notification period has run, an amended 14D-1 will be filed.

Schedule 14D-1

The Schedule 14D-1 which is filed contains the following information:

1. The name and address of the issuer, the title of the securities to which the statement relates, the amount of securities being sought, the price being offered, and the quarterly high and low sales prices for such securities in their principal trading market for the past two years

2. The name and business address or residence of each of the officers and directors of the offeror, their jobs over the past 5 years, the names and addresses of the places where employed and whether there were any criminal convictions or any violations of the securities laws over the past 5 years

3. Any transactions (including contracts) between the bidder and the target in an amount greater than 1% of the target's revenues or between the bidder and the target's officers or directors exceeding $40,000

4. Any contacts, negotiations, or transactions in the past 3 years between the bidder and the target concerning a merger, tender offer, sale of assets, or election of directors

5. The source and amounts of the funds being used for the offer, containing a description of any borrowing in connection with the deal (with the name of the bank kept confidential, if so requested)

6. The purpose of the offer, including any plans to acquire control, liquidate, sell the assets or merge the target, or to make other major changes in the business or corporate structure of the target, including any changes in dividend policy, capitalization, directors or listing of securities

7. The shares owned of the target by the officers and directors of the offeror and their associates and any trading done within the past 60 days

8. A description of contracts or understandings with any person regarding the securities

9. All persons retained to make solicitations for the securities and the terms of their employment

10. Any other material relationships between the bidder and the target and a description of any regulatory requirements, the applicability of the margin and antitrust laws and of any material pending legal proceedings relating to the offer

In addition, exhibits must be filed of all soliciting materials (ads, the Offer to Purchase, and related documents).

The major disclosure problems posed by these requirements will be discussed in connection with the description of the Offer to Purchase. Most of this information is either lifted from the Offer to Purchase or a cross-reference is made to it except for some of the background information on officers and directors. Curiously, the most difficult information to assemble for a 14D-1 is the most irrelevant: the employment records and various addresses required for officers and the directors. Many lawyers have discovered to their chagrin that some lead time is needed to assemble that information; you simply cannot find the address of a company for which an officer worked four years ago the night before the offer is to be announced when the officer is camping out in Yellowstone Park.

The Offer to Purchase

The actual offer to holders of the target's securities is not made through the 14D-1, but rather through an Offer to Purchase, which is mailed directly to the record holders. Traditionally, the Offer to Purchase has also been published in full in national newspapers, usually taking two to three full pages. Smaller ads may be used if a full Offer to Purchase is available. The names of the record holders are sometimes available from the target company under state laws, but because the record holders are often brokerage houses holding securities in street name for accounts and also to give notice to the market generally, the ads are thought to be necessary.

Rule 14d-1(c) states that all Offers to Purchase must state the following information:

- the name of the person making the tender
- the exact dates prior to which and after which persons tendering can withdraw their securities
- the date up to which purchases will be made pro rata, in the case of tender for a limited number of shares
- all the material information required for the Schedule 14D-1 other than the previous occupations for the past 5 years of the officers and directors of the offeror

The first part of the Offer to Purchase usually deals with the terms of the offer, including the price, and if applicable, the minimum shares required, the maximum commitment, the withdrawal dates, the date through which the proration obligation applies and the mechanics for tendering. Care must be taken in this section to state explicitly that the offer may be extended or amended.

General information is then provided about the offeror and the target. Although not required by Schedule 14D-1, the cases seem to indicate that this sort of disclosure is necessary. In most instances, the information about the target is quite simple. As explicitly stated in the Offer to purchase, the information is based on the publicly available filings of the target, particularly the Forms 10-K and 10-Q and the annual and quarterly reports to shareholders. The description is usually quite terse, consisting of brief capsule financial information, a summary description of the business lifted from the 10-K, and sometimes a quote from incumbent management about the company's prospects.

If the offeror, however, has any nonpublicly available information from the target such as projections, the situation becomes quite messy. To avoid liability for the failure to state a material fact, such material, even including projections, must be disclosed, although a disclaimer is usually put in stating that the offeror cannot attest to the information's accuracy. There is much to be said for deliberately avoiding knowledge of such inside information: The problems caused by its disclosure, including the possible reflection of those disclosed projections in a higher market price, often outweigh the utility of the information.

The description of the offeror is more sensitive because the depth of knowledge is obviously greater. Capsule descriptions are, again, generally used, but material facts not yet publicly available should be reflected. If the offeror is a foreign company, the disclosures become more extensive. For example, if the foreign accounting practices differ from generally accepted American accounting principles, the approximate aggregate effect of those differences should be disclosed. In addition, if public information is not readily available about an offeror, it should indicate where such supplemental material would be obtainable. Often, in fact, annual reports of foreign concerns are filed with the SEC for this purpose. In addition, as discussed, Schedule 14D-1 requires the financial statements of the foreign or private bidder.

Among the most difficult sections of the Offer to Purchase are those dealing with the purpose of the offer and the future plans of the offeror. The instinct of most offerors is to be as vague as possible. Although understandable, this tactic may be quite dangerous. Schedule 14D-1 specifically requires a detailed statement as to these items, and Section 14d-1(c) mandates that they be included in the Offer to Purchase. Unlike the rather cursory general financial disclosures, courts have been insistent that the description of future intent be specific, particularly in the case of offers for less than all the shares.

The judicial theory on a limited offering seems to be that there will necessarily be a continuing relationship between the stockholders who do not sell and the offeror, which requires full disclosure. However, logically even in an offer for all shares, security holders have a right to know what is the offeror's intent as to untendered shares and what will happen to the company if they remain shareholders.

Curiously, the impact of full disclosure may well help the offeror. By logic, the more negative the disclosures, the more stockholders should want to sell. The risk then to the offeror is less from revealing plans to pillage the company than from attempting to hide them.

The most pertinent question regarding future intent is whether there is a desire for control and whether there will be a merger in the future if control is achieved. To indicate the particularity of the courts on this question, one case, *Missouri Portland Cement,* actually stands for the proposition that an offeror for 50% of the outstanding stock should have explicitly stated that the purpose of the offer was control. Similarly, if the primary purpose of the offer is to frustrate the take-over by another party in a defensive alliance, full disclosure must be made.

Perhaps, the most difficult disclosure situation occurs when the offeror's management has studied a series of options but has not made any definitive commitment. In the *Otis* case, the court held that a plan should be disclosed if there was evidence of its adoption, explicit or implicit, by high corporate officers. For example, in *Otis,* a study was presented to the board of directors regarding a tender offer followed by a merger. The board explicitly approved the tender but did not act on the merger; however, the court held that the merger possibility should have been described. On the other hand, some courts have recognized that the purposes point has become a key target for dilatory litigation by target companies, and they have discounted the protestations of incumbent management accordingly.

Arrangements or understandings regarding the company's securities are often very simple to describe: there are none. Sometimes, however, there are options regarding the holdings of large holders or voting-trust agreements, and these, of course, must be fully described.

If there are any particular regulatory hurdles to implementation of a possible plan, they should be set out. Among the classic problems are foreign companies bidding for firms with radio licenses or defense contracts. Even though the licenses or the contracts may be only a small part of the target company's business, they may not be assignable to a foreign corporation. Therefore, the possibility that the target may lose some business or a license must be spelled out.

Similarly, if any other governmental approvals are required, including those of foreign governments (Canadian approval has often been a subject of contention) disclosure is required. In addition, the antitrust status of the transaction should be indicated: Was clearance sought; were any antitrust difficulties expected; was there notification under the Antitrust Improvements Act of 1976? The implications of the offer, if any, on the listing status of the target company's stock on the exchange on which the stock is traded should also be described.

The following clauses are typical of the way some of these disclosure problems are handled:

Tender period "The Purchaser will purchase all shares properly tendered at or prior to 5:00 P.M., New York City time, on January 11, 1978. The purchaser reserves the right to extend the offer by notice to the Depositary. Tenders are irrevocable except that shares tendered may be withdrawn, prior to 5:00 P.M., New York City time, on January 16, 1978, and unless theretofore purchased may also be withdrawn after March 2, 1978."

Basis for information about target "The following summary contains financial information taken from the 1976 10-K, which contained audited financial statements, and the September 1977 10-Q, which contains unaudited financial information. Such summary is qualified by reference to such reports and the financial information contained therein."

Inside information "The Purchaser has had various discussions with certain directors and major stockholders of the Company and received the following information from them: . . . The Purchaser takes no responsibility for the accuracy or completeness of this information."

Purpose "The Purchaser's objective in making the Offer is to acquire sufficient Shares to obtain control of the Company and eventually possibly 100% of the Shares. If the Purchaser acquires less than all of the outstanding Shares, it may acquire additional Shares following the expiration of the Offer through private purchases, market transactions or a subsequent tender or exchange offer. In addition, the Purchaser may seek to acquire the Company's assets (followed by a liquidation of the Company) or to effect a merger or similar combination with the Company."

Regulatory hurdles "Based on its examination of publicly available filings with the Commission, the Purchaser is not aware of any licenses or regulatory permits which appear to be material to the business of the Company except possibly the following:"

Sources of funds "Any funds required by the Purchaser will be borrowed from the XYZ Bank pursuant to an existing unsecured line of credit for $100 million which is presently available for borrowing at the prime rate."

Delisting "Published guidelines of the New York Stock Exchange, Inc., indicate that such Exchange would consider delisting the Shares if the number of publicly held Shares were less than 600,000, if there were fewer than 1,200 holders of 100 or more Shares (round lot holders) or if the market value of the publicly held Shares did not exceed $5,000,000."

Dealer-Manager Agreement

A Dealer-Manager Agreement is relatively simple and is mainly concerned with fees and indemnification. The basic compensation structure of the Dealer-Manager Agreement has already been discussed: There is a minimum guaranteed fee and a flat payment for success or a commission for each tendered share, and a participation in solicitation fees. Indemnification provisions are usually broad. Despite their simplicity, the lawyers seem to manage to squabble about these documents. In particular, the legal opinions and the scope of indemnification often raise questions. A dealer-manager should, however, insist on the right to approve all offering documents before they are used and should try to get the offeror's attorneys to indicate that to their knowledge, there are no material errors or omissions in the offer. Similarly, a dealer-manager should ask for as broad representations as possible.

If state filings or notification under the Antitrust Improvements Act is required, the dealer-manager for a proposed offer is often indemnified for any liability in a side letter before the dealer-manager agreement is executed at the time the actual offer is made. Alternatively, the dealer-manager agreement is executed at the time the proposed offer is announced.

Other Documents

Letter of transmittal and guarantee form The Letter of Transmittal is the form which accompanies tender shares. Usually standardized in its provisions, the information contained in it assists the depository and the offeror in keeping track of the progress of the offer. Some offers contain a separate guarantee of delivery form which brokers can sign when shares are being submitted at a later date.

The letter to brokers and dealers Another standard form addressed to brokers informs them of the solicitation fee and the procedure to be followed in response to the offer.

"To our customers" letter The offeror provides a form letter to be sent by the brokers to their customers explaining procedures.

Note to convertible security holders In case there are convertible security holders, a card is sent attached to the Offer to Purchase advising them of the offer.

State letters A broker has to attach a brief cover letter to the offer in several states such as Indiana and Ohio because a corporation can not make the offer itself. In addition, no offer can be made in Wisconsin without a simple filing in that state.

REACTING TO A TENDER

Although the incumbent management of a company may well treasure its independence for its own sake, both officers and directors have a duty to act in the best interests of the shareholders. However, it is also arguable that making a tender difficult militates in favor of a consensual deal at a higher price. For example, Prof. Ebeid concluded in his study that 42% of the resisted bids involved some litigation and that 68.4% of the contested bids which were litigated were unsuccessful. This lack of success was due less to victory in litigation that to the extra time it gives management to build its defense and, if desired, find an alternative bidder with a better deal. However, management often seems more preoccupied with its own prerogatives than with the welfare of the shareholders. But being too overt about self-protection can be quite dangerous: sensitivity, discretion, and a sense of how actions may appear in hindsight are advised.

On the other hand, management should realize that it may have potential liability if it does not resist tender offers which it believes are not in the best interests of the stockholders. This problem is particularly pertinent in situations where management has been offered some incentive to favor the deal not available to the public shareholders, such as favorable employment contracts. As an exercise in prudence, it is therefore useful for management to attempt to document the basis for its position.

Preoffer Tactics

The best time to fight a tender offer is before it begins, and the best tactic is good management and a high stock price. Nevertheless, there is a standard grab bag of tactics which can aid a defense.

Essentially, the preoffer strategy is to determine whether the company is a likely tender target and to try to fashion some characteristics which will make the likely target less attractive. Among the common maneuvers are the following:

- Stagger election terms to the board of directors. The theory is that the potential offeror would realize that even if effective control were obtained, it would be some time before it could be completely exercised. Care must be taken that the Certificate and state law do not permit a majority holder to bring about a new election for directors.

- Execute long-term employment contracts with key management. Other than feathering the nests of the incumbents, this again limits the flexibility of the potential offeror.

- Adopt certificate provisions requiring high votes for mergers. If a two-step merger is being contemplated, these provisions obviously make the procedure more difficult.

- Have authorized but unissued stock available. If stock is not authorized, management probably will not have time to enter into a defensive deal. With the unissued stock readily available, there are a number of potential possibilities—among them, sale of the stock to a friendly investor or its use in an acquisition of a firm controlled by a sympathizer. Some recent court decisions, however, have held that this was a misleading tactic.

- Keep a current list of potential investors, possible acquisitions, and merger candidates. Although it should not appear that a tender situation is the only reason for compiling such information, it is perfectly legitimate for a company to keep track of this sort of information, especially if it periodically does make a deal.

- Conduct activities in areas requiring regulatory approval. If a firm is doing defense business or has a radio license, the range of difficulties to an offeror is increased.

- Become subject to a tough state tender statute. Even without reincorporation in such a state, doing a sizable amount of business in a state such as Ohio may subject an offer to the local tender laws if it is arguable that the company's "principal place of business" is located there.

- Attempt to structure in antitrust problems for likely offerors. Since antitrust is one of the most common defenses in a tender, it is logical to attempt to build in a conflict with an unwanted offeror. Of course, this all assumes that the identity of a potential offeror can be discerned in advance. Sometimes this is possible; for example, when the potential offeror already owns a block of stock and has expressed interest in more. Management should use this tactic, however, only with the greatest of caution. With hindsight, making an ill-considered acquisition just to perpetuate incumbent management will look like a terrible decision.

- Keep the pension plan under tight control and have it purchase company stock. In essence, this keeps a large block of stock in friendly hands.

- Enter into contracts conditional on no changes in control. If any of these are major, it raises key disclosure and financial problems for the offeror.

- Boost the dividend rate. The hope is that the increase will raise the stock price or create more loyalty in the stockholders. Whether this appraisal is realistic depends on the facts of the situation.

- Establish an early warning system for tender offers. A daily review of trading in the company's stock to pick up any unusual activity is necessary, as well as periodic examination of the stockholder list. Because an offeror may acquire stock in a nominee name, these procedures are not foolproof, but often even the accumulation of less than 5% of the outstanding stock can represent a large percentage of the trading float, with resulting disturbances in the market. Perhaps the best device is regular checking with friendly institutional investors and traders who, from past experience, will often be able to detect unusual patterns. Of course, soon after 5% ownership is achieved, 13D's will be filed with the SEC.

- Develop a contingency defense plan. The development of a contingent defense plan is a difficult and controversial tactic. Some experts feel that it may well backfire in litigation indicating the premeditated recalcitrance of management. But realistically and historically, a strong defense has been possible only by a prepared team. The new state laws giving the target advance notice of the offer relieve the pressure somewhat, but not enough to completely vitiate the utility of some advance planning. First, the assembly of a possible defense team is necessary. In addition to counsel, an investment banker should be consulted, since the target company may well want an independent appraisal of the offer. Second, the mechanics for evaluating an offer should be anticipated: How will the board of directors be convened; will an evaluation be necessary; who will have particular responsibilities, etc.? It is vital that directors become sensitized to their responsibilities and realize their flexibility. An unsophisticated board is the weakest link in a defense. Third, a company may wish a blueprint for action in the event a tender is not acceptable. Some companies feel that draft press releases and letters to stockholders should be prepared in advance; most experts today feel that this "black bag" approach which was popular in the 1960s is now outdated and quite risky. It could be alleged that there was a lack of interest in the well-being of stockholders because it looks like any offer would be rejected, whether or not the acceptance of the offer was in the best interest of the stockholders.

■ Start using up excess cash. A company with excess cash is a prime target. Building up inventory, making capital investments, and paying off debt are all legitimate expenditures which make the target less attractive. Making sensible acquisitions for cash lowers liquidity and boosts earnings and, hopefully, a company's stock price. Otherwise, in effect, the offeror will use the target's cash to pay off the cost of the acquisition.

■ Develop effective public and stockholder relations programs. Effective publicity and knowledgeable stockholders may solidify a weak stock price.

■ Commence a stock-purchasing plan. Regular stock purchases absorb the float and help keep up the stock price.

The difficulty with many of these strategies is that they can easily backfire. Long-term contracts entrench management, regardless of competence; contracts conditional on control give enormous leverage to customers or suppliers; antitrust and regulatory problems may well block a favorable, as well as an unfavorable, deal. In addition, of course, none of these defense measures purports to be foolproof. The practical effect may be limited to raising the probability of a consensual deal.

Actions during the Tender

Recommendations Under Rule 14d-4, management must file a Schedule 14D if it recommends the acceptance or rejection of an offer. The Schedule 14D is quite simple; its main question is what was the basis of any recommendation. In the event of a surprise tender, however, Rule 14d-2(f) does permit management to urge security holders to defer any decision until management has had an opportunity to study the situation. Care should be taken that management in its enthusiasm does not make a material misstatement in its recommendation. Usually, the recommendation is mailed in a letter to stockholders and sometimes published in ads.

Litigation If a tender is unacceptable, the offer is often litigated as has been discussed. Most commonly the issues raised are the completeness of the disclosures (including an inadequate description of the purpose of the offer, the purchaser's intentions, the financing of the offer, confidential information received, regulatory hurdles, and the purchaser's past transactions in the target's stock), possible antitrust violations, and the lack of appropriate state filings. In order to get a preliminary injunction against an offer, there must be a finding of serious and irreparable harm, as well as a demonstration of the probability of ultimate success on the substantive issues raised. Thus, for example, if an antitrust point is raised, the burden is heavier on the target company than if the same suit were brought by the government after the acquisition was consummated. Furthermore, even if there is a litigation victory as to a disclosure point, the remedy is to redraft the offer. The deal is stalled—not stopped. A litigation defense, therefore, has its limits, but as has been pointed out, it does buy time and that opportunity for financial maneuvering may be critical for defeating an offer.

Paying for a Defense

The issue of whether management should be able to use corporate funds to defend against a tender offer has never been fully explored. As a rough rule of thumb, expenditures which are overtly for the purpose of perpetuating management in office are not legitimately payable by the target; costs related to some corporate policy are, however, compensable by the firm. These principles, derived from proxy contest litigation, are neat theoretically, but without much practical application. Any defense may be expressed in policy terms; whether that is form or substance is another question. Generally, not only has well-advised management been able to get the corporation to pay the expenses of a defense, but the target itself has received an ordinary tax deduction for these payments.

UNIQUE ASPECTS OF EXCHANGE OFFERS

The key differences between a cash tender and an exchange offer are the implications derived from the involvement of securities. The securities must be registered—a time-consuming process. The content of the registration statement itself must include all the information required by the applicable SEC form. However, Rule 434B also requires that the registration statement contain all the information required by Rule 14d-1(c) for inclusion in tender offers. In effect, the registration statement is a combined prospectus and an Offer to Purchase. A Schedule 14D-1 need not be filed under Section 13(d)(6) because a registration statement is being filed.

One recurrent problem is whether publicity regarding the offer is permissible before the registration statement becomes effective. Rule 135 states that limited announcements will not be registered as offers under the 1933 Act and permits the potential offeror to give notice that it intends to make an offer, including a description of the securities being registered and the basis upon which the exchange may be made. Despite the seeming clarity of 135, target companies often claim that the offeror's preregistration announcements were too broad and do not comply with the restrictions in the Rule. The most difficult problem is valuation. In order to make its proposal meaningful, the offeror usually thinks it must place a value on the securities being offered. On the other hand, such an appraisal is necessarily subjective and difficult to evaluate without a full registration statement regarding the security and the issuer.

ISSUERS REPURCHASING THEIR OWN SHARES

In recent years, it has become increasingly common for corporations to repurchase their securities both through the public market and through tender offers. The motivations for repurchases can vary widely. Some companies are anxious to soak up the float to avoid tenders. Others are merely trying to boost the stock price, and then there are firms attempting to "go private" at bargain prices in bear markets. The "going private" situation will be discussed in the next section.

The SEC has broad powers to regulate repurchases, but few rules have been adopted so far. Rule 13e-1 prohibits repurchases during tender offers by other parties. In addition, Rule 10b-6, which makes it unlawful for any participant in the distribution of securities, including an issuer, to purchase any securities of that class during the distribution, is pertinent in two respects. First, a company cannot hype a stock price during the registration of securities. Second, because technically a convertible security is perpetually in the process of distributing the underlying stock, a firm can't make repurchases when it has outstanding convertibles without an SEC exemption. As a matter of fact, the SEC grants the exemptions as a matter of course if certain criteria listed in proposed Rule 13e-2 are met and has proposed a rule automatically exempting repurchases complying with these criteria.

Proposed Rule 13e-2 addresses the question of how much stock can be purchased in the market without, in effect, manipulating the price. Before it was proposed, state and federal courts had a difficult time in determining whether stock repurchases were violations of fiduciary duty by bolstering the positions of management at general corporate expense and were a fraud on the purchasing public. The key provision of Rule 13e-2 is that the amount of securities purchased on any one day on a national securities exchange does not exceed 15% of the average daily trading volume in the preceding 4 weeks.

In December 1977, the SEC proposed Rule 13e-4 to regulate issuers' tender or exchange offers for their own securities. Under 13e-4, public companies would be required to have offers for their securities remain open for at least 15 business days. Security holders could withdraw their tenders during the first 10 days of the offer or, if the securities are not accepted, after 40 business days from the commencement date.

THE "GOING PRIVATE" PROBLEM

One of the most controversial areas of corporate finance law in the mid-1970s has been the ability of firms whose securities are held by public stockholders to become again privately held concerns. The "going private" issue arises in two contexts, incumbent management buying in shares and acquirers or insiders trying to eliminate dissident minorities by a merger.

With the drop in market prices in the early 1970s, some firms which went public at high prices during the 1960s, such as some advertising agencies, made controversial offers for their shares in the 1970s. Although the going-private-by-tender route has generally escaped sanction, there have been flurries of litigation, and the SEC did propose special "going private" rules in November of 1977 which, though not adopted, generated much heated discussion.

Under the SEC's proposed Rule 13e-3, a company or an affiliated corporation would not be allowed to purchase or make a tender offer for such company's stock which would cause a delisting from a national exchange, eligibility to delist from the reporting requirements under the 1934 Act, or loss of its over-the-counter quotation, unless specified requirements are met, including a fairness test. This test is based on multiple criteria, such as disinterested director approval, purpose of the transaction, financial considerations, and the adequacy of the representation of the independent shareholders. In addition, a filing on a proposed schedule and a waiting period prior to the effectuation of the transaction is required. The Schedule includes similar descriptions contained in Schedule 14D-1, any fairness opinion, and an opinion as to the legality of the deal.

The second type of "going private" situation, relates to the attempt to eliminate minority shareholders by merger. If a tender offer is successful and the offeror obtains control, it still has the problem of dealing with the remaining stockholders. The traditional approach has been a merger of the target into the offeror or one of its subsidiaries. Similarly, if insiders wanted to eliminate a minority, they could merge the company into another firm controlled by the insider group. The mechanics of these transactions work quite smoothly. For example, if more than 90% of the target's stock is owned by the offeror, the procedure in Delaware is simple. As has been discussed, the short-form merger may be used: Two companies may be merged without any stockholder vote required. If less than 90% of the stock is owned, a standard-merger procedure must be followed, and in Delaware, for example, 50% approval of stockholders is required.

In essence, this two step-process—tender, then merger—has a cramdown effect on dissident shareholders, although, as has been discussed, there is often an appraisal remedy. There is, however, little power to fight the merger itself.

In the mid-1970s, some court cases cast doubt upon the efficacy of the two-step merger when there was no legitimate business purpose for the transaction other than the elimination of a minority interest. The theory of these decisions was that the cram-down was inherently manipulative and, therefore, a violation of Rule 10b-5.

However, in the landmark 1977 decision, *Green v. Santa Fe Industries,* the Supreme Court held that a going private, freeze-out merger did not violate the federal securities laws. The Court's findings overturned a federal appeals court decision that a merger which eliminated minority shareholders violated Rule 10b-5 if there were no legitimate corporate purpose, even though there was full disclosure and compliance with all requirements of state law. In the Green situation, Sante Fe Industries acquired 60% of the Kirby Lumber Corporation in 1936 and, over the years, increased its control to 95%. Finally, in 1974, wishing to acquire 100% of Kirby, Sante Fe used the Delaware short-form merger procedure to freeze out the minority holders. The minority complained, among other things, that the cash being given to them for their shares was far below the value of their securities.

The *Green* holding is consistent with the Supreme Court's recent tendency to cut back on expansive readings of the federal securities laws. If the appeals court decision had been affirmed, the ground would have been set for a wide-ranging attack on the fairness of corporate transactions, even though they complied with state requirements. As the Court stated,

> Absent a clear indication of congressional intent, we are reluctant to federalize the substantial portion of the law of corporations that deals with transactions in securities, particularly where established state policies of corporate regulation would be overridden. . . . There may well be a need for uniform federal fiduciary standards to govern mergers such as that challenged in this

complaint. But those standards should not be supplied by judicial extension of section 10(b) and Rule 10b-5 to cover the corporate universe.*

In the wake of the *Green* decision, the SEC and the state courts have taken a more vigorous role in going private situations. A series of 1977 Delaware cases have established that a proper business purpose is required for a short- or long-form merger. In addition, it should be noted that proposed Rule 13e-3 would apply to these second-step mergers. Thus this area remains in flux and will be a point of controversy for the foreseeable future.

*Sante Fe Industries, Inc. v. Green, Supreme Court (March 23, 1977).

Bankruptcy Law

*Bankruptcy is perhaps the greatest and most humiliating
calamity which can befall an innocent man. The greater
part of men, therefore, are sufficiently careful to avoid it.
Some, indeed, do not avoid it; as some do not avoid the
gallows.*

—ADAM SMITH, *The Wealth of Nations* (1776)

*In addition to wiping out debt, bankruptcy proceedings are
carefully contrived to see that whatever assets are available
are distributed fairly. But in practice, the assets serve
essentially as a reservoir for the enrichment of a select
group of professionals—lawyers, accountants,
auctioneers, appraisers, et al.*

—SIDNEY RUTBERG, *Ten Cents on the Dollar:
The Bankruptcy Game* (Simon & Schuster, 1973)

SEVENTEEN

Bankruptcies
and Reorganizations

THE BANKRUPTCY ACT

In the boom years of the 1960s, bankruptcy law was of little interest to professionals in the corporate finance field. After all, other than "ma and pa" operations and garment center speculations as to next year's look, businesses simply didn't go bankrupt. Today, in the wake of Penn Central, W. T. Grant, Equity Funding, and countless real estate investment trusts, the situation has changed dramatically; knowledge of the bankruptcy and reorganization field is an imperative.

Beyond insights into how to handle a situation in an actual bankruptcy proceeding, however, a knowledge of the fundamentals of the bankruptcy and reorganization process gives an invaluable perspective for the handling of legal risk. After all, all the covenants and security devices found in standard legal instruments are designed to protect the investor in the event a deal turns sour. In essence, they are designed to reduce the downside risk. All too often, these provisions are relied upon without a sense of the practicalities of the bankruptcy process. Reams of paper can be quite valueless if the provisions in them do not work.

Under the Constitution, Congress has the power to establish uniform laws on bankruptcy. Until 1898, federal bankruptcy statutes were short-lived. However, that year a new federal bankruptcy act was passed and as amended, principally by the Chandler Act of 1938, is the governing statute today.

Under the Bankruptcy Act, there are three basic forms of bankruptcy which are the basic concern in the corporate finance field: straight bankruptcy and two procedures which contemplate the continued operation of the bankrupt, an arrangement of unsecured creditors under Chapter XI and a reorganization of secured and unsecured debt under Chapter X. In addition, recently Chapter XII, dealing with certain real estate arrangements, and Section 77, which covers railroad reorganizations such as the initial Penn Central situation, have also received attention, although they are beyond the scope of this book.

Bankruptcy law is a specialized field, with practices differing substantially from other federal laws. Under the Bankruptcy Act, federal district courts are considered bankruptcy courts. Many of the day-to-day decisions in a bankruptcy are made by bankruptcy referees, who are appointed for 6-year terms by the district judges and are themselves referred to as "bankruptcy judges." The decisions of a bankruptcy judge are appealable to the district court. In examining the law applicable to any of these proceedings, it is necessary to examine the Bankruptcy Act, the General Orders and Forms, which are rules and forms promulgated by the Supreme Court to implement the Bankruptcy Act, and the local rules of the pertinent federal district court, which can differ in important respects from district to district.

STRAIGHT BANKRUPTCY

Straight, or ordinary, bankruptcy involves the liquidation of the bankrupt corporation. The bankruptcy proceedings either can be initiated by the corporation itself voluntarily filing a petition with a federal district court, or can be made by certain creditors filing an involuntary petition if the corporation owes $1000 or more.

In order to force a corporation involuntarily into bankruptcy, three or more of its creditors, each of whom must have a claim for $500 above the value of the security they hold, (other than employees, stockholders, directors, or officers of the corporation) must sign the petition, unless there is a total of less than twelve creditors, in which case one such creditor may file. The involuntary petition must allege the commission of an act of bankruptcy within the last 4 months. Although seemingly simple, if a corporation is determined to fight bankruptcy proceedings, an involuntary petition can become quite a complicated imbroglio, centering around the question of whether an act of bankruptcy was ever committed.

Why should a corporation which seems to be doing badly fight bankruptcy? First, there is always the hope that with a little more time, everything will work out. This is not necessarily pie-in-the-sky optimism; it may have a rational basis.

There are, however, less obvious motivations. For example, it is possible that the owners of a business, realizing its ultimate failure, will want to run it for as long as possible to keep collecting their salaries. Or perhaps, the owners are feeding the assets out to affiliates at bargain rates, an old trick in the garment-business rackets. More honestly, an owner may fight a petition in order to have bargaining leverage with the creditors—maybe the creditors will extend the corporation more time or money or allow a reorganization instead of a liquidation.

For example, take a toy manufacturing company which a year ago had $100,000 in assets and $50,000 in senior debts when it received an unsecured subordinated loan for $25,000. The loan looked relatively solid at the time, with a cushion of some $25,000 in assets. But say that in the past year the company has lost some $30,000. Although this year the firm is optimistic, it is currently having problems paying its bills. The subordinated lender realizes that if bankruptcy proceedings were filed, it would be quite lucky to receive on a liquidation basis any money at all. Sure, it has a theoretical right to claims of $20,000 ($70,000 in assets today with senior claims of $50,000), but assets in bankruptcies usually are worth a fraction of their replacement or accounting values. So, the subordinated lender encourages the manufacturer to stay in business, hoping that things will turn around. The senior creditors, meanwhile, have decided that bankruptcy would best protect their position. They recognize that the manufacturer could well have a good year, but estimate that they will receive 100 cents on the dollar with a bankruptcy now, while if the manufacturer continues operations, it is possible that last year's performance could be repeated.

So fights over involuntary petitions can arise from numerous causes, and the law is complicated enough that motivated parties can easily find technicalities to squabble over, including whether an act of bankruptcy was committed.

The Six Acts of Bankruptcy

The transfer or concealment of property to defraud creditors As a practical matter this ground is rarely used, since the facts are difficult to ascertain or prove and solvency is a defense.

The preference of a creditor during insolvency If the corporation, while insolvent, transfers property to a creditor on the basis of prior debt, putting that creditor in a relatively preferred position, an act of bankruptcy has been committed. Note that the preferred treatment has to be made in relation to a prior, or antecedent, debt. If the corporation pays a creditor for goods and services being currently provided, it is not a preference. This is quite a frequently used act of bankruptcy, since such preferences are frequent, and insolvency, defined generally in the Bankruptcy Act to be when property is not at fair valuation sufficient to pay debts, need not, in this situation, have been known by the creditor.

Permitting certain liens   The corporation while insolvent permits a creditor to obtain a lien against its property through legal proceedings if not discharged.

General assignment   The corporation makes a general assignment of its assets for the benefit of creditors.

Appointment of receiver   While the corporation is insolvent or unable to pay debts as they mature, a receiver or trustee is appointed for the corporation.

Admission   The corporation admits in writing its inability to pay its debts and indicates its willingness to be adjudicated a bankrupt.

Although it may seem surprising, the fact that a corporation cannot pay its bills as they become due does not provide an adequate basis for an involuntary petition. Courts interpret the Bankruptcy Act quite rigidly. For example, a written admission of inability to pay debts is not sufficient; a willingness to be adjudicated a bankrupt must be indicated. Therefore, a creditor may have to seek a lien against the property of the debtor before an act of bankruptcy will have been committed. So a contested bankruptcy can be quite a sparring match, and creditors must be very careful, for if they made a mistake and no act of bankruptcy did take place, they may be liable for damages. If there are factual disputes, the issues are tried. Upon conclusion of the trial, either the corporation will be adjudicated a bankrupt or the petition will be dismissed.

The Bankruptcy Process

In order to collect any money in a bankruptcy, a proof of claim has to be filed within 6 months of the date of the first creditors' meeting, which is held shortly after an adjudication is made. Usually, the creditors elect a trustee to administer the estate. The election of the trustee is a key event, especially in a complicated case, because the trustee ferrets out undisclosed assets by investigation and examination of the officers of the bankrupt corporation and is responsible for getting the best possible prices for the assets from the creditors. As a practical matter, however, in many bankruptcies, the election of the trustee seems to be arranged through groups of creditors.

Under the Bankruptcy Act, the trustee is given broad powers to preserve the assets of the estate. A trustee may assume or reject any executory contracts which have not yet been fully performed, although the trustee cannot assume a contract which explicitly provides that it is terminated in the event of bankruptcy. The party to a rejected contract will then only have a claim as a creditor, and in the case of landlord, the damages are limited to 1 year's rent. In addition to the power to void fraudulent transfers and set aside all liens created within 4 months of the filing of the petition if the corporation was insolvent at that time, the trustee has the ability to undo the effects of the common last-minute grab by powerful creditors. For example, a transfer of property of a corporation while (1) it is insolvent (2) within 4 months before the filing of the bankruptcy petition (3) to a creditor for a past obligation (an antecedent debt) is known as a preferential transfer, or, more simply, as a preference. The creditor receiving the property is placed in a better position than similar creditors. Such preferential transfers can be recovered by a trustee if the creditor had reasonable cause to believe at the time of the transfer that the corporation was insolvent.

The issue of preferences is extremely complicated and yet very important, especially for lenders. Clearly, a lender receiving security at the same time the money is lent is not receiving a preferential transfer; however, if the loan was made, say, two weeks before the security was obtained, the transaction could be a preferential transfer, assuming the other key elements are present.

A common situation results when an unsecured creditor gets a court judgment that money is due and receives a judicial lien; the corporation, seeking to avoid the third act of bankruptcy, an outstanding lien, pays the creditor. The judicially created lien, as noted, is voidable if created within 4 months of the filing of the petition against an insolvent corporation which is ultimately adjudicated a bankrupt. By paying off that lien, within 4 months of the petition and while the lien creditor knew of the insolvency, a preferential transfer is made.

Meanwhile, while the unsecured creditors argue over acts of bankruptcy, the secured creditors often attempt to grab and sell their security. As a practical matter, it is a mad rush because there is always the fear of another party or the trustee asserting that a loan is not really secured or delaying the foreclosure proceedings. In fact, there is often a stay of proceedings. For example, a secured creditor may have a lien on some machinery in a plant in Philadelphia. Under Pennsylvania law, the landlord has broad rights to claim as security anything attached to the building. As a result, flabbergasted creditors find themselves without the security they thought they had. Grabbing the machinery does not solve any arguments, but it is an important source of leverage. Meanwhile, the bankruptcy court may well issue a stay preventing foreclosures.

If all this sounds cloak-and-dagger and a pretty tough way to practice law—it is. One reason most "white shoe" law firms avoid bankruptcy is its rough-and-tumble aspect. As a general rule, especially as far as the realization on assets which are security for loans, specialists are likely to be more effective than general practitioners. Even if the security seems ironclad, there may be debatable points. For example, the name of the company may have been slightly misspelled in the UCC filing, raising the possibility that other creditors could not easily find it in the proper records.

One of the key problems facing a secured creditor is delay. Even assuming court approval to foreclose, there must generally be public notice of an auction at a future date. Meanwhile, inventory will be getting old and equipment will be out of condition. The sluggish pace of bankruptcy proceedings is another reason why secured creditors must be very cautious in estimating the value of their security.

While disputes are being resolved, the trustee has the property appraised and begins to sell it upon notice to all creditors by public auction. The money collected is first applied to costs of administering the bankruptcy and then to creditors. The attorney for the creditors filing the petition and the corporation's attorney are entitled to compensation out of the funds allocated for administrative costs.

CHAPTER XI

Chapters X and XI are reorganization and arrangement procedures under the Bankruptcy Act. In contrast to straight bankruptcy, the assets are not completely liquidated; rather, the debt itself is restructured. The classic Chapter XI situation is a basically sound company which simply has incurred too much debt and has suffered business reverses. By modifying the terms of its debt, the firm is able to continue operations.

A Brookings Institution study of the bankruptcy process by David Stanley and Marjorie Girth, *Bankruptcy: Problem, Process, Reform,* indicates that in the past the arrangement process has not been very successful. For example, only one-third of the debtors utilizing Chapter XI were still operating their businesses 2 years after their proceedings were closed.

In Chapter XI, the corporation continues its business with a minimum of interference from the court; there is no requirement, unlike Chapter X, for the appointment of a trustee. The key advantage of Chapter XI to incumbent management, then, is that it allows them to retain their position. In addition, breathing room is obtained for a company relatively simply and cheaply. All suits may be stayed until a final decree is issued, providing a judicially imposed protective barrier against the onslaught of zealous creditors. Executory contracts may be rejected, and the other party will have only a claim as a creditor. In the case of a lease, however, unlike straight bankruptcy, where the damages are limited to 1 year's rent, the damages in a Chapter XI are limited to 3 year's rent.

To initiate a Chapter XI proceeding, a corporation may file a voluntary petition or convert an involuntary or voluntary straight bankruptcy proceeding or Chapter X reorganization into a Chapter XI arrangement. However, there is in most Chapter XI's a hearing as to whether the corporation should file an indemnity bond to cover creditors for any additional losses which may be incurred by continuing operations instead of liquidating the company.

The indemnity hearing is a key event because it gives the major creditors their first opportunity to negotiate with each other and the debtor and, if necessary, to attempt to block the reorganization procedures and liquidate the firm. Under the rules applicable to the Southern District of New York, which includes Manhattan, the ten largest creditors are notified of the indemnity hearing. At the hearing, the court may order the filing of a bond or allow the debtor to continue its business without it. Since the bond is difficult to obtain and the objections of the major creditors will influence the court as to how much the bond should be or whether it should be required at all, negotiations become quite intense. As a result of these negotiations, clear limits are often set on management compensation and policies.

Assuming the indemnity problem is solved, a meeting is held of all of the creditors. Generally, there is a discussion of general principles regarding an arrangement, and the management discusses its prospects. Although it is possible to submit an actual plan of reorganization at the first meeting, this rarely occurs. Aside from negotiations continuing with various creditors, the formulation of a plan may depend on future events. For example, a toy manufacturer enters a Chapter XI bankruptcy in April with a large inventory for the following Christmas season. The contours of the plan may vary greatly, depending on whether sales will be good later that year. Rather than voting on a plan not tailored to the facts of the situations, creditors and the firm may decide to submit a plan at a later date.

At the first meeting, the financial statements of the firm are examined and a creditors' committee is elected which bears the prime responsibility for negotiating with the management. Because all classes receiving payment must approve a plan, representatives of most important creditor groups are included on the committee. In addition to having a more direct role in negotiating the plan, the creditors' committee has another important function: selecting its attorney, who is paid out of the estate. It is not unusual to find attorneys maneuvering to get friends elected to the creditors' committee or various creditors making deals regarding the selection of the attorney. Usually, the creditors' committee directly solicits approval of the plan, accompanying the solicitation with a proof-of-claim form.

When a plan is finally formulated, it is submitted to a vote of the creditors whose claims have been approved by the court. A court will confirm the plan if it is approved in each class by a majority in number of all creditors and by a majority in amount of all claims in each recognized class and if it is feasible and in the best interest of the creditors. Even though the requisite creditors approve a plan, any individual creditor can object to the confirmation.

The actual plan is really a creation of the firm and the creditors; the court's review function is much more limited than in Chapter X. Precise contours of the plan are determined by the need to get the requisite approval. As part of the dealing, various classes of creditors may get more or less than their theoretical legal rights. For example, if there are two classes of creditors, senior and subordinated, unsecured creditors, and the subordinated creditors may under legal standards be theoretically entitled to 10 cents on the dollar, the senior creditors may have a big problem: The subordinated creditors can block the plan because their approval is required. As a result, it is not surprising that the plan which is approved may provide the subordinated class with 15 cents. Similarly, although theoretically a Chapter XI proceeding is not supposed to affect the position of secured creditors, there may well be modifications in the terms of secured instruments to induce a reorganization.

The determination of what exactly is a class of creditors is part of the art of devising a Chapter XI plan. Under the Bankruptcy Act, the only requirement is that classification be reasonable. Often, for example, small creditors are treated better than larger creditors to assure the requisite approvals.

CHAPTER X

Chapter X Procedures

Chapter X proceedings are financial reorganizations similar to Chapter XI arrangements, but are more complex and rigid. The dividing line between the appropriateness of the two procedures is fuzzy and, in some cases, produces vigorous debate. For example, in the *W. T. Grant* case, which resulted in the liquidation of the stores of a leading merchandiser, critics, including SEC officials, have asserted that if the proceedings had been conducted under Chapter X rather than XI, a successful reorganization, instead of a liquidation, might well have been accomplished. Among the factors favoring a Chapter X reorganization over a Chapter XI arrangement are general complexity, public security holders, the presence of alleged fraud, the lack of capability of incumbent management, and the need to modify the terms of secured debt.

A Chapter X proceeding may be initiated by the debtor firm or, unlike Chapter XI, involuntarily by the creditors. In addition, a Chapter XI reorganization or straight bankruptcy may be converted into Chapter X. Each petition must state that the firm is insolvent and why Chapter X is the appropriate relief. In addition, an involuntary petition by creditors must allege an act of bankruptcy or that a reorganization or bankruptcy proceeding is underway. In fact, the SEC will often intervene in a Chapter XI proceeding involving a large public company to urge that a Chapter X reorganization would be more appropriate.

The first major step in a Chapter X reorganization is the appointment of a trustee by the judge. This is a critical distinction from Chapter XI; the old management is out. Upon appointment, the trustee's first task is to investigate and report on the financial condition of the corporation, to recommend whether the continuance of operations is desirable, and to report all instances of fraud or mismanagement. In recent scandals such as Equity Funding, this can be quite a sizable task because the business prospects of the company and the scope of the fraud are most uncertain.

In order for a plan to be approved under Chapter X, it must be fair, feasible, and equitable, as those terms have been interpreted by the courts over time. Based on the trustee's report, the court must make findings as to the valuation of the estate, a prime requisite for a feasible plan. Hearings are held, and various experts testify as to the prospects of the corporation and its worth. Worth is analyzed on the basis of long-term prospects, not likely market value, on the date the reorganization is completed. As a practical matter, discounts of up to 50% on the reorganization evaluation may be reflected in the market price of the securities of a reorganized company. However, it is certainly possible, but by no means certain, that as the tarnish of a bankruptcy proceeding wears off, and if the reorganization projections were accurate, the price may equal or exceed the reorganization estimate. But even assuming that the stock price does equal the reorganization estimate a number of years later, one must keep in mind the effect of the time value of money, which dramatically lessens the value of 100 cents on the dollar if received years later.

The simple fact is that a Chapter X reorganization is usually very drawn out and expensive. A three-year period to reorganize is considered unusually swift, and the legal and administrative fees can mount into the millions.

After the trustee's evaluation, the negotiations begin in earnest. Although somewhat similar to the bargaining process in Chapter XI, there are distinct differences.

First, the trustee, rather than the old management, is taking the leading role. The skill of the trustee is crucial, for he or she must not only moderate between the creditors but also lead them to a common consensus. Yet in order to do this, the trustee must, unlike management in a Chapter XI, quickly absorb background about a company with which the trustee had no prior dealings.

Second, in order to confirm a plan, the requisite approval threshold is higher in amount than Chapter XI: Two-thirds of the amount of the claims allowed in each class must vote in favor of the plan, although there is no requirement about the number of creditors. As a result, a broader consensus is needed.

Third, Chapter X was specifically designed to be a "democratic" bankruptcy procedure, reflecting the fact that publicly owned concerns are usually involved. As a result, all creditors are encouraged to submit plans, and the possibilities for compensation of active creditors are broader than under Chapter XI. Large creditors may still be in control of some class votes, but smaller claimants more frequently interact in the proceedings. The one single official creditors' committee found in Chapter XI is not present in an X; rather, a Chapter X proceeding involves a diverse, fractious, but more democratic process.

Fourth, the SEC's role is crucial, limiting the flexibility of the major creditors and the trustee to reach an agreement at the expense of the small public stockholders and debt holders. Before any plan may be approved by the court in a major reorganization under Chapter X, the SEC submits an advisory report as to its views on the plan. Naturally, judges often defer to the expertise of the SEC and rely heavily on its report.

Over the years, the SEC has evolved its own common law of Chapter X reorganizations. For example, it dislikes complicated financial structures and, as a result, features such as warrants, convertible securities, or classes of stock are usually absent in approved Chapter X plans, even though they might under certain circumstances be useful.

When a plan is finally devised, hearings are held as to its fairness, feasibility, and equitability. These are terms of art, interpreted by a slew of court opinions, which, as of today, are really quite confusing. Originally, the idea of the early Supreme Court decisions in this area written by Justice Douglas was to avoid the rampant dealing without principle which preceded Chapter X, to result in reorganizations which followed the absolute priority rule: Senior creditors go first, then junior creditors, and then stockholders. As noted, in Chapter XI the exigencies of getting a plan adopted rapidly have often led to compromises. In Chapter X, there is the same impetus, despite the absolute priority principle, although the review of courts and the SEC is a constraining factor. As will be discussed, recently there have been a number of Chapter X plans in fraud situations which have compromised the absolute priority issue, and the trend is toward increased flexibility to promote a speedier reorganization.

After these initial hearings, the judge decides whether the proposed plan is of sufficient merit to submit to the SEC for its report which, although theoretically advisory in nature, is quite influential. After receiving the SEC report, the judge finds whether the plan is fair, feasible, and equitable. Upon an affirmative determination, the plan, the judge's findings, the SEC report, a proof-of-claim form, and a ballot (often combined with the proof-of-claim form) are forwarded to the classes of creditors. If the plan is accepted by the holders of two-thirds of the amount of claims in each class, the court, after a hearing, confirms the plan, and the reorganization is then consummated.

Equity Funding, a Case Study

To indicate the flavor of recent reorganization proceedings, it is highly instructive to briefly sketch the restructuring of Equity Funding Corporation of America.* Equity Funding was a go-go stock of the 1960s with a seemingly great concept: Insurance policies would be sold in combination with mutual funds; the growth in value of the mutual funds would help fund the insurance. Equity's results were impressive; an unbroken string of increased earnings. One day, however, a rumor swept Wall Street, based on a tip from a disgruntled employee to an insurance stock analyst: Equity was a fraud. Investors began to scramble, the stock price plummeted, the SEC and various insurance departments commenced investigations.

When the smoke cleared, it became apparent that most of the supposed assets of Equity Funding did not exist. Many of its insurance policies had simply been fabricated, and, in fact, its key real assets were insurance companies which had been recently acquired.

In April of 1973, Equity Funding entered Chapter X. A trustee was appointed, and he immediately began to investigate the fraud and the prospects of the company. His conclusion was that a reorganization was feasible because of the newly acquired subsidiaries.

Meanwhile, the creditors were tangling. A major bank, Class 4, purported to be a secured creditor because stock certificates of the various insurance subsidiaries of Equity had been pledged to it. Not so fast, the other creditors argued. Those certificates had been returned to the company shortly before the Chapter X filing and, even though subsequently returned, resulted in a loss of the bank's security. The stockholders who had recently sold the solid subsidiaries to Equity, Class 5, meanwhile claimed they should be entitled to get those good companies back because of the fraud. The senior unsecured creditors, Class 6, insisted that they were entitled to 100 cents on the dollar under the absolute priority

*For disclosure purposes, it should be noted that the author participated in these proceedings representing an indenture trustee.

doctrine, while the subordinated creditors, Class 7, replied that they were equal in status to Class 6 because the fraud vitiated the subordination provisions. But the critical problem was with the common stockholders, Class 8. Class 8 claimed that as victims of the undisputed fraud, they had the right to a judgment against Equity and therefore were equal in status to the unsecured creditors, Class 6. Furthermore, representatives of Class 8 sued the solvent subsidiaries, alleging that they had conspired in the fraud and should be liable for damages to all defrauded security holders. Adding to the complication were the array of different creditor representatives: indenture trustees, institutional investors, ad hoc investor committees, and contingent-fee, class-action lawyers. Meanwhile, suits were being litigated against former officers and accountants of Equity with major implications for the reorganization.

If all this sounds complicated, the fact is that it is a gross simplification of the issues. The essential point is that the claims of all the creditors were interrelated because if any issue were raised in litigation, it would take years for it to be resolved. By that time, the assets of the Equity Funding might well have been dissipated.

Three years after entering Chapter X, a compromise plan was conformed for Equity and was hailed as a speedy reorganization. The alleged secured creditors sacrificed postbankruptcy interest and modified the terms of their instruments; the senior unsecured creditors received about 80 cents on the dollar in securities in terms of the reorganization estimate of their value; the former owners of the subsidiaries received about 35 cents; and the stockholders received 12 cents. The trustee received a check for $1 million for his services over 3½ years, and his counsel received some $6 million. Millions more were disbursed to the other lawyers in the proceedings.

When the stock in the reorganized Equity Funding, known as Orion Capital Corporation, began trading, it sold for roughly half its estimated reorganization value. Soon, however, the price rose dramatically, as a series of major investors realized there was still solid value left in the company. In addition, the stockholders shared in more than $60 million recovered in settlements from the former auditors and officers of Equity Funding.

The Equity Funding reorganization was unusually complex and successful. Most reorganizations are simpler but take longer, and the results are worse. One possible lesson from all this is that a voluntary reorganization is preferable to a bankruptcy procedure. That is true, but often impractical. A reorganization or arrangement under Chapter X or XI has two important unique features: All creditors can be temporarily held at bay, and a plan accepted by the required creditors and approved by the courts can be imposed on dissenters despite their objections. In contrast, just one recalcitrant major creditor is enough to upset a voluntary reorganization.

There are currently before Congress a number of proposals to reform the Bankruptcy Act, particularly as it affects reorganizations, and it is anticipated that some revisions will be enacted before 1979. One suggestion is to merge Chapters X and XI and modify the absolute-priority principle. Certainly, some reform and clarification in the bankruptcy process would be useful. In any event, bankruptcy has now reemerged as a key element in corporate finance law.

Sample Certificate

(NOTE: *The material in brackets is for a corporation with two classes of common stock each of which is entitled to elect a number of directors.*)

CERTIFICATE OF INCORPORATION
OF
GREEN GRASS, INC.

The undersigned, for the purpose of forming a corporation pursuant to the provisions of the Delaware General Corporation Law, does hereby execute the following Certificate of Incorporation.

FIRST: The name of this corporation is Green Grass, Inc.

SECOND: The address of this corporation's registered office in the State of Delaware is 100 West 99th Street, in the City of Wilmington, County of New Castle. The name of its registered agent at such address is The Agent Company.

THIRD: The purpose of this corporation is to engage in any lawful act or activity for which corporations may be organized under the General Corporation Law of Delaware.

FOURTH: This corporation shall have authority to issue 1000 shares of common stock, each share to have a par value of one hundred dollars ($100) [of which 600 shares shall be designated Class A Common Stock and 400 shares shall be designated Class B Common Stock. The Class A Common Stock and Class B Common Stock shall have identical rights except that at each annual election of directors of this corporation, the holders of the outstanding Class A Common Stock shall be entitled to elect three directors, and the holders of the outstanding

Class B common Stock shall be entitled to elect two directors]. This corporation shall have a total of five directors. In the event of a vacancy on the Board of Directors, a successor director to serve until the next annual election shall be elected by the holders of the stock in the class of Common Stock that elected, or is deemed to have elected, the predecessor director as provided in the Bylaws of this corporation.

FIFTH: The name and mailing address of the incorporator is William Jones, One Chase Manhattan Plaza, New York, N.Y. 10005.

SIXTH: The powers of the incorporator shall terminate upon filing of this Certificate of Incorporation. The names and mailing addresses of the persons who are to serve as directors until the first annual meeting of stockholders or until their successors are elected and qualify are as follows:

Name   *Mailing Address*

[The first three of such directors shall be deemed to have been elected by holders of Class A Common Stock and the last two shall be deemed to have been elected by the holders of the Class B Common Stock.]

SEVENTH: The Bylaws of this corporation may be made, altered, amended, or repealed by a vote of at least three directors [at least one of whom shall have been elected by the holders of the Class B Common Stock, or the vote of the holders of at least 67% of the outstanding Common Stock].

EIGHTH: Unless and except to the extent that the Bylaws shall otherwise require, the election of directors of this corporation need not be by written ballot.

NINTH: Any director or any officer of this corporation may be removed at any time in such manner as shall be provided in the Bylaws.

TENTH: This corporation reserves the right at any time and from time to time to amend, alter, change, or repeal any provision contained in this Certificate of Incorporation, and other provisions authorized by the laws of the State of Delaware at the time in force may be added or inserted, in the manner now or hereafter prescribed by law by the vote of at least three directors [at least one of whom shall have been elected by the holders of the Class B Common Stock and the vote of holders of at least 67% of the outstanding Common Stock]; and all rights, preferences, and privileges of whatsoever nature conferred upon stockholders, directors, or any other person whomsoever by or pursuant to this Certificate of Incorporation in its present form or as hereafter amended are granted subject to the right reserved hereby.

IN WITNESS WHEREOF, I, the incorporator of this corporation, have signed this Certificate of Incorporation on the eighteenth day of January 1978.

William Jones

William Jones

Bylaws

(NOTE: *The material in brackets is for a corporation with two classes of common stock, each of which is entitled to elect a number of directors.)*

BYLAWS
of
GREEN GRASS, INC.

ARTICLE I
MEETINGS OF STOCKHOLDERS

SECTION 1. ANNUAL MEETINGS: The annual meeting of the stockholders of Green Grass, Inc. (the "Corporation") for the election of directors and for the transaction of any other proper business shall be held on such date and at such place, within or without the State of Delaware, and hour as shall be designated by the Board of Directors (the "Board") and stated in the notice thereof.

SECTION 2. SPECIAL MEETINGS: A special meeting of the stockholders of the Corporation for any purpose or purposes may be called at any time by any two directors, the Chairman of the Board, the President, or any other officer authorized to call such special meeting by the Board, and such meeting shall be held on such date and at such place, within or without the State of Delaware, and hour as shall be designated in the notice thereof.

SECTION 3. NOTICE OF MEETINGS: Except as otherwise expressly required by these Bylaws or by law, notice of each meeting of the stockholders shall be given not less than 10 nor more than 60 days before the date of the meeting to each stockholder of record entitled to notice of, or to vote at, such meeting, by delivering a written notice thereof to him personally or by depositing such notice in the United States mail, postage prepaid, directed to him at his address as it appears on the records of the Corporation. Every notice of a meeting of stockholders shall state the place, date, and hour of the meeting and, in the case of a special meeting, the purpose or purposes for which the meeting is called. Notice of any adjourned meeting of the stockholders shall not be required to be given if (1) the time and place thereof are announced at the meeting at which the adjournment is taken, (2) the adjourned meeting is held within 30 days thereafter and (3) a new record date for the adjourned meeting is not thereafter fixed.

SECTION 4. QUORUM: Except as otherwise expressly required by law, if stockholders holding of record two-thirds of the shares of stock of the Corporation entitled to be voted shall be present in person or by proxy, they shall constitute a quorum for the transaction of business at any meeting of the stockholders. In the absence of a quorum at any such meeting or any adjournment or adjournments thereof, a majority in voting interest of those present in person or by proxy and entitled to vote at such meeting, or, in the absence therefrom of all the stockholders, any officer entitled to preside at, or to act as secretary of, such meeting, may adjourn such meeting from time to time until stockholders holding the amount of stock requisite for a quorum shall be present in person or by proxy. At any such adjourned meeting at which a quorum may be present, any business may be transacted which might have been transacted at the meeting as originally called. The absence from any meeting in person or by proxy of stockholders holding the number of shares of stock of the Corporation required by law, by the Certificate of Incorporation or by these Bylaws for action upon any given matter shall not prevent action at such meeting upon any other matter or matters which may properly come before the meeting if there shall be present at such meeting in person or by proxy stockholders holding the number of shares of stock of the Corporation required in respect of such other matter or matters.

SECTION 5. ORGANIZATION: At each meeting of the stockholders, one of the following shall act as chairman of the meeting and preside in the following order of precedence:

(a) the Chairman of the Board (or such other person as he may designate);

(b) the President (or such other person as he may designate);

(c) any other officer of the Corporation designated by the Board;

(d) any other officer of the Corporation designated by a majority in voting interest of the stockholders present in person or by proxy and entitled to vote at such meeting; or

(e) a stockholder of record of the Corporation designated by a majority in voting interest of the stockholders present in person or by proxy and entitled to vote at such meeting.

The Secretary, or, if he shall be absent from or presiding over the meeting in accordance with the provisions of this Section, the person (who shall be an Assistant Secretary, if an Assistant Secretary shall be present at such meeting) whom the chairman of such meeting shall appoint, shall act as secretary of such meeting and keep the minutes thereof.

SECTION 6. ORDER OF BUSINESS: The order of business at each meeting of the stockholders shall be determined by the chairman of the meeting, but such order of business may be changed by the vote of two-thirds in voting interest of those present in person or by proxy and entitled to vote at such meeting.

SECTION 7. VOTING: Unless otherwise provided in the Certificate of Incorporation, each stockholder shall at each meeting of the stockholders be entitled to one vote in person or by proxy for each share of the stock of the Corporation which has voting power on the matter in question (the "voting stock") and which shall have been held by him and registered in his name on the stock record of the Corporation:

> (a) on the date fixed pursuant to the provisions of Section 6 of Article VII of these Bylaws as the record date for the determination of stockholders who shall be entitled to receive notice of and to vote at such meeting, or

> (b) if no such record date shall have been so fixed, then (1) at the close of business on the day next preceding the day on which notice of the meeting shall be given or (2) if notice of the meeting shall be waived, at the close of business on the day next preceding the day on which the meeting shall be held.

Shares of its own stock belonging to the Corporation or to another corporation, if a majority of the shares entitled to vote in the election of directors of such other corporation is held by the Corporation, shall neither be entitled to vote nor be counted for quorum purposes. Persons holding voting stock in a fiduciary capacity shall be entitled to vote such stock so held. Persons whose voting stock is pledged shall be entitled to vote such stock, unless in the transfer by the pledger on the records of the Corporation he shall have expressly empowered the pledgee to vote thereon, in which case only the pledgee, or his proxy, may represent such stock and vote thereon. Voting stock standing of record in the names of two or more persons or with respect to which two or more persons have the same fiduciary relationship shall be voted in accordance with the provisions of the General Corporation Law of the State of Delaware.

Voting stock may be voted at any meeting of the stockholders by the person entitled to vote the same in person or by proxy appointed by an instrument in writing delivered to the Secretary or an Assistant Secretary of the Corporation or the secretary of the meeting; provided, however, that no proxy shall be voted or acted upon after three years from its date unless said proxy provides for a longer period. The attendance at any meeting of a stockholder who may theretofore have given a proxy shall not have the effect of revoking the same unless he shall in writing so notify the secretary of the meeting prior to the voting of the proxy. At all meetings of the stockholders all matters, except as otherwise provided in the Certificate of Incorporation, in these Bylaws or by law, shall be decided by the vote of two-thirds in voting interest of the stockholders present in person or by proxy and entitled to vote thereat, a quorum being present. The vote at any meeting of the stockholders on any question, including the election of directors, need not be by ballot, unless so directed by the chairman of the meeting. On a vote by ballot, each ballot shall be signed by the stockholder voting, or by his proxy if there be such proxy, and shall state the number of shares voted.

[As to the election of directors, as provided in the Certificate of Incorporation, the holders of Class A Common Stock shall be entitled to elect three directors and the holders of the Class B Common Stock two directors. As to all other matters, except as provided by law, the voting rights of the Class A and Class B Common stockholders shall be identical and such holders shall vote together as one class.]

SECTION 8. LIST OF STOCKHOLDERS: It shall be the duty of the Secretary or other officer of the Corporation who shall have charge of the stock ledger, either directly or through another officer of the Corporation designated by him or through a transfer agent or transfer clerk appointed by the Board, to prepare and make, at least 10 days before every meeting of the stockholders, a complete list of the stockholders entitled to vote at such meeting, arranged in alphabetical order, and showing the address of each stockholder and the number of shares registered in the name of each stockholder. Such list shall be open to the examination of any stockholder, for any purpose germane to the meeting, during ordinary business hours, for a period of at least 10 days prior to the meeting, either at the place where said meeting is to be held or within the city where the meeting is to be held at such other place as is specified in the notice of the meeting. Such list shall also be produced and kept at the time and place of said meeting during the whole time thereof, and may be inspected by any stockholder who is present. The stock ledger shall be the only evidence as to who are the stockholders entitled to examine the stock ledger, such list, or the books of the Corporation, or to vote in person or by proxy at any meeting of the stockholders.

SECTION 9. CONSENT IN LIEU OF MEETING: Any action required to be taken at any annual or special meeting of stockholders of the corporation or by any class of stockholders, or any action which may be taken at any annual or special meeting of such stockholders, may be taken without a meeting, without prior notice and without a vote, if a consent in writing, setting forth the action so taken, shall be signed by the holders of outstanding stock having not less than the minimum number of votes that would be necessary to authorize or take such action at a meeting at which all shares entitled to vote thereon were present and voted. Prompt notice of the taking of the corporate action without a meeting by less than unanimous written consent shall be given to those stockholders who have not consented in writing, and any certificate filed shall state that such written notice has been given.

ARTICLE II
BOARD OF DIRECTORS

SECTION 1. GENERAL POWERS: The property, business, and affairs of the Corporation shall be managed by or under the direction of the Board.

SECTION 2. NUMBER AND TERM OF OFFICE: The number of directors which shall constitute the whole Board shall be five. (The term "whole Board" as used in these Bylaws shall mean the number of positions on the Board, regardless of the number of directors then in office.) Each of the directors of the Corporation shall hold office until the Annual Meeting of the stockholders next after his election and until his successor shall be selected and shall qualify or until his earlier death or resignation or removal in the manner hereinafter provided.

SECTION 3. ELECTION: At each meeting of the stockholders for the election of directors at which a quorum is present, the holders of Common Stock shall elect five directors. The five persons receiving the greatest number of votes shall be elected as directors. [The holders of the Class A Common Stock shall elect three directors and the holders of the Class B Common Stock shall elect two directors. The persons receiving the greatest number of votes in each class, up to the number of directors to be elected, shall be the directors elected by each such class.] Directors need not be stockholders of the Corporation or residents of the State of Delaware or of the United States of America.

SECTION 4. RESIGNATION, REMOVAL, AND VACANCIES: Any director may resign at any time by giving written notice of his resignation to the Chairman of the Board, the President or the Secretary of the Corporation. Any such resignation shall take effect at the time specified therein or, if the time when it shall become effective shall not be specified therein, then it shall take effect when received by the Chairman of the Board, the President or the Secretary of the Corporation. Except as aforesaid, the acceptance of such resignation shall not be necessary to make it effective.

Any director may be removed at any time for cause, or, if permitted by law, without cause, by vote of the holders of record of a majority of the class of voting stock which elected such director at a special meeting of such stockholders called for the purpose; and the vacancy in the Board caused by any such removal shall be filled by such stockholders at such meeting. Any director may also be removed at any time for cause by the vote of at least three members of the Board [at least one of whom shall have been elected by holders of the Class B Common Stock].

In the event of a vacancy or vacancies on the Board, a successor director or directors to serve until the next annual election shall be elected by the holders of the stock in the class or classes of Common Stock that elected the predecessor director or directors.

SECTION 5. MEETINGS:

(A) *Annual Meeting*   As soon as practicable after each annual election of directors, the Board shall meet for the purpose of organization, the election of a Chairman of the Board and of officers, and the transaction of other business.

(B) *Regular Meetings*   Regular meetings of the Board shall be held at such times as the Board shall determine. Notice of regular meetings need not be given. If any day fixed for a regular meeting shall be a legal holiday at the place where the meeting is to be held, then the meeting which would otherwise be held on that day shall be postponed until the next succeeding business day.

(C) *Special Meetings*   Special meetings of the Board, at which any and all business may be transacted, shall be held whenever called by the Chairman of the Board, the President or any two directors. The Secretary shall give notice to each director of each special meeting, including the time and place thereof and the nature of the business to be transacted. Such notice shall be mailed (by airmail if mailed outside the United States of America) to each director, addressed to him at his residence or usual place of business, at least ten days before the day on which such meeting is to be held, or shall be sent to him by telegraph, cable, wireless, or other form of recorded communication or be delivered personally or by telephone not later than five days before the day on which such meeting is to be held.

(D) *Time and Place of Meetings*   The Board may hold its meetings at such time or times and at such place or places within or without the State of Delaware, as the Board may from time to time determine or as shall be designated in the respective notices or waivers of notice thereof. A meeting of the Board or any committee designated by the Board pursuant to Article III may be held by means of a conference telephone or similar communications equipment by means of which all persons participating in the meeting can hear each other, and participation in such a meeting shall constitute presence at such meeting.

(E) *Quorum and Manner of Acting*   Except as otherwise expressly required by these Bylaws or by law, three of the directors then in office shall be present in person at any meeting of the Board in order to constitute a quorum for the transaction of business at such meeting, and the vote of three of the directors present at any such meeting at which a quorum is present shall be necessary for the passage of any resolution or for an act to be the act of the Board; [provided, however, that the following matters shall require the approval of at least three directors at least one of whom shall have been elected by the holders of the Class B Common Stock:

(a) Amendment of the Articles of Incorporation of the Corporation and amendment of these Bylaws;

(b) Increase or decrease of authorized capital stock or paid-in capital;

(c) Issuance of additional shares of stock or preference shares or any securities convertible into such stock or shares, or any warrants, options, or other rights to purchase or subscribe for such stock or shares;

(d) Acquisition or disposition of a material interest in, or a merger or consolidation with, any other firm or company;

(e) Creation of any debt obligation (including any revolving credit arrangement) having a maturity of more than one (1) year or the creation of any mortgage, lien, or encumbrance on plant or property of the Corporation in excess of two million dollars ($2,000,000) or the creation of any other debt obligation or guarantee in excess of four million dollars ($4,000,000);

(f) Adoption of annual operational and capital budgets;

(g) Declaration of dividends;

(h) Appointment of counsel and independent auditors;

(i) Election and dismissal of officers;

(j) Appropriation requests for any capital expenditure in excess of one hundred thousand dollars ($100,000) per annum;

(k) Making of contracts or amendments to or waivers of terms of contracts with shareholders;

(l) Liquidation or disposition of all or (other than in the ordinary course of business) a substantial portion of the assets of the Corporation; and

(m) Approval of any lease of real property for a term of more than ten years or of any lease of real or personal property for an annual rental of more than twenty thousand dollars ($20,000);].

In the absence of a quorum, a majority of the directors present may adjourn such meeting from time to time until a quorum shall be present. Notice of any adjourned meeting need not be given, but the Secretary of the Corporation shall make a reasonable attempt to inform all directors of the time and place of such adjourned meeting. The directors shall act only as a board and individual directors shall have no power as such.

(F) *Organization and Order of Business*   At each meeting of the Board, one of the following shall act as chairman of the meeting and preside, in the following order of precedence:

(a) the Chairman of the Board;

(b) the President; or

(c) any director chosen by a majority of the directors present.

The Secretary, or, if he shall be absent from such meeting, the person (who shall be an Assistant Secretary, if an Assistant Secretary shall be present) whom the chairman of such meeting shall appoint, shall act as secretary of such meeting and keep the minutes. The order of business at each meeting of the Board shall be determined by the chairman of such meeting.

(G) *Consent in Lieu of Meeting*   Any action required or permitted to be taken at any meeting of the Board or of any committee thereof may be taken without a meeting, if all members of the Board or committee, as the case may be, consent thereto in writing, and the writing or writings are filed with the minutes of proceedings of the Board or committee.

ARTICLE III
COMMITTEES

The Board may, by resolution passed by a majority of the whole Board, designate one or more committees, including an Executive Committee, each committee to consist of one or more of the directors of the Corporation. The Board may designate one or more directors as alternate members of any committee, who may replace any absent or disqualified member at any meeting of the committee. In the absence or disqualification of a member of a committee, the member or members thereof present at any meeting and not disqualified from voting, whether or not he or they constitute a quorum, may unanimously appoint another member of the Board to act at the meeting in the place of any such absent or disqualified member. Any such committee, to the extent provided in the resolution of the Board and permitted by law, shall have and may exercise all the powers and authority of the Board in the management of the business and affairs of the Corporation, and may authorize the seal of the Corporation to be affixed to all papers which may require it; but no such committee shall have the power or authority to approve any action which would require the vote of at least three directors [at least one of whom shall have been elected by holders of the Class B Common Stock], unless a resolution adopted by at least three directors [at least one of whom shall have been elected by holders of the Class B Common Stock] or the Certificate of Incorporation expressly so provides. Such committee or committees shall have such name as may be determined from time to time by resolution adopted by the Board. Each committee shall keep regular minutes of its meetings and report the same to the Board when required.

ARTICLE IV
OFFICERS

SECTION 1. ELECTION AND APPOINTMENT AND TERM OF OFFICE: The officers of the Corporation shall be a Chairman of the Board, a President, such number of Vice Presidents (including any Executive and/or Senior Vice President) as the Board may determine from time to time, a Treasurer, and a Secretary. Each such officer shall be elected by the Board at its annual meeting and shall hold office until the next annual meeting of the Board and until his successor is elected or until his earlier death or resignation or removal in the manner hereinafter provided.

The Board may elect or appoint such other officers (including one or more Assistant Treasurers and one or more Assistant Secretaries) as it deems necessary, who shall have such authority and shall perform such duties as the Board may from time to time prescribe.

If additional officers are elected or appointed during the year, each of them shall hold office until the next annual meeting of the Board at which officers are regularly elected or appointed and until his successor is elected or appointed or until his earlier death or resignation or removal in the manner hereinafter provided.

SECTION 2. RESIGNATION, REMOVAL, AND VACANCIES: Any officer may resign at any time by giving written notice of his resignation to the President or the Secretary of the Corporation. Any such resignation shall take effect at the time specified therein or, if the time when it shall become effective shall not be specified therein, then it shall take effect when accepted by action of the Board. Except as aforesaid, the acceptance of such resignation shall not be necessary to make it effective.

An officer or agent elected or appointed by the Board may be removed, either with or without cause, at any time by the Board.

A vacancy in any office may be filled for the unexpired portion of the term in the same manner as provided for election or appointment to such office.

SECTION 3. DUTIES AND FUNCTIONS:

(A) *The Chairman of the Board*   The Chairman of the Board shall preside at meetings of the Board of Directors and stockholders. [The Chairman shall be initially elected by the directors elected by the Class B stockholders and the following year by directors elected by the Class A stockholders and thereafter in annual rotation among the directors elected by each such class.]

(B) *President*   The President shall be the chief executive officer of the Corporation and shall have general charge of the business and affairs of the Corporation and shall have the direction of all other officers, agents, and employees. The President shall preside at meetings of the Board of Directors and of the stockholders in the absence of the Chairman of the Board. The President may assign such duties to the other officers of the Corporation as he deems appropriate.

(C) *Vice Presidents*   Each Vice President shall have such powers and duties as shall be prescribed by the President of the Board.

(D) *Treasurer*   The Treasurer shall have charge and custody of and be responsible for all funds and securities of the Corporation.

(E) *Secretary*   The Secretary shall keep the records of all meetings of the stockholders and of the Board and the Executive Committee. The Secretary shall affix the seal of the Corporation to all deeds, contracts, bonds, or other instruments requiring the corporate seal when the same shall have been signed on behalf of the Corporation by a duly authorized officer. The Secretary shall be the custodian of all contracts, deeds, documents, and all other indicia of title to properites owned by the Corporation and of its other corporate records (except accounting records).

ARTICLE V
CONTRACTS, CHECKS, DRAFTS, BANK ACCOUNTS, ETC.

SECTION 1. EXECUTION OF DOCUMENTS: The Board shall designate the officers, employees, and agents of the Corporation who shall have power to execute and deliver deeds, contracts, mortgages, bonds, debentures, checks, drafts, and other orders for the payment of money and other documents for and in the name of the Corporation, and may authorize such officers, employees, and agents to delegate such power (including authority to redelegate) by written instrument to other officers, employees, or agents of the Corporation. Such designation may be by resolution or otherwise, and the authority granted may be general or confined to specific instances, all as the Board may determine.

SECTION 2. DEPOSITS: All funds of the Corporation not otherwise employed shall be deposited from time to time to the credit of the Corporation or otherwise as the Board or the President or any other officer of the Corporation to whom power in that respect shall have been delegated by the Board shall select. For the purpose of deposit and for the purpose of collection for the account of the Corporation, checks, drafts, and other orders for the payment of money which are payable to the order of the Corporation may be endorsed, assigned, and delivered by any officer or agent of the Corporation.

SECTION 3. PROXIES IN RESPECT OF STOCK OR OTHER SECURITIES OF OTHER CORPORATIONS: The Board shall designate the officers of the Corporation who shall have authority to appoint from time to time an agent or agents of the Corporation to exercise in the name and on behalf of the Corporation the powers and rights which the Corporation may have as the holder of stock or other securities in any other corporation and to vote or consent in respect of such stock or securities; such designated officers may instruct the person or persons so appointed as to the manner of exercising such powers and rights; and such designated officers may execute or cause to be executed in the name and on behalf of the Corporation and under its corporate seal, or otherwise, such written proxies, powers of attorney, or other instruments as they may deem necessary or proper in order that the Corporation may exercise such powers and rights.

ARTICLE VI
OFFICES AND BOOKS AND RECORDS

SECTION 1. REGISTERED OFFICE: The registered office of the Corporation in the State of Delaware shall be in the City of Wilmington, County of New Castle, and the registered agent of the Corporation in said state shall be The Agent Company.

SECTION 2. OTHER OFFICES: The Corporation may also have an office or offices other than said registered office, either within or without the State of Delaware.

SECTION 3. BOOKS AND RECORDS: The Corporation may keep its books and records in such place or places within or without the State of Delaware as the Board may from time to time by resolution determine.

ARTICLE VII

SHARES AND THEIR TRANSFER: FIXING RECORD DATE

SECTION 1. CERTIFICATES FOR STOCK: Every owner of stock of the Corporation shall be entitled to have a certificate certifying the number of shares owned by him in the Corporation and designating the class of stock to which such shares belong, which shall otherwise be in such form as the Board shall prescribe. Each such certificate shall be signed by, or in the name of the Corporation by, the President or a Vice President and by the Treasurer or an Assistant Treasurer or the Secretary or an Assistant Secretary of the Corporation. Such signatures may be facsimile if such certificate is countersigned by either a transfer agent other than the Corporation or an employee of the Corporation, or by a registrar other than the Corporation or an employee of the Corporation. In case any officer who has signed or whose facsimile signature has been placed upon a certificate shall have ceased to be such officer before such certificate is issued, it may nevertheless be issued by the Corporation with the same effect as if he were such officer at the date of issue. Every certificate surrendered to the Corporation for exchange or transfer shall be canceled, and a new certificate or certificates shall not be issued in exchange for any existing certificate until such existing certificate shall have been so canceled, except in cases provided for in Section 4 of this Article.

SECTION 2. RECORD: A record (the "stock ledger") in one or more counterparts shall be kept of the name of the person, firm, or corporation owning the stock represented by each certificate for stock of the Corporation issued, the number of shares represented by each such certificate, and the date thereof, and, in the case of cancelation, the date of cancelation. Except as otherwise expressly required by law, the person in whose name shares of stock stand on the stock ledger of the Corporation shall be deemed the owner therof for all purposes as regards the Corporation.

SECTION 3. TRANSFER OF STOCK: Registration of transfers of shares of the stock of the Corporation shall be made only on the stock ledger of the Corporation by the registered holder thereof, or by his attorney thereunto authorized by power of attorney duly executed and filed with the Secretary of the Corporation or with a transfer clerk or transfer agent appointed as in Section 5 of this Article provided, and upon surrender of the certificate or certificates for such shares properly endorsed and payment of all taxes thereon. Whenever any transfer of shares shall be made for collateral security, and not absolutely, such fact shall be so expressed in the entry of transfer if both the transferer and the transferee request the Corporation to do so when the certificate or certificates shall be presented for transfer.

SECTION 4. LOST, STOLEN, DESTROYED, OR MUTILATED CERTIFICATES: The holder of any stock of the Corporation shall immediately notify the Corporation of any loss, theft, destruction, or mutilation of the certificate therefor. The Corporation may issue a new certificate for stock in the place of any certificate theretofore issued by it and alleged to have been lost, stolen, or destroyed or in substitution for any such certificate which has been mutilated, and the Board may, in its discretion, require the owner of the lost, stolen, destroyed, or mutilated certificate or his legal representative to give the Corporation a bond, or other indemnity, in such sum, limited or unlimited, in such form and with such surety or sureties as the Board shall in its discretion determine, to indemnify the Corporation against any claim that may be made against it on account of the alleged loss, theft, destruction, of mutilation of any such certificate or the issuance of any such new certificate.

SECTION 5. REGULATIONS The Board may make such rules and regulations as it may deem expedient, not inconsistent with these Bylaws, concerning the issue, transfer, and registration of certificates for stock of the Corporation. The Board may appoint or authorize any officer or officers to appoint one or more transfer clerks or one or more transfer agents and one or more registrars and may require all certificates for stock to bear the signature or signatures of any of them.

SECTION 6. FIXING DATE FOR DETERMINATION OF STOCKHOLDERS OF RECORD: In order that the Corporation may determine the stockholders entitled to notice of or to vote at any meeting of the stockholders or any adjournment thereof, or to express consent to corporate action in writing without a meeting, or entitled to receive payment of any dividend or other distribution or allotment of any rights, or entitled to exercise any rights in respect of any change, conversion or exchange of stock, or for the purpose of any other lawful action, the Board may fix, in advance, a record date, which shall not be more than 60 nor less than 10 days before the date of such meeting, nor more than 60 days prior to any other action. A determination of stockholders entitled to notice of or to vote at a meeting of the stockholders shall apply to any adjournment of the meeting; *provided, however,* that the Board may fix a new record date for the adjourned meeting.

ARTICLE VIII
SEAL

The Board shall provide a corporate seal, which may be impressed or affixed or reproduced or other use made therof by the Secretary, any Assistant Secretary or any other officer authorized by the Board.

ARTICLE IX
FISCAL YEAR

The fiscal year of the Corporation shall end on the last day of December in each year.

ARTICLE X
INDEMNIFICATION

SECTION 1. RIGHT TO INDEMNIFICATION: Any person who was or is a party or is threatened to be made a party to or is in any other way connected with or involved in any threatened, pending, or completed action, suit, or proceeding (whether civil, criminal, administrative, or investigative), by reason of or arising out of the fact that he was or is a director, officer, or employee of the Corporation, or was or is serving at the request of the Corporation in any capacity in or with another corporation, partnership, joint venture, trust, or other enterprise, shall, subject to the provisions of Section 2 of this Article and except as prohibited by law, be indemnified by the Corporation against all liabilities and reasonable expenses incurred by him in connection with such action, suit, or proceeding, whether brought by or in the right of the Corporation or such other corporation, or otherwise. As used in this Article the term "expenses" shall include attorneys' fees and disbursements and all other expenses (except any liability) relating to any such action, suit, or proceeding, and the term "liabilities" shall include judgments, fines, penalties, and amounts paid in settlement.

SECTION 2. LIMITATIONS AND STANDARDS: To the extent that a person referred to in Section 1 of this Article has been successful on the merits or otherwise (including the expiration of a reasonable period of time after the making of any claim or threat of an action, suit, or proceeding without the institution of the same, without any payment or promise made to induce a settlement) in connection with an action, suit, or proceeding, or a claim, issue, or matter therein, he shall be entitled to indemnification. To the extent that a person referred to in Section 1 of this Article has not been so successful, he shall be entitled to indemnification only if a Referee, who shall be independent legal counsel (who may be regular counsel for the Corporation) or other disinterested person or persons, selected and compensated by the Board (whether or not a quorum of disinterested directors exists), shall deliver to the Corporation his written finding that the person claiming indemnification acted in good faith and in a manner he reasonably believed to be in or not opposed to the best interests of the Corporation and, with respect to any criminal action or proceeding, had no reasonable cause to believe his conduct was unlawful. The termination of any claim, action, suit, or proceeding by judgment, order, settlement (with or without court approval), or conviction, or on a plea of guilty or *nolo contendere* or its equivalent, shall not, of itself, create a presumption that a person did not meet the foregoing standards of conduct. When indemnification hereunder requires a written finding of a Referee, the person to be indemnified shall, at the request of the Referee, appear before him and answer questions which the Referee deems relevant and shall be given ample opportunity to present to the Referee evidence upon which he relies for indemnification. The Corporation shall, at the request of the Referee, make available to him facts, opinions or other evidence in any way relevant for his finding which are in the possession or control of the Corporation.

SECTION 3. ADVANCE OF EXPENSES: Expenses incurred in connection with a civil, criminal, administrative, or investigative claim, action, suit, or proceeding may be paid by the Corporation in advance of the final disposition of such claim, action, suit, or proceeding as authorized by the Board (whether or not a quorum of disinterested directors exists) upon receipt of an undertaking by or on behalf of the person to be indemnified to repay such amount unless it shall ultimately be determined that he is entitled to be indemnified by the Corporation.

SECTION 4. ADDITIONAL RIGHTS AND LIMITATIONS: The rights of indemnification provided in this Article shall be in addition to any rights to which any person referred to in Section 1 of this Article may otherwise lawfully be entitled. Irrespective of the provisions of this Article, the Board may, at any time or from time to time, approve indemnification of any person to the full extent permitted by the provisions of the General Corporation Law of the State of Delaware at the time in effect, whether on account of past or future transactions.

SECTION 5. CONTINUANCE OF INDEMNIFICATION: The indemnification provided or authorized by this Article shall continue as to a person who has ceased to be a director, officer, or employee and shall inure to the benefit of the heirs, executors, and administrators of such person.

SECTION 6. INSURANCE: The Corporation, as authorized by the Board, shall have power to purchase and maintain insurance on behalf of any person who is or was a director, officer, employee, or agent of the Corporation, or is or was serving at the request of the Corporation in any capacity in or with another corporation, partnership, joint venture, trust, or other enterprise, against any liability asserted against him and incurred by him in any such capacity, or arising out of his status as such, whether or not the Corporation would have the power to indemnify him against such liability under the provisions of this Article or otherwise.

ARTICLE XI
WAIVER OF NOTICES

Whenever notice is required to be given by the Certificate of Incorporation, by these Bylaws, or by law, a waiver thereof in writing, signed by the person entitled to such notice, including stockholders, directors, or members of a committee of directors, shall be deemed equivalent to notice, whether given before or after the time specified therein and, in the case of a waiver of notice of a meeting, including regular or special meetings of the stockholders, Board, or committee of the Board, whether or not such waiver specifies the purpose of or business to be transacted at such meeting. Attendance of a person at a meeting shall constitute a waiver of notice of such meeting, except where the person attends the meeting for the express purpose of objecting, at the beginning of the meeting, to the transaction of any business because the meeting is not lawfully called or convened.

ARTICLE XII
AMENDMENTS

These Bylaws may be altered or repealed by the vote of at least three directors [at least one of whom shall have been elected by the holders of the Class B Common Stock] subject to the power of the holders of 67% of the outstanding stock of the Corporation entitled to vote in respect thereof, by their vote given at an annual meeting or at any special meeting, to alter or repeal any Bylaw made by the Board.

Bibliography

This bibliography is designed to provide a basis for further reading to supplement the text. In addition, it provides the full citations to all cases, articles, or books referred to in the text. Since much of this book is based upon personal observation and experience, the number of useful supplementary sources is necessarily limited.

The "latest edition" of works are referred to when there are frequent publications of revised editions. The reader should also be aware that the New York Law Journal Press and the Practising Law Institute each year publish a series of valuable handbooks and seminar outlines. Although some of these are listed in this bibliography, the titles differ slightly each year, and these organizations should be contacted regarding their latest offerings.

PART ONE: STARTING A BUSINESS

HISTORICAL BACKGROUND

W. Cary, *Corporations* (4th ed., 1969)
> (The classic casebook containing some good historical information)

L. Loss, *Securities Regulation* (1968)
> (The now-outdated bible on securities regulations, still useful for research on origins of policy)

R. Nader, M. Green, and J. Seligman, *Taming the Giant Corporation* (1976)
> (Contains interesting historical material and articulates the need for reform)

Cary, *Federalism and Corporate Law: Reflections upon Delaware,* 83 Yale Law Journal 663 (1974)

Williston, *History of the Law of Business Corporations before 1800,* 2 Harvard Law Review 105 and 149 (1888)

FORMING A BUSINESS

M. Bittker and J. Eustice, *Federal Income Taxation of Corporations and Shareholders* (latest edition, as supplemented)
  (The definitive tax treatise)

W. Cary, *Corporations* (4th ed., 1969)
  (Has strong sections on alternative means of restricting controls)

J. Chommie, *Federal Income Taxation* (latest edition, as supplemented)
  (A comprehensible text)

J. Crane and A. Bromberg, *Partnership* (treatise, 1968)

R. Deer, *The Lawyer's Basic Corporate Practice Manual* (American Law Institute, looseleaf manual)
  (Strongest section deals with setting up businesses)

E. Folk, *The Delaware General Corporation Law* (latest edition)

J. Grimm, R. Knauss, and B. Goodwin, *Small Business Financing Library* (Institute of Continuing Legal Education Project Book, 1966)

H. Henn, *Law of Corporations* (text, 1970)
  (Especially good on analyzing the forms of business organizations and their consequences)

C. Israels, *Corporate Practice* (Practising Law Institute, lastest edition)
  (Text on organizing and running a corporation)

J. Mulder, *The Drafting of Partnership Agreements* (American Law Institute paperback, latest edition)

F. O'Neal, *Close Corporations* (a supplemented text)

K. Pantzer and R. Deer, *The Drafting of Corporate Charters and By-Laws* (American Law Institute paperback, latest edition)

Prentice-Hall, *Corporation Statutes*
  (Looseleaf service containing all state corporation statutes)

C. Rohrlich, *Organizing Corporate and Other Business Enterprises* (looseleaf text)

White on New York Corporations (looseleaf-supplemented text)

Business Organizations (Matthew Bender)
  (A solid, multivolume encyclopedia, covering the full sweep of corporate law)

Fletcher Cyclopedia of Corporations (supplemented text)
  (A general reference)

The Journal of Accountancy, *Tax Consequences of Incorporation* (July 1976, p. 32)

THE ROLE OF DIRECTORS

A. Berle, Jr., and G. Means, *The Modern Corporation and Private Property* (1933)

Duties and Responsibilities of Outside Directors (Practising Law Institute handbook, latest edition)

M. Mace, *Directors: Myth and Reality* (1971)
  (An elegant study of what directors in fact do)

Melcher, *A Primer on Convertible Securities,* Mergers & Acquisitions (Summer 1971)

New York Law Journal, *Outside Counsel: Inside Director* (latest edition)
  (Indicates the lawyers on boards and what their law firms were paid)–Stirling Homex Corporation: *Report of Investigation Relating to Activities of the Board of Directors, Securities Exchange Act Release No. 4516* (July 2, 1975)

Leech and Mundheim, *The Outside Director of the Publicly Held Corporation* 31 The Business Lawyer 1800 (1976)

Preventing Directors' Liability under the Securities Laws (Practising Law Institute handbook, latest edition)

M. Schaeftier, *The Liabilities of Office: Indemnification and Insurance of Corporate Officers and Directors* (1976)

The Business Lawyer, *Corporate Director's Guidebook* (pamphlet, 1976)

Business Week, *Why Lawyers and Bankers Desert the Board* (March 29, 1976, p. 100).

Forbes, *Will the Directors Speak Up?* (May 15, 1976, p. 75)

Wall Street Journal, *As Suits Rise, Firms Scramble to Increase Insurance for Directors* (July 12, 1976, p. 1)

Guth v. Loft, Inc., 5 A 2d 503 (1939)

SEC v. Texas Gulf Sulphur Co., 401 F 2d 833 (2d Cir. 1968)

CAPITAL STRUCTURE

American Bar Association, *Commentaries on Model Debenture Indenture Provisions* (1971)
   (Contains both model indenture provisions and an analysis as to the reasons for and impact of restrictions)

V. Brudney and M. Chirelstein, *Corporate Finance* (1972)
   (A legal textbook with some good summaries of the business aspects of capital structure)

B. Graham and D. Dodd, *Security Analysis* (latest edition)
   (The classic, with emphasis on fundamentals)

E. Helfert, *Techniques of Financial Analysis* (latest edition)

H. Henn, *Law of Corporations* (text, 1970)

Understanding Financial Statements (Practising Law Institute handbook, latest edition)

J. Van Horne, *Financial Management and Policy* (latest edition)
   (An excellent book for the theoretical aspects of financial structure)

Kaplan, *Piercing the Corporate Boilerplate. Anti-Dilution Clauses in Convertible Securities*, 33 University of Chicago Law Review 1 (1965)

Klein, *The Convertible Bond: A Peculiar Package*, 123 University of Pennsylvania Law Review 547 (1975)

Modigliani and Miller, *The Cost of Capital, Corporation Finance and the Theory of Investment*, American Economic Review 48 (June 1958)

Ratner, *Dilution and Anti-Dilution*, 33 University of Chicago Law Review 494 (1966)

The Journal of Finance often has excellent, although sometimes technical, articles on capital structure.

Business Week, *Preferred Stocks Are Not What They Seem* (July 12, 1976, p. 52)

SECURITIES LAW BACKGROUND

Annual Institute on Securities Regulation (Practising Law Institute, latest edition)

H. Bloomenthal, *Securities and Federal Corporate Law* (looseleaf text)

Bureau of National Affairs, *Securities Regulation & Law Report* (looseleaf service)

Commerce Clearing House, *Blue Sky Law Reporter* (looseleaf service)

R. Jennings and H. Marsh, Jr., *Securities Regulation* (casebook, 3d ed., 1972)

Loss, *Securities Regulation* (1968)
   (Still useful on policy background)

Prentice-Hall, *Securities Regulation* (looseleaf service)

L. Rappaport, *SEC Accounting Practice and Procedure* (latest edition)

R. Sobel, *NYSE: A History of the New York Stock Exchange 1935–1975* (1975)
   (Describes practical and legal underpinnings of stock exchange practice)

SEC Annual Reports
   (The agency's annual reports discuss recent developments)

E. Thomas, *Federal Securities Act Handbook* (American Law Institute paperback, latest edition)

The SEC Speaks
  (Material for the annual Practising Law Institute Symposium)
Standard & Poor's, *The Review of Securities Regulation*
  (A biweekly service featuring essays on current topics)
SEC Docket
  (The SEC's weekly publication containing all of its releases)

PRIVATE PLACEMENTS AND VENTURE CAPITAL

J. Dominguez, *Venture Capital* (1974)
S. Goldberg, *Private Placements and Restricted Securities* (looseleaf text)
Nierenberg, *The Art of Negotiating* (1968)
SEC, *Disclosure to Investors—A Reappraisal of Federal Administrative Policies under the '33 and '34 Acts* (The Wheat Report, 1969)
Barron's, *Animal Spirits Rising: Venture Capital Has Begun to Flow Again* (June 14, 1976)
S. M. Rubel & Company, Venture Capital (a monthly magazine)
Zinbarg, *The Private Placement Loan Agreement,* Financial Analysts Journal (July-August 1975)
Doran v. Petroleum Management Corp., 545 F. 2d 893 (5th Cir. 1977)
SEC v. Continental Tobacco Co., 463 F. 2d 137 (5th Cir. 1972)
SEC v. Ralston Purina Co., 346 U.S. 119 (1953)

ALTERNATIVE MEANS OF FINANCING

Bender's Uniform Commercial Code Service (looseleaf text)
ESOPS: Employee Stock Ownership Plans (Practising Law Institute handbook, latest edition)
J. Grimm, R. Knauss, and B. Goodwin, *Small Business Financing Library* (Institute of Continuing Legal Education Project Book, 1966)
W. Hawkland, *A Transactional Guide to the Uniform Commercial Code* (1964)
Leveraged Leasing (Practising Law Institute handbook, latest edition)
J. Levie (ed.), *Commercial Finance and Factoring* (Practising Law Institute handbook, latest edition)
J. Van Horne, *Financial Management and Policy* (latest edition)
  (Contains a brief summary of alternative means of financing)
Barrons, *Smelling Like a Rose?: Air Pollution Control Bonds Benefit Buyers and Sellers* (April 25, 1977, p. 9)
Nichols, *ESOTS: A Tool for Divestiture,* 11 Mergers & Acquisitions 4 (Winter 1977)
Simmons, *Drafting of Commercial Bank Loan Agreements,* The Business Lawyer 179 (November 1972)

PART TWO: PUBLIC FINANCINGS

(See the books under securities law background)

American Stock Exchange, Company Guide (looseleaf service)
A. Bromberg, *Securities Law: Fraud; SEC Rule 10b-5* (looseleaf text)
V. Brudney and M. Chirelstein, *Corporate Finance* (1972, textbook)
P. Hoffman, *Lions in the Street* (1973)
  (A description of the work of Wall Street lawyers)
New York Stock Exchange, Company Guide (looseleaf service)
G. Robinson, *Going Public* (looseleaf text)
H. Sherwood, *How Corporate and Municipal Debt Is Rated* (1976)
Institutional Investor, Annual Financing Directory
  (An extremely useful statistical profile of transactions, including a listing of which investment bankers serve which corporations)
Securities and Exchange Commission, *Report of Advisory Committee on Corporate Disclosure* (September 8, 1977)

Securities and Exchange Commission, *Report of Special Study of Securities Markets* (1963) (Describes the hot issues market of the early sixties)

Kripke, *A Search for a Meaningful Securities Disclosure Policy,* 31 Business Lawyer 293 (1975)

The New York Times, *White & Case Agrees to Settle SEC Suit in Anti-Fraud Action* (May 3, 1977, p. 59)

Blue Chip Stamps v. Manor Drug Stores, 421 U.S. 723 (1975)

Ernst & Ernst v. Hochfelder, 425 U.S. 185 (1976)

Escott v. Bar Chris Construc. Corp., 283 F. Supp. 643 (S.D.N.Y. 1968)

Globus v. Law Research Serv. Inc., 418 F 2d 1276 (2d Cir. 1969)

Lanza v. Drexel, CCH Federal Securities Law Reporter, Para. 92,826 (S.D.N.Y. 1970)

Santa Fe Industries v. Green, CCH Federal Securities Law Reporter, Para. 95914 (S. Ct. 1977)

TSC Industries, Inc. v. Northway Inc., CCH Federal Securities Law Reporter, Para. 95,615 (S. Ct. 1976)

United States v. Morgan, 118 F. Supp. 621 (S.D.N.Y. 1953) (An excellent source for the history of investment banking)

Part Three: MERGERS, ACQUISITIONS, AND TENDER OFFERS

American Bar Association, *Antitrust Law Developments* (1975, periodically supplemented)

E. Aranow, H. Einhorn, and G. Berlstein, *Developments in Tender Offers for Corporate Control* (1977)

Bureau of National Affairs, *Antitrust and Trade Regulation Report* (looseleaf service)

A. Choka, *Buying, Selling and Merging Business* (American Law Institute paperback, latest edition)

Commerce Clearing House, *Trade Regulation Reporter* (looseleaf service)

Department of Justice, *Merger Guidelines* (reprinted in American Bar Association, Antitrust Law Developments [1975] in the supplement)

Federal Trade Commission, *Economic Report on Corporate Mergers* (1969)

J. Flom, M. Lipton, and E. Steinberger, *Takeovers and Takeouts—Tender Offers and Going Private* (a New York Law Journal Handbook, 1976)

J. Freund, *Anatomy of a Merger* (Law Journal Press, 1975)

M. Green, B. Wasserstein, and B. Moore, *The Closed Enterprise System: The Nader Report on Antitrust Enforcement* (1972)

Georgeson & Co., *Tender Offers* (A looseleaf service which includes all of the state takeover statutes)

J. Herz and C. Baller (eds.), *Business Acquisitions: Planning and Practice* (Practising Law Institute text, latest edition)

E. Kintner, *Primer on the Law of Mergers* (1973)

J. McCord, *Course Materials on Buying, Selling and Merging Businesses (1977)*

The Business Lawyer, *Corporate Takeovers* (May 1977)

Ebeid, *Tender Offers: Characteristics Affecting Their Success,* 11 Mergers & Acquisitions 21 (Fall, 1976)

Ferris, Melnik and Rappaport, *Cash Tender Offer Pricing,* 12 Mergers & Acquisitions 9 (Spring 1977)

Gunther, *Financial Reporting for Mergers and Acquisitions Revisited,* 12 Mergers & Acquisitions 4 (Spring 1977)

Forbes, *Ruthlessness by the Rules* (February 1, 1976, p. 24)

A. Fleischer, Jr., *Defensive Tactics in Tender Offers,* The Review of Securities Regulation 853 (1976)

Hayes and Taussig, *Tactics of Cash Takeover Bids,* Harvard Business Review (March-April 1967, p. 135)

Cash Tender Offers, 83 Harvard Law Review 377 (1969)

Siegel, *How a Target Is Picked for a Tender Offer,* New York Law Journal (July 14, 1976, p. 1)

Troubh, *Purchased Affection: A Primer on Cash Tender Offers,* 54 Harvard Business Review 79 (July-August 1976)

Brown Shoe Co. v. United States, 370 U.S. 294 (1962)

Brunswick Corp. v. Pueblo-Bowl-O-Mat, Inc., 45 U.S. Law Week 4138 (S. Ct. 1977)

FTC v. Consolidated Foods Corp., 380 U.S. 592 (1965)

FTC v. Procter & Gamble Co. (Clorox), 386 U.S. 568 (1967)

General Foods Corp. v. FTC (S.O.S.), 386 F. 2d 936 (3d Cir. 1967) (1968)

Great Western United Corporation v. Kidwell, CCH Federal Securities Law Reporter, Para. 96, 187 (N.D. Tex. 1977)

Kennecott Copper Corp. v. FTC, 467 F 2d 67 (10th Cir. 1972)

Otis Elevator Co. v. United Technologies Corp., 405 F. Supp. 960 (S.D.N.Y. 1975)

Purex Corp. v. Procter & Gamble Co. 453 F.2d 288 (9th Cir. 1971)

United States v. Aluminum Co. of America (Alcoa-Rome), 377 U.S. 271 (1964)

United States v. General Dynamics Corp., 341 F. Supp. 534 (N.D. Ill. 1972)

United States v. International Tel. & Tel. Corp. (Canteen), CCH Trade Regulation Reporter, Para. 73,619 (N.D. Ill. 1971)

United States v. International Tel. & Tel. Corp. (Grinnell), 306 F. Supp. 766 (D. Conn. 1969)

United States v. Marine Bancorporation, Inc., 418 U.S. 602 (1974)

United States v. Penn-Olin Chemical Co., 378 U.S. 158 (1964)

United States v. Philadelphia Nat'l Bank, 374 U.S. 321 (1963)

United States v. Standard Oil Company (Potash), 253 F. Supp. 196 (D.N.J. 1966)

United States v. Von's Grocery Co., 384 U.S. 270 (1966)

Stanley Works v. FTC, 469 F. 2d 498 (2d Cir. 1972)

Missouri Portland Cement v. H. K. Porter Co., CCH Securities Law Reporter, Para. 95,864 (S. Ct. 1977)

BANKRUPTCY

Commerce Clearing House, *Bankruptcy Law Reporter* (looseleaf service)

Commerce Clearing House, *Blue Sky Law Reporter* (looseleaf service)

L. Forman, *Compositions, Bankruptcy, and Arrangements* (American Law Institute handbook paperback, 1971)

S. Rutberg, *Ten Cents on the Dollar* (1973)

D. Stanley and M. Girth, *Bankruptcy: Problem, Process, Reform* (1971)

A. Quittner, ed., *Current Developments in Bankruptcy* (Practising Law Institute text)

Index

Accountants, 140–141, 177–179, 219–220
Accounting, purchase, 218–219
Accounts receivable:
  assignment of, 99
  factoring of, 98
Acquisitions (*see* Mergers and acquisitions)
Alex. Brown, 122
Aluminum Co. of America (Alcoa-Rome), United States v., 195–196
American Bar Foundation, Corporate Debt Financing Project, 46, 47, 49
American Law Institute, Federal Securities Code Project, 180
American Stock Exchange, 27, 204, 235
Andersen, Arthur & Co., 140, 179
Antitrust aspects of mergers, 190–201
  conglomerate mergers, 197–199
  horizontal mergers, 194–196
  merger guidelines, 195–199
  private suits, 200–201
  vertical mergers, 197
Antitrust Division, Department of Justice, 191–193, 195–200
Appraisal rights, 206
Arkansas tender offer statute, 237
Arnold, Thurman, 193

Bache Halsey Stuart, 123

Bain, Joe, 184
Bank loans, 97–98, 100–101
  lines of credit, 97–98
  revolving credit agreements, 100
  term loans, 100–101
Bank mergers, 200
Bankruptcies and reorganizations, 255–267
  Bankruptcy Act, 256
  bankruptcy process, 258–260
  Chapter X, 64, 256, 260–267
  Chapter XI, 64, 256, 260–264, 266–267
  Chapter XII, 256
  Equity Funding, case study, 265–267
  six acts of bankruptcy, 257–258
  straight bankruptcy, 256–260
BarChris Construction, 138–141
Bentnam, Jeremy, 4
Blackstone, William, 9
Blue Chip Stamps v. Manor Drug Stores, 141
Blue-sky laws, 60–62
Blyth Eastman Dillon & Co. Incorporated, 122, 128
Board of directors (*see* Directors)
Board of directors meetings, minutes of, 16–17
Boot, "real," 209–210
Brandeis, Louis D., 62
Brown, Wood, Fuller, Caldwell & Ivey, 128
Brown Shoe Co. v. United States, 194, 196–197
Brunswick v. Pueblo Bowl-O-Mat, 201

"Business judgment" rule, 24
Bylaws, 15–16
  sample, 271–283

California corporation statute, features of,
  16
Capital structure, 34–59
  common stock, 40–42
  convertible securities, 56–58
  debt (*see* Debt)
  leverage (*see* Leverage)
  preferred stock, 42–45
  warrants, 58–59
Cary, W., 11*n.*
Certificate of incorporation, 13–15
  sample, 269–270
Class actions, 29
Clayton Act:
  Section 7, 200
  Section 16, 200
Cold comfort letter, 150–151
Commercial paper, 97
Common stock, 40–42
Consolidated Foods Corp., FTC v., 198
Continental Tobacco Co., SEC v., 68–69
Convertible securities, 56–58
Coopers & Lybrand, 140
Corporate opportunity doctrine, 24
Corporation(s):
  control devices, alternative, 17–20
    classes of stock, 17–18
    close corporation statutes, 19–20
    irrevocable proxies, 18–19
    restrictive covenants, 19
    voting agreements, 18
    voting trusts, 19
  current ratio, 39
  name of, 13, 14
  origins of, 9–10

Davis Polk & Wardwell, 128
Debevoise, Plimpton, Lyons & Gates, 128
Debt, 45–56
  covenants, 49–54
    debt limitations, 51–53
    disposition of assets limitation, 54
    dividend and redemption restrictions,
      53–54
    information requirements, 50
    insurance, 50
    mergers, 54
    pledge clauses, 50–51
  events of default, 54–55

Debt (*Cont.*):
  interest, 55
  repayment provisions, 55
  security, 47–48
  subordination, 55–56
Delaware corporation statute:
  appraisal rights, 206
  certificate of incorporation, 13, 14
  close corporation, 19, 20
  features of, 11–13, 16, 23
  history of, 10
  mergers, acquisitions, and asset sales, 204
  tender offer provisions, 236–237
Dewey, Ballantine, Bushby, Palmer & Wood,
  128
Directors, 22–33
  liability for issurance of securities, 135
  meetings of, minutes of, 16–17
  reporting requirements of, 25–26
  responsibilities of, 23–24, 30–33
  role of: in sale of securities, 24–25
    in short sales and arbitrage
      transactions, 26
    in short swing trading, 26
Disclosure system, federal, 174–180, 191
  contents of disclosure, 177–179
  disclosure approach, 174–175
  disclosure audience, 176–177
  timing of disclosure, 180
Doran v. Petroleum Management Corp., 69
Douglas, William O., 45, 62, 174
Drucker, Peter, 106
Due diligence, 138–142, 165–166, 169

Earn-outs, 215
Ebeid, Fred, 232–233
EBIT (earnings before interest and taxes)
  diagram, 37–39
Employee Retirement Income Security Act
  of 1974, 105
Employee stock ownership plans (ESOP's),
  105–106
Equipment financing, 100
Equity Funding, case study, 265–267
Ernst & Ernst, 140
Ernst & Ernst v. Hochfelder, 141
Exchange offers, 248–249
  (*See also* Tender and exchange offers)
Executive committee, 16, 23

Federal corporate chartering, 11, 12
Federal Trade Commission (FTC), 191–193
Financial Accounting Standard No. 13, 103
Financial Accounting Standards Board, 103,
  178

Financing:
  bank loans (*see* Bank loans)
  equipment, 100
  ESOP's, 105–106
  guarantees, 110
  intermediate, 100–101
  inventory, 99–100
  joint ventures, 109–110
  lease (*see* Lease financing)
  pollution bonds, 107–108
  project, 108–109
  secured loans, 98–100
  short-term, 97–98
  (*See also* Debt; Public offerings)
First Boston Corporation, The, 122–124,
    128
Freedom of Information Act, 159, 206

Galbraith, John Kenneth, 184
General Dynamics, United States v., 196
General Foods Corp. (S.O.S.) v. FTC, 198
Georgensen & Co., 228
Gilbert brothers, 22
Glass Steagall Act, 125
"Going private," 249–251
Goldman Sachs & Co., 122–124
Grace, J. Peter, 32
Grace, W. R., & Co., 32
Green, Santa Fe Industries v., 141–142, 251
Guth v. Loft, Inc., 24n.

Hart-Scott-Rodino Antitrust Improvements
    Act of 1976, 191, 228–229, 236
Haskins & Sells, 140
Heizer Corporation, 123
Hot issues, 125
Hutton, E. F., & Company Inc., 123

Idaho tender offer statute, 237
Indemnification:
  of directors, 29
  of underwriters, 149–150
Insider trading, 27–28
Installment purchases, 213–214
Insurance:
  of directors, 29, 30
  of mortgage assets, 50
Internal Revenue Code:
  Regulation 1502, 31, 217
  Section 103, 107
  Section 279, 229
  Section 334, 218
  Section 337, 214
  Section 341, 214

Internal Revenue Code (*Cont.*):
  Section 351, 21
  Section 355, 218
  Section 368(a): (1) (A), 203
    (1) (B), 207
    (1) (C), 209
    (2) (D), 207
    (2) (E), 207
  Section 368(c), 207
  Section 381, 216
  Section 382, 217–218
  Section 453, 213
  Section 483, 214
  Section 1244, 8, 111
  Subchapter S, 7, 8, 18, 111–112
  tax-free reorganizations, 203–210
    A reorganization, 203–204, 216–218,
      221
    B reorganization, 207–209, 216, 218,
      221, 229, 232
    C reorganization, 209–210, 216–218,
      221
    D, E, and F reorganization, 218
    triangular mergers, 207, 221
Inventory financing, 99–100
Investment bankers, 122–128
  choosing, 125–128
Investment Company Act of 1940, 231–232
ITT antitrust litigation, 199

Joint ventures, 109–110
Jones & Laughlin, 190

Kennecott Copper Corp. v. FTC, 198
Kheel, Theodore W., 31
Kidder, Peabody & Co. Incorporated, 122
King, D. F., & Co., Inc., 228
Kuhn, Loeb, 122, 128

Lawyers, securities, role of, 128–130
Lease financing, 102–105
  accounting treatment, 103
  tax treatment, 103–104
Lehman Brothers Kuhn Loeb Incorporated,
    122, 128
Letter stock, 73
Leverage, 35–39
  EBIT diagram, 37–39
  theory of, 35–37
Lines of credit, 97–98
Liquidation upon sale of assets, 214–218
Long-term debt (*see* Debt)
Loss, Louis, 180
Loss carry-overs, 215–218
LTV Corporation, 189, 190

Mace, Myles L., 30
McLaren, Richard W., 197
Madison, James, 9, 12
Margin rules, 235–236
Marine Bancorporation, United States v.,
    196
Mergers and acquisitions, 183–201
    accounting for, 218–220
        pooling, 219–220
        purchase treatment, 218–219
    antitrust aspects of (*see* Antitrust aspects
        of mergers)
    earnings and other advantages, 188–
        190
    efficiencies produced by, 184–188
    forms of: asset purchases, 210–211
        statutory merger, 203–207
        stock for assets, 209–210
        stock for stock exchanges, 207–209
        merger and acquisition agreement, 205,
            211–213
    tax aspects of, 202–221
Merrill Lynch, Pierce, Fenner & Smith,
    Incorporated, 122–123, 128
Metcalf, Lee, 178
Metcalf Report, 178
Milbank Tweed, Hadley & McCloy, 128
Miller, Merton, 36
Missouri Portland Cement v. H. K. Porter Co.,
    241
Mitchell, John, 108
Modigliani, Franco, 36
Morgan, J. P., 4
Morgan Stanley & Co. Incorporated, 122–
    124, 128
Mortgages, 48

Nader, Ralph, 11
National Association of Securities Dealers,
    160, 167–169, 230
National Student Marketing, 129
Negotiation strategy, 78–84
New Court Securities Corporation, 122
New Jersey corporate statute:
    features of, 13
    history of, 10
New York corporate statute:
    certificate of incorporation, 14
    features of, 11
New York Stock Exchange, 23, 31, 162, 166,
    168, 172, 204, 235

Offering Memorandum, 87–88
Ohio tender offer statute, 236–237
Otis Elevator v. United Technologies, 242

Peat, Marwick, Mitchell & Co., 138, 140
Penn Central, 14, 42–45, 102
    call provisions, 44
    convertibility, 44
    dividends, 43–44
    liquidation rights, 44
    sinking funds, 44
Penn-Olin, United States v., 200
Philadelphia Bank, United States v., 194, 196–
    197, 200
Piper v. Chris Craft, 238
Pollution bonds, 107–108
Preferred stock, 42–45
Preliminary prospectus, 131–132, 167
Price Waterhouse, 140
Private, going, 250–251
Private placements, 67–73, 86–94
    Offering Memorandum, 87–88
    purchase contract, 88–94
        closing conditions, 89–90
        covenants, 89
        registration provisions, 90–94
        representations, 88–89
Procter & Gamble Co. (Clorox), FTC v., 196,
    198
Project financing, 108
Prospectus, 153–159
    preliminary, 131–132, 167
Public offerings:
    deciding on an initial offering, 117–122
    documents for (*see* Registration
        statement; Underwriting
        agreements)
    expenses, 159–161
    under the 1933 Act, 131–142
        defenses, 136–138
        exemptions, 132–134
        illegal sales of securities, 135–136
        (*See also* Due diligence)
    partnerships, 6–8
    proxy statement, 25
    timetable for, 162–173
Purchase accounting, 218–219
Purchase contract (*see* Private placements,
    purchase contract)

Qualification to do business, 13
Quick ratio, 39

Ralston-Purina, SEC v., 67–68
Ratio analysis, 38
"Red herring" preliminary prospectuses,
    132, 167
Registration rights, 90–94
    demand rights, 91–93
    piggyback rights, 93–94

Registration statement, 152–159
  acceleration request, 170
  price amendment, 170–171
  review of, by SEC, 169–170
  summary of the prospectus, 153–159
Replacement costs requirements, 177–178
Repurchase of shares, 249
Restricted securities, resale of, 73–75
Rodgers & Wells, 128
Roosevelt, Franklin D., 62, 193
Root, Elihu, 5

Salomon Brothers, 122, 125
Schumpeter, Joseph, 184
Scully, Sister June, 32
Secured loans, 98–100
Securities and Exchange Commission (SEC),
    24, 31
  accounting policy, 178–179
  Accounting Series Release No. 177, 179
  Advisory Committee on Corporate
      Disclosure, 153, 176
  disclosure approach, 174–180
  Division of Corporate Regulation, 64
  Division of Corporation Finance, 64
  Division of Enforcement, 64
  Division of Market Regulation, 64
  Guides for Preparation and Filing of
      Registration Statements, 152–155
  Office of the Chief Accountant, 64
  organization of, 64
  origins of, 62–63
  projections of, attitude toward, 179–180
  regulation S-X financial statement re-
      quirements, 157–158, 164, 177
  and small business, 65–73
    intrastate issues, 65
    private offering exemption, 67–73
    Regulation A issues, 65–66
    Regulation 240, 66
    simplified registration, 67
  statutory responsibilities of, 63–64
Securities Act of 1933, 63
  defenses to liability, 136–138
  exempt securities, 132
  exempt transactions: brokerage trans-
      actions, 133–134
    dealer transactions, 134
    intrastate offerings, 65
    private offerings, 67–73, 134
  Form 1-A, 68–69
  Form S-1, 152–159, 163, 208
  Form S-2, 152
  Form S-7, 152, 153, 163, 168, 208
  Form S-8, 152
  Form S-14, 152, 205, 206, 208

Securities Act of 1933 (*Cont.*):
  Form S-16, 152
  liabilities, 135–136
  Regulation A, 65–66, 113, 133
  Regulation C, 167
  Release 5170, 168
  Release 4936, 167–168, 170
  Release 5180, 132
  Release 5231, 167, 170, 171
  Rule 144, 73–74, 91–92
  Rule 146, 68, 70–73, 86–87, 112, 134
  Rule 147, 65, 112, 132, 133
  Rule 237, 74–75, 91
  Rule 240, 66, 112
  Rule 402, 167, 171
  Rule 404, 167
  Rule 405, 133
  Rule 424, 172
  Rule 434B, 248
  Rule 458, 168
  Rule 460, 170
  Rule 461, 170
  Rule 471, 171
  Rule 472, 172
  Section 2, 132, 133
  Section 3, 132
  Section 3(a), 11, 65
  Section 3(b), 65
  Section 4, 132, 133
  Section 4(2), 67, 134
  Section 5, 131, 135, 167
  Section 11, 66, 135, 137, 138, 140, 141,
      149, 173
  Section 12, 66, 135
  Section 15, 135
  Section 16, 135
  Section 17, 66
  Section 20, 135
  Section 24, 135
  simplified registration procedures, 67
Securities Exchange Act of 1934, 64
  Form 3, 25, 120
  Form 4, 25, 120
  Form 8-K, 119, 163, 173
  Form 10-K, 119, 153, 163–165, 177
  Form 10-Q, 119, 163
  Release 9395, 231
  Rule 10b-4, 230
  Rule 10b-5, 27–28, 107, 223
  Rule 10b-6, 249
  Rule 10b-7, 145
  Rule 10b-13, 235
  Rule 13e-1, 249
    proposed Rule 13e-2, 249
    proposed Rule 13e-3, 250
    proposed Rule 13e-4, 250
  Rule 14f-1, 235

Securities Exchange Act of 1934 (*Cont.*):
  Schedule 13D, 234, 246
  Schedule 14D, 247
  Schedule 14D-1 (*see* Tender and
    exchange offers, Schedule 14D-1)
  Section 10(b), 27, 140, 141
  Section 13, 234
  Section 13(d), 234
  Section 14, 234
  Section 14(d), 234–235, 248
  Section 14(d)-4, 247
  Section 14(e), 234
  Section 15(c), 144
  Section 16(a), 25, 27
  Section 16(b), 26–27, 224, 235
  Section 16(c), 26
  Section 16(e), 27
  Section 18(a), 25
  Section 20, 25
Seidler, Lee, 180
Shearman & Sterling, 128
Small business (*see* Securities and Exchange
  Commission, and small business)
Small Business Administration, 94
S.O.S. case, 198
Soss, Wilma, 22
South Sea Bubble, 3
South Sea Bubble Act of 1720, 3, 9
South Sea Company, 3, 9
Stabilization, 145
Standard Oil (Potash) case, 197
Stanley Works, FTC v., 195
State blue-sky regulations, 60–62
Stirling Homex, 31
Supreme Court, 141–142

Tax Reform Act of 1976, 104, 203, 217, 232
Tax treatment of mergers and acquisitions,
  202–221
Tender and exchange offers, 222–252
  arbitrageurs, 230–231
  "bear hugs," 228
  dealer-manager, 226–228
  dealer-manager agreement, 243–244
  defense tactics, 244–247
  definition of, 223–224
  federal securities regulation of, 234–236
  letter of transmittal, 244
  offer to purchase, 240–243
  pricing, 232–233
  Schedule 13D, 234, 246
  Schedule 14D, 247
  Schedule 14D-1, 234, 238–244, 248–250
  solicitation fee, 233–234
  soliciting agent, 228

Tender and exchange offers (*Cont.*):
  soliciting dealers, 230–231
  state regulation, 236–238
  target selection, 224–225
  terms of offer, 229–234
Texas Gulf Sulphur Co., SEC v., 28
Touche Ross & Co., 140
Trade credit, 97
Trust Indenture Act of 1939, 45, 46, 50, 63–
  64, 152, 159
TSC Industries, Inc. v. Northway, Inc., 141

UCC (Uniform Commercial Code) Form 1,
  98
Underwriters (*see* Investment bankers)
Underwriting agreements, 143–152
  Agreement Among Underwriters, 144–
    145
  Purchase Agreement, 146–152
  Selected Dealer Agreement, 145–146
Underwritings:
  compensation for, 145, 146
  expenses, 159–161
  forms of, 146–147
  pricing, 147, 171
  timetable, 162–173
Uniform Commercial Code, 98
Uniform Partnership Act, 6
Uniform Securities Act, 61

Vagts, Detlev, 32
Venture capital, 76–95
  negotiation strategy, 78–84
  selling the deal, 84–86
  venture deal documents, 86–95
    Offering Memorandum, 87–88
    purchase contract (*see* Private
      placements, purchase contract)
Von's Grocery, United States v., 195

Warehouse financing, 99
Warrants, 58–59
Wearly, William L., 32
Wheat, Francis, 73
Wheat Report, 73
White & Case, 128–129
White Weld & Co. Incorporated, 122
Wiesen, Jeremy, 180
Williams Act, 223, 234
Wilson, Woodrow, 10

Young, Arthur, & Co., 140